THE END
THE BOOK

PART TWO
YOU HAVE BEEN WARNED

J.L. ROBB

" ll these are the beginning of sorrows"
Matthew 24:8 KJV

Printed in the United States of America

NOTE FROM THE AUTHOR

The End The Book series is a fictional account of the predicted apocalypse as outlined in the *Bible*. Several readers have asked me, "Is it true?"

It is true that the Biblical *end* will happen, but I have written this series as a counter-weight to the apocalyptic fiction coming out of Hollywood, like *Armageddon* and *2012*, that fail to mention God and His role. Any similarities between things that are occurring now and things written in this series are purely coincidental. It would be impossible to write a "true" account of the Biblically described *End Times*.

I hope all readers will find this series thought provoking, as well as thrilling, and might make us think about some of the things we believe and why we believe them.

In *Part Two: You Have Been Warned*, Jeffrey Ross continues his journey of unbelief from one tragedy to another, disaster lurking just moments away.

What would you do if you woke up one morning, turned on the TV to get the latest weather and the screen showed only an announcement: *Please Standby for Homeland Security*

You try other channels, but all are the same. What would you do if you found out the end really *was* near, and there wasn't a thing mankind or science could do about it? What if the electricity went out and never came back on? Could you make it?

I hope you enjoy reading *Part Two* as much as I enjoyed writing it for you.

J.L. Robb is an author and free-lance writer with a degree in zoology. A U.S. Navy veteran and cancer survivor, he lives in the Bible-Belt with his Great Dane and two kitties.

PREFACE

"They made pomegranates of blue, purple and scarlet yarn and finely twisted linen around the hem of the robe. And they made bells of pure gold and attached them around the hem between the pomegranates. The bells and pomegranates alternated around the hem of the robe to be worn for ministering, as the Lord commanded Moses." Exodus 39:24-26 NIV

Jerusalem

"What do you think he meant by that?"

"By what?" James had no idea what John was talking about; the question came out of the blue. John did that sometimes.

"What do you think he meant when he said the temple would be destroyed and then rebuilt in three days?" John loved his little brother, but sometimes James just couldn't seem to keep up.

Judas followed the conversation, contemplating. He had a lot of questions himself. Standing up, he shook the desert sand, cooled by the night air, took off his sandals and removed the sand-brier lodged in his heel. He finally spoke.

"You know, the rabbis, especially Caiaphas, say the Teacher is crazy as a loon, just another fake Messiah. They do seem to be coming out of the woodwork. Look at that teacher in the desert, what was his name, Bar-Abba? He had hundreds of followers. There have been others who have claimed to be the Messiah."

Judas had a tendency to speak out more than the brothers James and John, as well as Andrew.

"Some of the things he says make no sense to me," he continued.

"Judas! What are you saying?" John whispered the question. The garden was deserted except for them, no one could hear; but John was beginning to notice a change in Judas. "Be quiet or the Teacher will hear you!" he whispered, this time emphatically.

"I'm just saying, like you said, what did he mean about the Temple being destroyed; and then it reappears in three days? Does that not sound a little crazy to you?"

Judas was animated but whispered quietly. He continued.

"King Herod would have a stroke if someone destroyed his Temple. Then he would kill all of us! Don't you see that? Herod needs no reason to kill Jews. Think about it," Judas continued, pausing a moment to look around the perimeter of the garden, the cicadas suddenly silent against the night sky. Y'shua sometimes seemed to just appear, Judas knew. He loved Y'shua and wouldn't want to disappoint him, but . . .

"He said that before the day of God's wrath, nations would rise against nations and wars would be everywhere. Do you really think that could happen? Who would possibly go to war against Rome? They rule the world, and they rule it with a mighty sword. Who could stand up to Caesar, I ask?" Judas was in rare form today, agitated even more than usual.

James looked at John, and then Judas. There were no other followers of the young rabbi around, at least none in sight.

"The Teacher also said other things Judas. He didn't mention anything about Rome. Maybe it's not the last days. He said there would be storms and earthquakes like never before. That hasn't happened. The seas would 'roar' like never before is what he said. That hasn't happened. The Mediterranean is no worse than ever before, except maybe during the Great Flood. The Sea of Galilee has bad storms, but no worse than before! You have misread the prophecies of the Ancients, Judas." James scolded Judas, as he had done many times before.

"Let's go to Pomegranates and have a hot tea."

James addressed the invitation directly to Judas; and the four followers of Jesus left Gethsemane, walking under the trees of the olive grove around the Mount of Olives and into Jerusalem, the City of David, as it was often called. The trail was dusty from the prolonged droughts of recent years, the dust evolving into a small cloud suspended in the air a few inches above their sandals.

A brief forty minute walk later, John, his brother James, Andrew and Judas entered the side entrance of Pomegranates and took a seat on the hard benches in the back by the portal. The portal was the only window in the dingy place, and the stained granite table offered a limited view of the street. James knew a limited view was better than no view, better to keep a lookout for the feared Roman Guard.

The tall and olive-skinned Philistine servant approached the four men and bowed to each before asking their pleasure.

"Bring a pomegranate mint tea for myself and my three friends." James ordered.

"Sir, do you want the Pomegranate Mint Tea or King Herod's Mint?" The servant seemed anxious and glanced over his shoulder at the two guards in the front of the dark, dry café. James noted the silent tip and said, "King Herod's of course!" He spoke loudly enough for the two guards to hear. They paid no heed.

James was wise beyond his years and knew to accept any brand of tea other than King Herod's Mint would bring unwanted scrutiny by the two guards, large men with plated leather gear for protection, and great big swords. Judas said nothing; and James held his breath, knowing how John sometimes was, hoping he would make the right tea choice. He did.

After the servant brought the men the hot tea, James looked at Judas and asked, "What's up with you Judas? You seem to be having doubts that Y'shua is who he says he is."

"That's the question, James. Who does he say he is? The Son of Man? What's that? I'm confused, James. The rabbis are the real teachers, and they all say that Y'shua's 'miracles' are a fraud from Satan himself."

"Judas! You have seen the wonders with your own eyes. My God, man, what's wrong with you? Do you not believe your own eyes?"

"I didn't see him walk on water. No one can walk on top of the water James, don't you see that?"

"I saw it," Andrew said, softly.

"Peter and Andrew saw it? Peter tried it himself, was successful for a moment, according to Andrew, then sunk like a rock. But Andrew said Peter walked on top of the Sea too, about 30 cubits. Do you think they just made up that story?"

"We didn't make it up. Why would we?" Andrew asked.

"I don't know." Judas was suddenly sullen, stressed. "I just get confused, James. I want so much to believe that he is the Messiah, *The* Messiah. Know what I mean? He was supposed to come and liberate us from our misery, and I think the prophets meant Rome. But he walks around Judah preaching love and peace, love your enemy as yourself. That's the most ridiculous thing I've ever heard. Love your enemy? Love the Roman Legion?? Love the Arabs? I don't think so."

"I think Y'shua is just saying," James paused as John listened intently. "I think he just means that if everyone in the world would love each other, the Commandments would fall in place naturally. He knows that's not going to happen, according to Matthew at least."

The three sat silently for a moment, and James pondered what Matthew had said, that Y'shua did not mean for us to turn the other cheek indefinitely, that Y'shua himself would return again, this time with a sword to judge mankind, not a kiss.

"It's not going to be pretty," and James had a feeling Matthew was right.

"Judas, I know the scriptures said that the Messiah will free us from oppression, but it's not Roman oppression he is freeing us from, don't you see? That's not what he is talking about!"

"What then? What is he going to free us from? And when in Yahweh's name will it happen?"

James understood Judas' frustration and angst. The Jews had been waiting a long time for this prophesied savior, hundreds of years. This was him, James knew that for sure. He had seen Jesus cure that blind man, with his own eyes, in an instant. He had seen the miraculous feeding of thousands of hungry followers with a few loaves of bread. He had seen Jesus call out to Mary and Martha's brother Lazarus, dead in the tomb four days, the atrocious smell of death flowing from the tomb like honey from a hive.

When Jesus' friends, Mary and Martha, had first sent the message that Lazarus was deathly sick, Jesus was heart-broken and felt for the two sisters. You could just tell in his eyes. Still, he waited for two days, continuing to cure the sick and heal the lepers. There were so many miracles, too many to count, much less remember. The apostles had wondered why Jesus waited so long. When Jesus finally did show up, the sisters were almost angry.

"If you had just come earlier, Y'shua, Lazarus would still be alive," and Martha was visibly distraught. Mary wept nearby. James spoke.

"Moses freed us from the slavery of Egypt, Judas. Y'shua is here to free us from the slavery of death. That is if we don't kill him first. Most Jews hate him with a passion and think the miracles are not from Yahweh. I don't know how he's going to do it, but Y'shua is here to save us from ourselves, can't you see that?

"The time is not right for the last days. I'm not sure what he meant about the Temple being restored in three days. I know it sounds impossible but so is curing a man from blindness since birth. Y'shua is the first person in our history who has ever done such a thing. It is not possible, but Y'shua did it! Think about it. I believe future generations will look back and understand perfectly.

"If great earthquakes suddenly start happening more often, if the oceans roar and rise above the shore more than normal, if the winds begin to roar exceedingly and if hail storms proliferate the land, when the sun turns hotter over the land and the world warms beyond normalcy, then we will know: the end *is* near. It will get much hotter!"

"So why did Jesus wait so long to save Lazarus when he could've just issued the word; and Lazarus would have been healed, right?"

"Judas, maybe he did it to prove to us who he really is, something you are having a hard time believing. Maybe Jesus waited until Lazarus was dead, so he could bring him back to life. That was pretty impressive, don't you think?"

The Roman guards turned to leave, when one noticed the four apostles were whispering. He turned to walk their way.

"What are you Jews whispering about? Aren't you followers of that prophet, the one who heals lepers?" The Roman soldier was large, but he appeared even larger in his leather armor.

"No Sir. We don't know who you're talking about." Judas denied Jesus that night, long before Peter did the same. The other three followers said nothing.

"I would like to learn about this Jesus. I saw one of his miracles."

The guard turned away from the men, disappointment on his face.

LIST OF MAIN CHARACTERS

Alphabetical by First Name

Abe the Bartender: Key character. General Manager and bartender at *The Divide Disco & Café*.

Aboud Rehza: a.k.a Vinny, a.k.a. Ricky, a.k.a. Jean Philippe. In charge of U.S. Operations for *Jihad's Warriors* and various other Islamic Jihadist groups. Twin brother of Mohammed Rehza.

Aludra Khalid: Muhammed's sister. Lives with Muhammed, leader of terrorist Jihad's Warriors, in the Korengal Valley, Afghanistan-Pakistan border.

Amber Michelle: Investigative reporter with al-Jazeera USA.

Betty Davis: Also known as Betty Davis Eyes. Bartender at American Legion Post 251 in Duluth, GA.

Bill "Wild Willy" Briggs: Master of Nanotechnology, Georgia Tech Nanotechnology Research Center, Atlanta. Ex-U.S. Navy, CIA and Homeland Security. Works closely with Israel's Mossad. His cover is high dollar repo man.

Chad "Chadbo" Myers: Assistant Director, Near Earth Object and Heliospheric Laboratory, Goddard Space Flight Center, Greenbelt, MD.

Chuck Hutz: a.k.a. Hutz the Putz. After accident, speaks fluent Hebrew and witnesses to others while in a trance.

CJ: Bartender at American Legion Post 251 in Duluth, GA. Helped capture terrorist wannabe that attacked the Post.

Condi Zimmerman: Independent news anchor/reporter and Atlanta contract correspondent with FOX News Network and OLNN.

Dan Brunson: Nuclear physicist and public speaker.

Dennis Duncan: Geophysics Professor and public speaker.

Dmitry Ustinov: Chechnyan-Russian arms dealer. Brokered the sale of 5 high-yield nuclear weapons and delivery systems from Pakistan to Iran. Arranged high jacking of Nerpa 155 nuclear submarine.

Dr. Joseph Rosenberg, PhD: Public Speaker and Professor of Apocalyptic Religions, Candler School of Theology, Emory University.

Edgar Allen Poe: Homeless veteran who discovers terrorist plot.

Erica P. Robbins: Freelance reporter and U.S. War Correspondent.

Gray and Andi Dorey: Close friends of Jeff and Melissa Ross. Philanthropists and owners of Dine for Dollars.

Jack Russell: United States Senator from Cumming, Georgia and ranking member on the Military Finance Committee. Married to Samarra Russell.

Jeffrey "Jeff" Ross: Main character. Ex-husband of Melissa Ross. Father of three daughters, Jami and Jenni (twins) and Audry. U.S. Navy SEAL until discharged with injury after the Vietnam conflict.

Jill Haskins: Wife of Leon "Bubba" Haskins and Samarra Russell's closest friend.

Judi Ellis: Director of Paleobiology, Emory Primate Research Center, Atlanta.

Judy Blanton: Lives in Lukeville, Arkansas. Previous owner of J. Blanton concrete Company.

Kara Mulherin: Missionary to Haiti and future girlfriend of Scott Johnson.

Kari K. Vermi: News anchor with OLNN, Omega Letter Network News. Columnist with www.omegaletter.com

Kipper T and Missy T: Angels

Kyoto Kushito: Founder and Director of *The Foundation*, a shadowy, suspected worldwide terror think tank, based in the Hiroshima, Japan area. *The Foundation* funded the hijacking of the Nerpa 155 nuclear submarine.

Leon "Bubba" Haskins: Owns the largest minority contracting firm in Georgia and a tourist submarine facility at Lake Lanier Islands, Georgia. Married to Jill Haskins.

Mehdi: Chief of Security and Jihad Planner for Muhammed Khalid. Lives in Korengal Valley along the Afghanistan-Pakistan border.

Melissa Ross: Also Melissa Ross-Jeremias. Divorced from Jeff Ross, mother of twins, Jami and Jenni, and adopted daughter, Audry. Recently married Robert Jeremias, later killed in a plane crash. May have been raptured.

Mohammed Rehza: Ruthless Islamist in charge of European operations for *Jihad's Warriors*. Twin brother of Aboud Rehza (a.k.a. Vinny and others)

Muhammed Khalid: Islamic Jihadist and founder of the extremely secretive *Jihad's Warriors*. Lives in Korengal Valley with his sister, Aludra.

Naomi: Old Jewish woman who carries a cross necklace. Helps Aludra escape Korengal Valley through Tajikistan.

Pam MacLott: Owner of *The Divide Disco & Café*.

Richard "Rich" Badey: Investigative reporter.

Robert Jeremias: Missionary, philanthropist. Married Jeff's ex, Melissa Ross, before he was killed (or missing) in a plane crash.

Russ Ivies: Chief of Security, Centers for Disease Control and Prevention, Atlanta. Actor and producer. Suffered one of first Spanish Flu cases.

Samarra Russell, PhD: Director of Research of Communicable Diseases, Centers for Disease Control and Prevention, Atlanta. Married to Senator Jack Russell.

Scott Johnson: Assistant manager of *The Divide Disco & Café*.

Sheryl Lasseter: Director of the United States Public Relations Liaison. Works directly for the U.S. President.

Terry and Toni Fahey: Next door neighbors of Jeffrey Ross.

The Admiral: Justin P. McLemore. A graduate of the U.S. Naval Academy and retired four-star Admiral. Director of Near Earth Object and Heliospheric Laboratory, Goddard Space Flight Center, Maryland.

Three Wild Women: Wanda, BJ and Beverly from the American Legion Post 251, skilled in self-defense and sharp-shooting.

Vinny: A truly bad man, his real name is Aboud Rehza, a product of wealthy Saudi parents. He and his twin brother, Mohammed, had been child prodigies and both speak several languages, fluently. A man of many aliases. Vinny resides in the United States after infiltrating across the Mexican border. Aliases include Vinny, Ricky, Jean Philippe, and others.

PROLOGUE

December 20, 2012

Jeff was in a remarkably good mood, and Abe the Bartender was glad to see him finally socializing. It had been awhile. Abe didn't know Samarra, but wasn't surprised at her beauty. Jeff seemed to do that. Samarra sat next to Jeff at the bamboo-topped bar, as magnificent as ever.

"Hey man. Glad you decided to come party." Abe winked at Samara and continued. "You know Jeff, I've always wondered how you know so many beautiful women. I mean, you're just not that hot."

Samarra smiled.

"Thanks Abe, I'll come over and Round-Up your camellia bushes. Think we're gonna make it through the night?" Jeff asked, sipping the cool glass of Duckhorn merlot.

He wasn't making light of the prediction of a December 21, 2012, calamity. The crowd at *The Divide* grew, everyone waiting for midnight, December 20. That's when the real partying would begin, all over the planet, twenty-four hours of December 21st revelry, unless the Mayans and Hopis were right.

Abe the Bartender pondered while serving Judi Ellis a dirty martini, still astounded by her remarkable and quick recovery, and her gorgeous legs. He was happy with his new relationship. *Judi Ellis and Abe the Bartender; who would've ever figured?*

"We are if Hutz the Putz is right, and he seems to be right a lot."

"Why, what did he say?" Judi asked.

"He was ranting again about parents and how they are so permissive with their kids. He does that a lot and has really ticked off a lot of people. Wait, there he is."

Abe turned the TV volume up, and the small crowd gathered around. Hutz was speaking Hebrew, as usual; and Audry Ross interpreted for the crowd.

"Yahweh, the God of Israel and the universe, is not happy. Why do you let your children dye their bodies with drawings and paganistic symbols. Do you not know what Yahweh said in Leviticus 19:28? Let me tell you:

'Do not cut your bodies for the dead or put tattoo marks on yourselves. I am the LORD.'

"What do you think he meant by that? Do you think it's alright to disobey Yahweh because it applied to Jewish Law and not Christianity? Didn't Jesus himself say he didn't come to change the Law? This is what Jesus said in Matthew."

Chuck paused and sipped his iced tea. He was perspiring profusely, and beads of sweat spilled onto his blue and white seersucker coat.

"Do not think that I have come to abolish the Law or the Prophets; I have not come to abolish them but to fulfill them. For truly I tell you, until heaven and earth disappear, not the smallest letter, not the least stroke of a pen, will by any means disappear from the Law until everything is accomplished. Therefore anyone who sets aside one of the least of these commands and teaches others accordingly will be called least in the kingdom of heaven, but whoever practices and teaches these commands will be called great in the kingdom of heaven."

Chuck held a Bible up, opened to Matthew, chapter five.

"Israel, did Yahweh rescue you from the depths of the holocaust and restore your bones? Did Yahweh take you back to the land he gave Moses, just like Ezekiel prophesied in chapter thirty-seven? And how do you show Yahweh your respect?

"You don't keep the Sabbath holy, and you are sanctifying men marrying men. Do you not remember Sodom and Gomorrah? And now you kill your children while still in the womb, rejecting their chance at life in this world. But Yahweh takes these children directly to his Kingdom, the children you did not want. Where does this logic come from, Yahweh wants to know? He blesses you from the First Book of the Torah, yet you kick him in the face."

The vision of Chuck Hutz was interrupted by a loud explosion, but Chuck kept talking.

"People of the world, hear what I say. The dust of the dark comet will come to you and poison your waters, and your thirst will be quenched with bitterness

and death. The day is coming when the ships of the Great Sea will sink at the pleasure of Yahweh, and your military-might will disappear.

"Let the world hear what I say. A time is coming soon, O' Israel, a time of great distress.

"You have been warned."

Chuck Hutz the Putz slumped in his seat, exhausted and drenched; and Kari, the OLNN news commentator, looked concerned, though this was the normal routine.

"There you have it. The latest from Mr. Hutz. Not sure what the explosion was; but as soon as we hear, you will hear.

"Now to Noah's Ark. Archeologists state that they are ninety-nine percent certain that the find on Mt. Ararat could be the remnants of Noah's Ark. The large ship is remarkably preserved, and no one is certain why. The DNA analysis has puzzled many microbiologists. Apparently much of the DNA is from unknown life forms."

"Do you believe that?" Jeff asked, interrupting Kari and the news. "Haven't they found Noah's Ark many times in the past, just to find out they were wrong?"

"That's true," Samarra said, "only this time there is DNA. That's different. Would you start believing if they really have found Noah's Ark?" Samarra whispered in Jeff's ear, her breath warm and . . . sexy; and she was happy for the first time in a long time. She found Jeff Ross to be quite dreamy.

"Maybe." He answered, and held her hand. Judi made note of the possible budding romance.

Across the club, Chad, The Admiral and Sheryl were in deep conversation, their demeanor animated and serious. Judi and Samarra motioned, the way ladies do; and they both headed to the rest room. Abe poured Jeff another glass of Duckhorn.

"Abe, did I ever tell you about my dreams?"

". . . in Brazil. The Parliament has legitimized the young religion through their more recent liberalizing of social morés. The Temple of Molech will be built next year. If you recall from an OLNN exclusive report last year, Brazil also lowered the consent-for-sex age to ten years old."

Kari knew the worship of Molech wasn't a "young" religion and actually predated Judaism. Molech, the stone god that accepted every parent's first sacrifice, their first born child, burned to death on the altar of Molech. She hoped the Molechites in Brazil wouldn't be burning their babies alive and continued. *"Pakistan is reporting a security breach at a nuclear weapons lab. Reuters is trying to verify that as many as four nuclear warheads may be missing.*

"Now to Morgellons disease. *Cases of this very strange illness are being reported throughout Asia, and scientists are studying the possibility that comet dust or lunar dust could be the culprit.*"

"I don't think so. What dreams?"

Abe thought about the near-death experience from the Spanish Flu, and he again wondered if Jeff had seen the light that so many spoke of.

"I've been having these dreams since the flu, and they are the weirdest things. I thought maybe it was just part of my *experience*, but I keep having them. I think there's more to it."

"Are they *bad* dreams?" Abe asked.

Another scuffle appeared on the Towne Green, and Abe kept vigilant. People were everywhere with their TEIN signs, large and small displays of *The End Is Near! Repent!*

"No. Not yet at least. I keep seeing the same two people, Missy T and Kipper T; and I can't quite figure out their relationship."

"Well, it's just a dream. I want to ask you, did you see the light that so many see when they have a near death experience? So many NDEs are consistent with that."

"No. I didn't see a specific light at the end of a tunnel. There wasn't a tunnel; but there were multi-colored lights everywhere. There is this series of rooms, and each has its own color; and there is a door, a black door. I have dreams of going through the black door and never returning." Jeff was talking faster than normal.

Samarra and Judi returned to the bar, talking about the lady they met in the ladies room.

"You met a lady in the bathroom?" Jeff asked.

"Yes, we do that. You men go in, do your business and leave. We like to talk, make friends." Samarra winked at him and smiled. Her hand slid into his.

"She was an immunologist," Judi chimed in, "from NIH."

"Yes, and she was telling us about the HIV breakout in Tajikistan and throughout Asia. Apparently there is widespread concern at the National Institutes of Health that the disease is spreading through flea infestations. Since the droughts, there have been numerous infestations; fleas, mosquitos, mice."

"I thought they were talking about mosquitos carrying the disease." Abe said.

"They were, but now it appears to be getting totally out of control. HIV is spreading like wildfire throughout China."

Diana Hendricks, young and blonde, was the head waitress at *The Divide* and motioned to Abe. He walked from around the bar to see what she needed. She was an expert at spotting potential drunks.

"See the ladies sitting at the hi-top in the corner?"

Abe recognized the three.

"Yep. That's Wanda, BJ and Beverly from the American Legion Post."

"The *Three Wild Women*?" Diana had heard of them many times and would go introduce herself.

"Yep, that's them. Nice ladies, but you wouldn't want to mess with 'em. Tough as nails. One is a sharp-shooter, and they all have black-belts."

"Well, there's a guy who keeps hitting on them; and they are getting annoyed. He is well on his way to drunkville. He thinks he's so suavé bollo, but they are so not interested. We need to keep an eye on him."

"Go find Scott. He can handle it. Those ladies will chew that guy up and spit him out. I'm a lover, not a fighter." Abe grinned, ear-to-ear. A news alert flashed across the numerous flat screens.

"*Astronomers in Chile have spotted an intermittent, bright object in the sky; and they have confirmed that it is Blip, the bright light reported by people all over the world. Astronomers are trying to determine the origin and why it's there. Spectroscopic analysis indicates that the chemical makeup may be organic.*

"*Now to the giant chunks of ice that fell from the sky today.*"

"It's been a helluva year, hasn't it my friend?" Abe placed a glass of water in front of Samarra.

"It's been a helluva year, Mr. Abe the Bartender," and Jeff's thoughts drifted back to January."

Midnight crawled westward.

CHAPTER ONE

"It's not the fall that kills you; it's the sudden change in direction." Hutz the Putz

One year earlier

A be the Bartender opened early, anticipating some kind of New Year's Eve crowd. *The Divide Disco and Café* had become quite a hit in Duluth, in spite of all the worldly goings-on. In spite of the dark comet, a one hundred mile wide near Earth object on a collision course with planet Earth in a couple of weeks.

"Hey Pam. You're early! I told you Scott and I would open."

"Couldn't sleep. I keep having the weirdest dreams."

"What kind of weird?" Abe asked. He hadn't expected the owner. Two days ago, Pam was planning on taking a little vacation with her husband. She needed a break. The year had been stressful.

"Weird, like nightmares, about floods and devastation, and . . . all these bodies. Very disturbing, so I decided to forget Hilton Head and stay home."

Pam glanced out the front doors of the club; and a crowd was already gathering on Duluth, Georgia's Towne Green, kids playing in the fountain with temperatures in the eighties. The New Year's Eve celebration was a huge event for Duluth, as thousands gathered to watch the famous glass Disco Ball rise, instead of fall, at midnight.

"What kind of crowd do you think?"

"Who knows? There were hardly any people on Grand Cayman last week. I'm glad I went, I love that place; but it was kinda eerie with no

1

tourists. Melissa told me that Jeff may close his dive shop and just maintain the one in Jamaica."

"How did it go with Jeff and Melissa?"

"Oooh La La," Abe said, holding his heart.

"Really? Do you think they'll get back together? Jeff would be in heaven." Pam was happy as punch.

"Jeff doesn't believe in heaven." Abe said matter-of-factly. "But I will say this. The day before I left, they were snuggled up like a bug in a rug. Don't think they could get much closer without being sexual." He winked and grinned.

Pam grabbed the remote from the bamboo bar counter, turned to the new eighty inch big screen, and clicked the on button. Her heart was pitter-pattering, maybe in disbelief, maybe in joy for Jeff. He really never got over the divorce, she knew that, no matter how many women Duluth's most eligible bachelor went out with. His heart was still with Melissa, and everyone knew . . . except the ladies he went out with. He never talked about his ex when on a date. That he learned the hard way, and Pam chuckled quietly at *that* story.

"How long are Jeff and Melissa staying on Cayman? Are Gray and Andi still there?

The TV was on, but there was no sound.

"They'll probably stay until the comet hits, at least that's the plan. Jeff told me they would rather bite-the-dust on Grand Cayman than in Atlanta, Georgia."

"Do you think it will hit, Abe?" Pam's smile faded, and she realized that the coming doom may be the reason for the nightmares.

"That's what all the great minds say. People are partying all over the world, Hong Kong, Bangkok, London, Paris."

"And Duluth." They laughed, as Scott Johnson, the head bartender and other things, emerged from the office.

"That kind of blows the whole Mayan thing don't you think? Their calendar doesn't end until December 21." Scott had researched the Maya 2012 so-called predictions.

The TV remained silent, and a News Alert icon was the only thing showing across the screen. Scott walked around the club, turning on the other fifteen televisions, each tuned to a different news channel. That was the theme of *The Divide*, not a sports bar but a news bar. His mind wandered, thinking about his new sweetie, Kara Mulherin. Who would've ever thought that he would fall in love with a missionary?

"All the channels have Breaking News alerts." Scott called from across the restaurant.

"Try Al Jazeera."

"Same thing," Scott replied, walking back to the bar and handing Pam the control.

Pam, Abe the Bartender, Scott and the first customer to come through the door this day, stared at the sixteen flat screens. Suddenly, the sound came on sequentially, different TVs losing their Breaking News icons at different times. The beautiful Condi Zimmerman appeared on the screen, a foxy lady who had once been with Fox News before going independent. Condi always smiled, a cheerful and positive, *my glass-is-half-full* type of lady. Today she looked grim.

"Folks, this is not good news."

Condi thought that almost laughable. There had been nothing but bad news for the past two years it seemed.

"Montserrat, once the jewel of the Caribbean, had been a British island, high-dollar resorts, romantic beaches, until . . ."

The commentator was breathless.

"Soufrière Hills has erupted again!

"The island of Montserrat in the Caribbean has exploded, according to Reuters. The Soufriere Hills volcano has been erupting on-and-off for several years you may recall, completely burying the capital in deep ash. The island population has relocated to the far side of Montserrat over the years.

"About one hour ago, the volcano exploded and fell into the sea. Eye witnesses report that there were only a few minor tremors before the mountain 'leaped into the sky' and crashed into the ocean. A large tourist ship trying to bring tourism back to the island disappeared as the mountain landed directly on top of the ship. Tsunami warnings have been issued for all of the Caribbean, Bahamas, Cancun and the Mexican Riviera and the east coast of the United States. As we get more information, we will surely pass it on.

"Now to Ronn Aronson, our European correspondent. Ronn, it looks like Europe is realigning once again, since Greece's default and bankruptcy. What do you hear?"

"That's right Condi. Greece was already in dire straits last year, when the government suddenly decriminalized pedophilia and exhibitionism. These acts were reclassified as 'disabilities' which meant the state picked up tremendous additional health care costs . . ."

3

Abe the Bartender, Pam and Scott, mouths agape, said nothing initially and tried to absorb the news they just heard. A tsunami in the Caribbean?

Grand Cayman was in the Caribbean, and so were their close friends. In a flash, they started dialing or texting. The first customer of the day walked out the front door and disappeared into the still-growing crowd on the Green and glanced at the western sky. It was still too bright to see the Earth-bound comet; but he was sure he'd seen it the night before, a brief glimpse of bright light in the dark, North sky.

Melissa Ross fell over the top of Cayman Grand Hotel, washed over the side actually, toward the dark asphalt parking lot forty feet below. The fall seemed surreal. She wasn't sure how long the descent would take and was awed at all the thoughts that crossed her mind in the few seconds before she would lose consciousness.

Where had that wave come from? That was one thought. It had been so sudden . . . and *where was Jeff* . . . The wave had been almost silent, an eerie beauty along the distant horizon. She was sure, had the electricity on Grand Cayman Island not been out, Jeff the news-junkie would have known; and she recalled the news reports from yesterday, something about the Soufrière Hills Volcano erupting. Could that have caused *this*?

Falling, she again thought of Jeffrey and feared their reunion would be short-lived. They were holding hands when they ran to the edge of the roof and looked out to sea. What had earlier appeared as a gray ribbon stretched across the horizon, the dark wave had grown immensely and was approaching the shore *so* fast. She had never seen a tsunami, except in news reports, and was briefly amused at the beauty. *So beautifully terrifying.* She had not expected that the giant wave would actually wash *over* the roof of one of Cayman's taller hotels; but she knew that forty feet wasn't all that high off the soon-to-be-flooded ground below.

Falling face down, Melissa tried to rotate her body in the air; but the BC hindered her coordination. She was glad to have the Buoyancy Compensator strapped on, one of the last things she and Jeff had done before running to the edge to watch doom approach. Should the fall not kill her, at least she would stay afloat. Maybe that would keep her alive until the comet hit, and she wished she hadn't recalled *that*.

Miraculously, her acrobatics worked; and the sunlight hit her squarely in the eyes as she completed her rotation. She noted the coconuts as she passed through the thick fronds of the palm tree. At least when they found her body, her face wouldn't be all smashed up; and she laughed at her vanity just before crashing onto the hood of the black Mercedes limousine parked below. Her last thoughts before darkness set in was how hot the hood of the car was, and *where* was Jeffrey?

Jeff watched Melissa wash over the edge of the hotel roof. He felt the wave would breach the rooftop and squeezed Melissa's hand tightly. He knew the power of the water would destroy the grip, and she was gone in an instant.

They had remained at the edge of the roof, almost hypnotized by the specter of the rapidly approaching wave, at least until the bright blue cabanas, jet skis and paddle boats started slamming against the stucco siding of Cayman Grand. There was nowhere to go, but they went anyway. Holding Melissa tightly, they hid together behind one of the large, green rooftop air conditioners and waited. It seemed the seconds were creeping by. Jeff leaned over and kissed Melissa softly on her lips. The ambient noise was so great by now, he mouthed, "I love you Melissa. Always have." And then she was gone, ripped from his grip by the salty tsunami and washed over the side, into the parking lot below.

Jeff didn't have time to mourn his great loss as he lost his grip on the roof exhaust fan and raced the green air conditioning system to the edge. He hoped the air conditioner would win this race, because he knew that landing on the HVAC system would probably be better than the HVAC system landing on him.

A blur of blue *something* flew toward him, caught in the wave like so much other debris; and he recognized the bright blue cushions that had recently adorned the white oak chaise lounges on Seven Mile Beach below, just a few seconds earlier. His instinct and quick reaction allowed the catch; and he held the cushion tightly, heading perilously toward the north edge of the roof. Now floating a good six feet above the roof's surface, something slammed into him. Dazed, his mouth full of Caribbean saltiness, he tried to protect himself with the cushion when he suddenly recognized the object that collided with him. Earlier it had been the little old man from France who always walked up and down the beach, greeting everyone he met with a *bonjour* and a smile. Now the Frenchman was wet and dead, twisted in two like a pretzel, deep wounds turning his face into streams of crimson. They raced for the edge, the torrent heading north toward Rum Point and the open sea.

The air conditioner, the dead man and Jeff washed over the edge at the same time; and the water below now completely covered the parking lot. Jeff barely missed the black Mercedes limousine with the hot hood, now floating across what had been bright pink and red bougainvillea bushes edging along the sidewalk. He pulled himself tightly into a ball, not very easy with the inflated BC strapped tightly to his torso, and landed with the blue cushion stretched out in front of him. The cushion hit at just the right angle; and Jeff surfed over the parking lot, floating higher with each second as the flood grew. Nearly a half mile inland, he slammed into the top of a coconut palm about twenty feet above the cars and the two-person Pedi-cabs below. He lost all consciousness in an instant. He had no last thoughts as he passed from an otherwise beautiful Cayman Island's sunset into blackness, darkness, comfort. It was like he suddenly fell asleep.

"Reports are still coming in, but heavy damage has been reported from the Bahamas to Barbados and now the Cayman Islands and Jamaica. Cuba is in the big wave's sights, and the eastern coasts of Florida will be hit within an hour. Beaches along the entire Gulf and Atlantic coasts are being evacuated. We have no news from the Cancun area or the Mexican Riviera because of continuing power outages.

"This could be devastating for Mexico's tourist industry, already gearing up for the End-of-the-World parties this coming December 21, 2012."

Sitting in Duluth's newest sensation, *The Divide Disco and Café*, Abe the Bartender listened to the six o'clock news. Condi Zimmerman, the news babe, projected in high-definition from the flat screen above the bar. Tonight Condi's beauty was far from Abe's mind. His thoughts were with Jeff and Melissa, and their friends, Gray and Andi. He had flown back from Grand Cayman just a day earlier to handle the New Year's Eve crowd at the new club. He had to admit, as he sat on the plane, it did occur to him: *What's the use?*

For the life of him, he couldn't figure out why so many people were coming to celebrate the New Year; and it was happening at clubs everywhere, not just the United States. Big *End of the World* parties were being thrown along the French Riviera; and Hong Kong's famous Privé Club was totally booked at $15,000 per person, champagne and room included. London and Las Vegas gamblers were betting on where the comet would hit and at what precise second. It seemed that no one really believed, or else it was mass denial. Abe was still undecided. *Would the comet hit before the world ended?* and he smiled at the irony.

Abe was a self-taught Jewish and Christian *Bible* scholar, of sorts. He couldn't match up to the *real* experts and had never attended professional theology schooling, but he had come a long way since his days of *disbelief.* An Israeli, he had studied the Jewish prophecies thoroughly but didn't remember anything about God destroying the world with a comet. There *was* that prophecy in *Revelation 8* about a burning mountain falling from the sky and hitting the great ocean, or something like that; but if his memory was correct, that was one of the latter things that happened in God's plan of destruction and renewal. Hail and fire would be thrown at the Earth first, then the burning mountain falling into the sea . . . *could that be Soufrière Hills?* . . . then the star blazing like a torch that fell to Earth. *Is that the dark comet?*

Condi continued.

"*This just in, a retired admiral, Justin P. McLemore, and the United States Public Affairs Liaison, Sheryl Lasseter, were the victims of an armed robbery attempt today when at least three 'Pants on the Ground' gang members followed them from the Fox Theater in Atlanta to a Ponce de Leon Street parking garage.*

"*Unfortunately for the street thugs, the admiral turned out to be a retired Navy SEAL-team member; and Ms. Lasseter had just won the military's top civilian honor in pistol sharp-shooting, the coveted <u>Crosshairs Trophy</u>. As the admiral chased one perpetrator up Ponce de Leon, Ms. Lasseter fired through the bottom of her purse, blowing the gun out of the perp's right hand. The taller gang member lunged at Ms. Lasseter with a knife, and she shot him in the chest, squarely in the sternum. Before the other gang member could react, Ms. Lasseter pointed her gun at his . . . well, can I say 'private parts' on TV, and told him not to do anything silly. He did not.*

"*The police arrested the three young men and are looking for others. The 'Pants on the Ground' gang has been connected to several armed robberies, including some possible homicides. Admiral McLemore was released from Emory with a foot injury after kicking one fugitive in the head.*"

"Hey Abe. What's up? Have you heard anything yet?"

"Oh, hey Pam; you startled me. The owner's not supposed to be here early. No, I haven't heard anything from anybody. I did just hear on Channel 5 that Admiral McLemore and Sheryl were robbed or something down by the Fox. I was daydreaming and only caught part of the story."

"You're kidding!"

"No. I'm sure there will be an update in just a few minutes. Sounds like they're OK. I bet those guys wish they had chosen another target."

"Do you think we'll have a crowd tonight? I mean, with all the terrible things that are happening. I heard Jamaica has at least 30,000 deaths and counting. Not sure how much of that's true. You know how first reports are."

Pam considered if she should've told Abe about the number of deaths, but she knew that he had probably heard as much news as she had. They both knew the estimates would be higher. The ejection of the Soufrière Hills Volcano into the Caribbean Sea and the subsequent earthquake was sure to cause more death and destruction before this day was over.

Pam glanced out the open french doors adorning the entrance of *The Divide*. The day had been unusually warm for December 31. A crowd was beginning to gather on the Duluth Towne Green, children running up and down the yellow brick path that designated the geography of the Eastern Continental Divide that ran straight through the center of downtown. Pam had never thought promoting the Continental Divide as a tourist attraction would work for the city, but it had. The crowd was early; and the sun was setting, darkness racing westward at a thousand miles-per-hour.

"With the President admitted to the National Naval Medical Center in Bethesda, Maryland, it is suspected that he has also contracted the Spanish Flu. With the deaths of much of the White House staff and much of the Senate and Congress, the Spanish Flu continues to take its deadly toll, though the CDC claims this particular strain is not as contagious as the original Spanish Flu of 1918. The entire Senate, House and Justice Department have been temporarily quarantined until the spread of the virus is investigated. The CDC has a bio-lab crew on sight at the White House as we speak. The President's family is in China on vacation and has been advised to stay there until the source of the carrier can be found, which according to CDC is not likely. Homeland Security is suggesting that it could be the result of terrorism, and now, this: A man identified as a member of TACS has been found in a local D.C. hospital where he passed away yesterday. The hospital is now under quarantine.

"The Army of the Christian Soldier, whose sole intent is the overthrow of the U.S. government and the installation of a Christian theocracy, has been

connected to various computer hacking incidents. Some of you will remember the traffic light incidents last year that caused so many deaths and injuries. It appears that this particular ACS member visited the White House with a tour group last month.

"The dark comet continues heading toward Earth, and most of the world's nuclear ICBM missiles have been launched on an interception course . . ."

Pam gave Abe a conciliatory hug and kiss on the cheek.

"I'm sure we will hear something soon. It looks like the crowd's starting early tonight. I wonder how many'll make it to midnight to see the Duluth Disco Ball go up? Last year they gave it a standing ovation. How many disco balls have ever gotten a standing ovation?"

Pam greeted some of the employees on the way back to her office, but she couldn't contain her amusement at all the revelry. Florida was getting ready to get creamed by a tsunami, a comet was hitting Earth in less than three weeks, street gangs were roaming the streets, rapes were up big time; and all these people seemed in total denial.

"Ghana has reported its 34th case of mosquito-borne HIV. This is devastating news, as if there weren't enough. Spraying of the dreaded pesticide DDT has begun in large areas of the African coastal regions.

"Famine and drought continue in the western and central United States as well as large areas of Europe.

"On a different note, people of Semite origin do not seem to be as susceptible to the Spanish Flu virus as others; and the CDC is doing research on this puzzling bit of information."

Abe left Condi Zimmerman's reporting at the bar and started mingling with the crowd, welcoming the revelers to what could be the last New Year's Eve party. He thought again about *Revelation 8* and the mountain that would fall into the sea. That prediction says a *third* of sea life will be destroyed and a third of the world's ships. He would watch the news.

Abe circled the bar, taking note of the mumblings about the Mayan calendar and December 21, 2012, and whether we would even make it until that date. Abe figured he would know on December 22, as his thoughts drifted back to Jeff and his friends at Grand Cayman Island and whether they were still alive.

CHAPTER TWO

"W̲ho you calling fat boy, hero?" Sheryl laughed as she retold the story of the attempted mugging to her friend Judi.

Judi Ellis heard the news report while driving home from Emory and called her friend Sheryl right away, mostly out of concern but also curiosity.

"Yeah, Justin chased that poor guy up the street; and when he turned around, Justin kicked him right in the head. I've never seen anything like it Judi. For an old man he moves quite well. Of course now he can't walk!"

"Yes. Some news reports have designated you two as the *Over the Hill Gang*."

They both laughed, but Judi couldn't help but notice . . . *Justin?* Sheryl had never called The Admiral *that* before. She smiled, her mind working like an inquisitive mind will, and thought maybe there might be just a little hanky-panky going on. Women knew these things.

"Justin?" she queried.

Sheryl felt her face flush and was glad there was a land-line between them, not really understanding her sudden blush. She found herself feeling like a school girl, something she hadn't felt for years. She ignored the query.

"Judi, have you heard anything from Jeff? We didn't even know about the disaster in the Islands until we were leaving the hospital. *We*, she and Justin. She liked the sound of that.

"Nope. Haven't heard anything yet. There has been no news from any of the Cayman Islands and just a few tidbits from the others. Apparently Jamaica has had a really bad day, at least the eastern part. I heard something about a large cruise ship that was totally capsized and washed back out

11

to sea near St. Thomas. It's awful. All the news is awful." Judi was not her usual, jovial self. Who could be? Her doorbell rang and she carried her cell phone to the front door. She was expecting a package from Dr. Rosenberg.

"Hold on Sheryl. Let me see who this is. Joe is sending me a synopsis of tomorrow's speech."

Sheryl and Judi had often worked together with Dr. Joseph Rosenberg, a professor of apocalyptic religions at Emory. An interesting man to say the least.

Sheryl heard the doorbell ring once more followed by a knock and Judi saying, "I'm coming. I'm coming. Cool your cookies," followed by a scream and the sound of breaking glass, then silence as the phone went dead.

The light was bright, extraordinarily, even brighter than the dentist's light that always manages to blind you even with your eyes closed. Jeff could actually see his blood vessels winding their way through the pinkness of his closed eyelids and tried to open his eyes but couldn't. Then it was gone. Slowly he tried again, annoyed at whatever was sticking into his back. He vaguely remembered . . . something . . . water maybe? His head was killing him. It was eerily quiet, except for the sounds of the splashing water beneath him; and he was surrounded by darkness, clinging to him like a fog.

"Where the hell *am* I?" he asked out loud. There was no one to hear his question, not even the sound of nocturnal insects screaming for a mate clouded the night. Total silence, except for the water. Then he fell from the palm tree to the waters below, even before he could force his eyes open. Jeff slid into a world of unconsciousness and dreams, drifting closer to Rum Point and Stingray City.

Jeff's injuries were internal, so there was no blood to attract shark, barracuda or other predators of the sea. He alternated between unconsciousness to semi-consciousness, back and forth throughout the night. At times he was sure he saw a flash of light because his eyelids would turn pink, just for an instant. He finally forced his eyes open after one such experience only to see a sky full of stars, a Milky Way as clear as it used to be on the farmlands surrounding Charleston when he was a kid.

He continued his horizontal voyage toward the north side of the island, often bumping into *something* that floated into him, maybe a log, a table, a body. Gradually he began to recall the day's late afternoon events, the wave, Melissa washing out of his grip and over the side of the building. *Me..lis..sa* . . . He tried to shout her name, but only silence exited his salt-ridden throat. For the first time in many years, Jeffrey Ross cried and silently wondered why God was such a tease.

Gray and Andi Dorey had been close friends with Jeff and Melissa when they were married, when they were divorced, when Melissa remarried and after Melissa's new husband, a missionary, was killed in a plane crash off Puerto Rico. Before heading out to sea on their ultra-quiet, electric jet skis earlier in the day, they were convinced that whatever Jeff and Melissa once had, a special fondness, was back. They were happy for them. They were happy for themselves. There were many memories between the foursome, most good. It suddenly seemed darker, and Gray motioned Andi to head back in.

"What *was* that? Did you *feel* that, Gray?"

"I did." Gray answered his wife's question as she asked it; but he knew what had just happened wasn't normal, the sudden rise in the ocean's surface. They were stopped less than a mile out to sea, their electric jet skis nearly silent except for the occasional slap from a passing wave assaulting the yellow and green fiberglass housing.

"What do you think that was?"

"I'm not sure, but it was odd."

Gray looked back toward Seven Mile Beach, George Town just to the right. George Town, the capital of Grand Cayman, had been bustling earlier with activity, shopping and high finance. The crowds on the beach were small for the Christmas season, primarily because of the Spanish Flu; and many Europeans were not traveling because of the smallpox outbreak. The crowds, though small, were running inland. Then Gray lost sight of the beach, of George Town, the entire island had disappeared; and he rubbed his eyes in disbelief.

"Andi, I think it was a tidal wave," and in the few seconds since Andi asked the *what was that* question, the massive wave began to grow as it rushed to shore. Everything disappeared behind the height of the now towering wall of water; and then it crashed inland, skirting between the rows of buildings, pine trees ripped from the beach.

"Do you think Jeff and Melissa were still diving?" Andi was notably distressed, and the end of div-*ing* was almost an octave higher than the rest of the question.

"I hope not," was all Gray could say as the quiet, still air was insulted by the sounds of the thunderous wave crashing inland, carrying mounds of beach chairs, umbrellas, jet skis, pine trees and sea life with it. The Cayman Grand held its stature against the onslaught, as did most of the structures; the island had strict building codes and little poverty.

"What are we going to do?" Andi and Gray were stunned, almost dizzy, from the sudden turn of events. The sight was totally surreal.

"Let's go. We have to find Jeff and Melissa. Andi, we're not going to like what we see; so try to prepare yourself. There will be bodies, carcasses, ants, snakes, no telling what, floating in the water. Then there's the debris. Let's get closer, but be prepared. Most of the time there are two or three waves, often more."

As they made their way slowly and deliberately toward what had been Seven Mile Beach, the mist grew in the eyes of both Gray and Andi. They were almost sure their friends were dead, whether they were resting on the beach or had been doing a shore dive. Darkness had crept through the afternoon quickly, the sun setting in the west. It was going to be a long night.

By eight o'clock, Gray and Andi gave up their search, reluctantly. Andi was sick, and the darkness set in, the only lighting coming from the stars above. Andi threw up again.

"You OK sweets?" Gray knew she wasn't OK, who could be? The wave had not been followed by other waves, unless they were too small to detect. Seven Mile Beach was Seven Mile Beach again, George Town was only slightly flooded, but the night was silent, except for the occasional groan, or a cry from out of the distance.

"I'm not OK, Gray. Are *you*?" She wasn't angry, just worried.

The devastation looked worse than the Indonesian tsunami of 2004, at least it appeared so when viewing *live and in person*. Hundreds, maybe thousands of bodies, floating in the sea along the shore line with many just resting on the streets, in a final sleep.

"Gray, I've never seen so many dead animals. This place is going to be a field day for the birds. It's already beginning to smell. Where are we going to stay tonight?" Andi was calm.

"I would say we go back to Seven Mile Beach, see if there are any top floor rooms available that aren't heavily damaged. Or we could go to the Ritz."

"*Going to the Ritz,*" and Andi sang the jingle with a nervous laugh. "I say Cayman Grand; because I know, if Melissa and Jeff were on the beach, they would've known right away what was happening. As soon as the ocean drained out to sea, they would've headed to higher ground."

They turned their jet skis back toward Cayman Grand, moving slowly in case they hit unseen debris, or worse. Andi again felt nauseous. The indicators told the story of the jet skis' batteries; less than two hours of charge left. Gray kept his eye out for floating jet skis, battery powered or otherwise. That could very well be their only mode of transportation until they found Jeff and Melissa. *If* they found them. Then there were questions: *How were they going to get back to the United States? Was the Cayman airport damaged? How much damage would the tsunami cause to Florida and the other coasts? And what about that comet or what-ever?*

"Andi, do you think the world's ending?"

"No Gray, it's not ending. We've talked about this. Things are just *bad* right now." Andi was the ultimate optimist.

Making their way onto the very dark Seven Mile Beach, they pulled the jet skis onto shore and took the starter keys with them. Entering the hotel was not easy, the outdoor lobby now filled with dead fish, squid, people and beach chairs. There was a small dog waiting at the rear entrance, and they couldn't believe their eyes. Neither could the dog, as he came bounding into their arms, licking Andi all over her face. Every cloud has a . . . Andi thought, and the small dog brought immense joy to their hearts. *How could that dog have survived, the only life they had seen in more than three hours?*

Had Andi and Gray looked across the back parking lot still covered in four-and-a-half feet of salty sea and up into the trees, they might have spotted Jeff hanging in the very top of a palm, supported by the dark blue strap of his buoyancy compensator.

Jeff floated with the help of the inflated BC and chaise lounge cushion that had remained entangled around his leg, northward toward Stingray City off the North Shore. He also floated in and out of consciousness, mostly out. Occasionally he would awaken, sure that someone was shining a flashlight in his eyes but would see nothing except a jet-black sky with a crystal chandelier that only God could make, enhancing God's ceiling with a jewelers delight. Only he didn't believe in God, in spite of all Abe's counseling, bless his heart, the last year. These disasters were purely coincidence. Besides, he had actually prayed to God a few days earlier, to bring his best friend and his only true love, back into his life. He had actually gotten on his knees for Pete's sake. His first prayer in many years, though he knew it was nonsense. And it hadn't happened. It almost had, at least it seemed. Now she was gone, drowned probably, in a forty foot wave that came out of nowhere. Melissa . . . he drifted back into dreamland, still floating northward toward Rum Point and Stingray City. He was sure something was nibbling on his toes. One minute 'til midnight.

"JEFFREY ROSS!!!"

"Did you *hear* that?" Andi jumped out of the damp, queen-size bed of the third-floor room, a room with at *least* a semi-dry bed. She almost collided with Gray as they rushed out the sliding glass doors, now warped in a half-open position, and onto the Roman tiled balcony. The night was dark, but the Milky Way was no longer visible due to the intensity of the light in the distant sky. It was an unusual light, almost blue-white. Gray knew it was no star or supernova, at least from what he had learned last summer at the Duluth Library's *Conference on Astronomy*.

"What do you think that is Gray?" Andi had about had it with natural wonders, and her anxiety showed. "Could it be a search helicopter?" She knew that couldn't be. As quiet as it was, she would surely hear the motor in the distance.

"Nope, can't hear the motor," Gray answered. Andi couldn't help but note how smart her hubby was. "What was the noise we heard? It nearly shook me out of bed. I swear the radio on the night stand was vibrating." Gray seemed shaken. The noise had been *very* loud, much louder than thunder.

"It sounded like a loud band instrument of some kind, maybe a trombone, or trumpet, except . . ." Gray recalled his marching band days and his old high school buddy, Darrell Edwards. They would grab a trombone, a baritone, a trumpet, a tuba, any brass instrument they could find and see who could blow it the loudest and the longest without taking another breath. Used to drive his parents crazy, as well as Mr. Southwick the band director . . . He briefly wondered about his old friend Darrell but figured he was probably a famous trumpet player somewhere, maybe in Austria or Sweden, or maybe a famous symphony like the one in Charleston, where Jeff grew up. He snapped out of the day dream.

"I thought it sounded like a voice. I know it sounds crazy, but I am absolutely sure it was a voice. It was like a *shout*."

"Sounded like a horn to me." Andi insisted. "Never heard anything like it."

There was silence between them as they continued to watch the light. It really couldn't be a star, because it wasn't actually *shining* in their eyes. As intense as it was, it was more like a spotlight at the opera; focused, a beam almost like a fat blue-white laser of some kind, and very high in the sky.

CHAPTER THREE

"But about that day or hour no one knows, not even the angels in heaven, nor the Son, but only the Father." Mark 13:32 NIV

"**A**be, do you think the world is going to end in December? Everybody's talking about it, December 21, 2012; the Mayans, the Hopi Indians and Nostradamus. Every time I turn on TV there's something about the end of the world."

Pam was having serious doubts that the world would even make it to January 21, 2012, much less December 21. Everyone seemed in total denial, and Pam could see a quiet hysteria clouding the world.

"No one here seems worried about it tonight," Abe answered, observing the rapidly growing deluge of people. He considered the 1500 or so missiles journeying through space toward the dark comet. *Would it work? Could the nuclear missiles actually affect the comet's trajectory?* He would know soon. They all would.

"And don't forget the whackos who predicted May 21 would be the return of Jesus, then October 21 would be the end of the world. Bet they were surprised October 22 when they were still here." Abe chuckled but knew these sorts of things, these *false predictions*, turned unbelievers further from God. "Maybe they just didn't make the cut."

"Yeah, they put up billboards. How embarrassing."

Pam scanned the bar and dining areas, man-made fog flowing across the neon dance floor, already filled with pretty girls in gorgeous disco dresses, dancing the night away. Donna Summers sang *MacArthur Park*; and no one really seemed worried about December 21, just 11 months away. No one seemed the least-bit concerned that a 100 mile-wide comet was supposed to make a direct hit on Earth in about two weeks and end civilization, again. Sixty-five million years earlier, an asteroid killed off all the dinosaurs. It could certainly happen again. Pam smiled, as though she had a hint at what was coming. The asteroid that ended the dinosaurs was only 6 miles wide.

"No, I don't think so," Abe said. "I think 2012 could be a significant year in the whole scheme of things. There is that planetary and star alignment that only occurs every 26,000 years. That's supposed to happen December 21 and may have a gravitational effect of some kind. However, if the *Bible* is correct, and I think it is, we're at least seven to ten years away from *the end*. This comet hitting Earth is not supposed to happen until a lot of other stuff happens, if then. And the other stuff hasn't happened."

"No, but it's happening right in front of our eyes. Look at the hail storms, the outbreak of Morgellon's Disease and all the fires. Greece's olive orchards are torched, again; unprecedented forest fires in the west and midwest. More people than ever are starving because of famine." Pam was getting depressed and poured herself an early glass of champagne.

"Hollywood's version of *2012* was a fantastic movie; but in the biblical version of the end, Earth isn't here one day and gone the next. According to the people who study this stuff a lot more than I do, before the world ends there is to be a seven year period called the tribulation; a time of *great distress*, and the distress will get worse each year. You know, hail storms, hurricanes, earthquakes, volcanos . . ."

"Comets and tsunamis," Pam interrupted. "Abe, I'm not a religious scholar by any means; but there is a specific mention of a star, flaming like a torch, that falls to earth in the *last days*. It was described in John's writings two thousand years ago. That could easily be a comet. Comets look like stars falling. That's why they call meteorites 'falling stars.'"

Abe remembered the verse well. He'd been hooked on end times prophesies for a long time and the *trumpets* that would hail their oncoming disasters. He recited it in his head: *Then the third angel sounded: And a great star fell from heaven, burning like a torch, and it fell on a third of the rivers and on the springs of water.*

"And you are correct again Ms. Pam, *Revelation 8:10*. But if that were to happen now, it would not be in the prophesied time frame. I've been studying prophecies for years, and they all seem to come true. In exactly the sequence predicted. The apostles asked Jesus when *the end* would be, 2000 years ago. You know what he said, don't you?"

"He said he didn't know, that no one knew except God."

"Well, there ya go. *No one* would include the Hopis, the Maya and Nostradamus. 'No one' is pretty specific, so I don't doubt it. Like I said, they all come true. It wouldn't surprise me if we blow that comet right out of the sky. I'm a lot more worried about Jeff and Melissa," he paused, "and their friends."

"Abe, do you ever think you might be wrong?"

"About what?"

"About your religious beliefs? I know you are a *Messianic* Jew, but I'm not real sure what that is. When you were little, what made you think your beliefs were wrong?"

"I didn't think my beliefs were wrong then. One day I decided to read the *New Testament*. Then I researched the *Old Testament* references and decided my family was wrong, that they had missed the Messiah. Of course, they think I'm wrong and were really distraught when I changed my mind. You do know that all the first believers in Christ were Jewish, not gentile?" Abe paused.

"I never really thought about it. Do you ever think *your* religion is wrong, that possibly Jesus really *wasn't* the predicted Messiah?" Jeff asked.

"No. Not really. I just find myself wanting to learn more."

"Well, therein lies the problem. Everyone with a belief system thinks they're right and everyone else is wrong. It's the nature of the beast."

Abe checked his trusty Timex, 11:45. Just fifteen minutes 'til midnight. The evening had flown by.

"Let's move outside and mingle, get ready for the New Year's Disco Ball." Abe faked jubilation.

"You go ahead, Abe. I need to find Scott and tell him to give everyone free champagne at midnight. I'll meet you over by the amphitheater."

Pam turned from Abe, scanning the crowd for Scott Johnson, the assistant manager. At six-foot five, he should be easy to spot; and he was. She made her way through the unexpectedly large crowd toward the manager's office. On the way she thought about what Abe had said and wondered how much grief the little Jewish man ended up taking for converting to a Christian. She decided she would ask when the time was right. People were funny about *religion*, but Pam felt in her heart that Abe probably had a heck of a story.

Walking out of the club through the open, hand-carved, persimmon doors, Abe couldn't believe how warm the night was. The A/C had been running all night in *The Divide*, and the air inside was still a little stuffy.

He subconsciously looked up into the northern sky. The dark comet, as everyone called it after the Hutz statement, was clearly visible now, even over all the city lights. Glancing over his shoulder, he thought he heard his name, Abe blindly ran straight into the arms of Admiral McLemore and almost knocked Sheryl onto the all-brick patio.

"My goodness, I didn't know you cared so much Abe. You should've told me." They laughed out loud, and the din of the crowd grew stronger. The waitresses were working the outdoor patios and gardens, the free champagne flowing.

"Look at the crowd," The Admiral commented. "It's surprising."

"Yeah, it's huge." Abe confirmed.

"That's not what I meant," Admiral McLemore responded. "They're all looking up."

Abe noted that no one was looking toward the soon-to-ascend Disco Ball but up into the north sky, many pointing toward the comet. Abe considered the comet's brightness. It had been invisible to the naked eye just a couple of days earlier. It wasn't a *pretty* comet like the ones Abe had seen in pictures and movies. It was a dull white, more gray than white, with no tail.

"Heard anything from Jeff or Melissa?" Sheryl interrupted the sky gazing.

"Not yet. We borrowed a ham radio from Woody's Nursery. Scott's been monitoring it, but the only broadcasts he's getting from the Islands have been from Jamaica and Haiti. Seems like there have been few deaths at either place, which is hard to believe, especially in Haiti. I guess the two hours of warning gave everyone time to head to higher ground. The bad news is, one report said Grand Cayman Island had suffered a major power outage caused by solar flares. That's not good. They may have had no warning at all."

"Well, the Cayman Navy made it out of port; so *someone* knew something." The Admiral always had inside knowledge on anything *military*.

"Abe, do you know Judi Ellis?" Sheryl asked.

"I do. Dirty martini girl. Why?"

"She was attacked today at her own home by four men and is at St. Joseph's. Can you believe that? They stole both her laptops. One was Jeff's."

"Actually, I do believe it. There are youth gangs everywhere. *They're* certainly not worried about any comets hitting Earth. Is she alright?" Abe didn't know Judi well but had always admired her poise, and her legs. She did wear some short dresses sometimes, but why not? If you have the wheels, show them.

"I don't know the story. I was on the phone with her when it happened. I called the Roswell police, and they rushed to her home; probably saved her life. Thankfully, they were there in about two minutes. Never found the four guys, and Judi was only shaken. One of the four told her it was a warning to Dr. Rosenberg."

"Dr. Rosenberg?" Abe asked.

"Joe's a religious scholar who Judi works with at Emory. She schedules conferences for him."

Abe thought he had heard, or seen the name before. "By the way, how's that foot doing Admiral?" Abe winked at Sheryl. "Heard you saved an angel in distress."

"My foot's fine. I haven't kicked anyone in the head in years. And don't give me any grief, or I'll hit you with my crutch."

They ambled toward the Disco Ball, The Admiral hobbling along with Sheryl offering support; and Abe thought he might detect a romance being born. It was 11:59.

Jeff continued his voyage northward, the warm Caribbean Sea slapping against his body; and occasionally, something else. And there *was* something else, something wrapped in plastic, maybe a baggie, lying on his chest. He opened his eyes as soon as he heard his name, and the light was blinding. Just like the light he had seen the year before in Villa Rica. Out of reflex his eyelids slammed shut, reacting to the intensity. Jeff was reminded of the previous sighting of this *blip* of light and how it reminded him of the old Kodak Brownie cameras with the flash cube. If someone took your picture, you couldn't see for five minutes. He could still see the blood vessels through his closed eyelids.

"Let's go!" Gray grabbed Andi's hand and led her down the three flights of stairs. "Let's get the skis and get over there."

"Are you sure?" Andi worried about running into things in the darkness, like dead bodies. She also worried that the batteries in the jet skis might not last.

"We have to. I think Jeff's out there. The battery gauge says two hours. I'll use my headlight, and you follow me."

"Why do you think Jeff is out there?" Andi heard the same noise that Gray had heard. *JEFFREY ROSS.*

Gray hesitated, then answered. "Did you think the noise we heard sounded more like a voice or a trumpet, maybe *some* kind of horn?"

"It sounded like a loud French horn, maybe. But whatever it was, it didn't play music. It said *Jeffrey Ross*. At least that's what I heard."

"Yeah, me too. That's why we have to go."

Gray and Andi pulled the heavy jet skis into the water. The batteries that powered the craft were made of lithium, not as heavy as lead but still heavy. The silent motors started as soon as the keys were turned. Gray turned on his headlight, and they headed toward the light. There was no noise, only silence and the water that slid by the skis.

"You know what that light looks like?" Andi asked as she looked at the distant light.

Gray and Andi had been married thirty two years and were always on the same wave-length; and Gray replied, "*The Star of Bethlehem*, at least from the drawings I've seen over the years," and he admired the intensity and the narrow focus of the beam. It was truly awesome, a pin-point spotlight.

Jeff was beginning to find the light annoying. There had been no other sounds, other than his name; and now he wasn't even sure he heard his name. He may have been dreaming. Then the light spoke again, softly this time.

"Your prayer was answered."

The light went out just as Gray and Andi saw Jeff, spotlighted in the bright beam like a moth in a light.

CHAPTER FOUR

"Now I have come to explain to you what will happen to your people in the future, for the vision concerns a time yet to come." Daniel 10:14 NIV

The Nerpa 155 nuclear attack submarine wasn't in the news, at least unclassified news, but was in the mind of the navies across the world. It had suddenly disappeared a few weeks earlier in the Pacific, an apparent victim of an internal explosion while traversing the depths of the Marianas Trench. Except, Russian subs couldn't go nearly as deep as the Trench. The bottom was seven miles deep. Only one manned vessel had ever been to the bottom, the U.S. Navy *Trieste Bathyscaphe* in January, 1960.

The Marianas Trench was the deepest area in all the oceans, so finding the submarine would not be easy. Debris, clothing, a few bodies and oil had been discovered soon after the sub's disappearance. The U.S. Navy didn't buy the story for a minute, as was the case with the Israeli and British navies.

The Nerpa 155, though built in Russia, had been sold to the Indian Navy. It was Russia's most advanced nuclear attack sub. Loaded with stealth technology, most stolen from Uncle Sam, the submarine had a propulsion system that was second to none. Especially worrisome was the sub's stealth, it was *so* quiet, virtually undetectable; and the transformer-like nuclear missile pods.

The submarine crew was mainly from the Chechen Republic, a part of the old Soviet Union. Chechnya had long been a thorn in Russia's side, and Chechen Islamists had caused many deaths among the Russians. The Chechen Republic was 94% Islamic with a large, radical base. That was even more troubling.

As it approached midnight on December 31, the Nerpa-class submarine had a rendezvous planned with the Panama Canal. After that encounter, she would soon be gliding smoothly and silently through the Atlantic toward the Mediterranean, the Suez in her sights.

Diego Garcia was located in the Indian Ocean and was the home base of large U.S. bomber fleets, including the B-52 Stratofortress and the B-1B Stealth Bomber. Both had created great havoc in Iraq and Afghanistan, with Iran in their future.

Earlier the submarine had deployed a missile pod in the Atlantic off the coast of Florida, similar to the pod off Diego Garcia, consisting of two independently-guided nuclear warheads contained in the single missile, 2.5 megatons each. Two and a half million tons of TNT would cause tremendous damage, but the radiation would make the island uninhabitable for years to come.

The missile systems had been pre-programmed for midnight and would destroy much, if not all, of the Naval Submarine Base at Kings Bay, Georgia, insha'Allah.

The K-155 submarine, at a depth of 200 feet, edged closer to the Atlantic coast of Panama just before midnight. Her crew was anxious.

The night was moonless and clear, a perfect night for alligator hunting on Gatun Lake just a few miles away. Commander Julio Kadyrov had no interest in hunting anything other than that which would hurt the Americans and the Jews, like the Panama Canal.

Kadyrov *was* compassionate and had purposely chosen the Pedro Miguel Locks, because those were located in the least populated area of Panama. He had nothing against the Panamanians, but they were a sacrifice that had to be made in this Holy War. Jihad was the way; the *only* way. The Commander ordered the sub to begin surfacing. They would stop at sixty feet.

To the west, two Panamanian men, crowded in a small boat, listened for the sounds of gators swimming through the swamps.

"Hand me another beer, Gonzalo."

Gonzalo and Jorge worked together at the Gatun Lock, a part of the Panama Canal closest to the Caribbean Sea. Gatun Lake, one of the world's largest man-made lakes, was completed in 1913 specifically for the construction of the Panama Canal. The lake was one of the few recreational areas and a favorite fishing and alligatoring spot for the locals. There was a small dance hall on the south shore, along the main highway, that was the hottest spot around for socializing. It was the only spot around.

Gonzalo reached into the cooler and handed another Balboa to Jorge. "Don't get too drunk Jorgio. It's almost midnight. The wives will be home from the New Year's Eve celebrations long before we get home."

"Me get too drunk? You're the one who's drunk my friend. I can always tell when you start calling me 'Jorgio.'" They both laughed.

As Jorge turned up Panama's most famous beer for another big swig, he saw in the moonless sky the brightest light he had ever seen. "A shooting star Gonzalo. Look!"

They were mesmerized as the shooting-star progressed across the dark sky, outlined by a myriad of stars.

"That's not a shooting-star Jorgio. It's too low. Must be an airplane or somethin' man. I can hear it. You need another beer my friend."

Gonzalo explored the cooler once again and opened another beer. The cruise missile continued westward, less than a quarter mile above the surface of Gatun Lake. The fishermen's wives did not see the missile but may have heard something during the celebrations, a roar like a jet engine flying low over their small, Catholic Church.

The warm, December night welcomed the celebrants as they slowly made their way across the Duluth Towne Green toward the LED-lit Disco Ball. The Admiral was not so good on crutches, even with Sheryl's support; and he managed the steps, barely. Just 45 seconds from midnight, the large Disco Ball began its ascent. The higher it went, the more the crowd cheered, and drank. Abe could only wonder at all the jubilee this year, much more than last. *Were people in denial about the comet?*

At the stroke of midnight from the Big Ben-like clock that graced the top of Duluth's City Hall, the mayor toasted the City; and the couples kissed, as couples have done for so many years on New Year's Eve. This year was somewhat different, as three gay couples sat on the hill behind the playground and kissed passionately at midnight. The conductor, Darrell Edwards from *The Symphony*, struck up the band; and Auld Lang Zyne reigned loudly across the square, as couples of all varieties, and couples with kids, slow danced into the New Year. As many held each other tightly, moving mystically to the music, most knew the coming three weeks would be trying, waiting for Dark Comet to hit . . . somewhere.

The Admiral and Sheryl danced the best they could, at least with crutches in the picture. Just a few bars into the music, Sheryl felt light-headed. She was really beginning to like this man; and she gave him a little extra *squeeze*, sort of an *I really like you* kind of squeeze. That's when she saw the sky light up over the trees to the north of town.

The light was so bright, everyone stopped dancing; and Director Edwards brought the band to a halt. The night sky to the north continued to brighten as though it was the East and the sun was rising. The light was soon followed by a sound, a distant roar that only seemed to get louder, a sound almost of thunder but not quite. The Admiral was sure he felt the ground shake, just a bit, like a mild earthquake.

Just twenty miles north of Duluth, while the Disco Ball was rising above City Hall in the Towne Green, the two guards atop the Buford Dam had noticed a soft light deep in the water below the dam.

"What the hell's *that?*" the senior guard questioned.

"Maybe it's the submarine, you know; the tour sub at Lake Lanier Islands. They have special permission from the Corps tonight for a night dive."

"They don't have special permission to be *there!*" the senior exclaimed. He grabbed his radio; but before the call button could be pressed, both guards vanished in a flash of heat that was hotter than the surface of the sun. They would have certainly been blinded by the light had they not been vaporized first.

Buford Dam, as thick and well-constructed as any dam in the country, began to crack at the base, underwater. The top half of the dam had disappeared with the two guards.

A few midnight fishermen graced some of the rocks in the Chattahoochee River downstream, some in Suwanee and some in Duluth. It was a New Year's Eve ritual for many. They were all startled when the warning sirens went off shortly after midnight, an automatic warning system to let those downstream know when the dam was releasing water. But the dam wasn't supposed to be releasing water at midnight. Everyone who knew anything about the river knew that.

The two fishermen on one large rock at Jones Bridge Park looked at each other. "Musta been a mistake," one said; and they threw their lines back in the water.

The roar on the Chattahoochee grew louder as the large mass of Lake Lanier was finally free from the constraints that had held it back for so many years.

Atlanta and many communities downstream would never be the same after this night.

The Chattahoochee roared.

CHAPTER FIVE

January 3

"*This is Condi Zimmerman reporting from Duluth, Georgia's WJLR-Newsradio. I am at a Duluth icon, the famous Rexall Grill. I say 'famous' because a few years back, during the Runaway Bride event that everyone seems to want to forget, the Rexall Grill became the meeting place for all the press. Suddenly, the Rexall Grill became an international name.*

"*Some of you may remember that I was in Tel Aviv at that time; and right there, on Israeli television, was the Rexall. I never thought I would be here, and I certainly do wish I was here for the Chicken 'n Dressing instead of the devastating news that brought me.*

"*At midnight on New Year's Eve, the Buford Dam, about 20 miles north of Duluth, was severely damaged by what now has been confirmed as America's first nuclear attack on U.S. soil.*"

The thought briefly crossed Condi's mind, had there been a first nuclear strike on *non-U.S.* soil?

"*The top half of Buford Dam was found about a quarter mile away, and fractures along the base of the dam have required evacuations of all remaining citizens and pets along what is now the new, expanded banks of the Chattahoochee River. Farm animals will be the next priority.*

"*Homeland Security has given no statement on the yield of the nuclear weapon; but Dr. Dan Brunson, a physicist and graduate of Georgia Tech, is joining us at the Rexall Grill.*

"*Dr. Brunson, you have viewed the damage at Buford Dam. Can you assess the size of the nuclear explosion, and how exactly do we know it was a nuclear explosion?*"

Dan Brunson moved to the front of the room from one of the blue, vinyl booths adorned with *Coca-Cola* and *Gone with the Wind* memorabilia.

"Ms. Zimmerman, I really cannot estimate the explosive yield from a flyover, but it took a mighty explosion to cause the visible damage; and the damage to the base of the dam is being reviewed at this time by the Army Corps of Engineers. A 'best guess' would be 2-3 kilotons. That's about a fifth the size of the Hiroshima event. As far as how do we know it was nuclear; it only takes a Geiger Counter. Radiation levels are high around the dam."

Condi thanked Dr. Brunson for his brief statement, and continued.

"The damage that has occurred downstream from the dam, along the Chattahoochee flood plain, is significant. Large parts of Suwanee, Duluth, Roswell, all North Atlanta suburbs, have been heavily damaged. Large areas of western sections of Atlanta are underwater. Damage further downstream has occurred in Columbus, where the downtown is underwater, Eufaula, Alabama and of course, Apalachicola, Florida, where the Chattahoochee terminates.

"The number of folk drowned is unknown but will be in the hundreds, if not thousands. There are dead cattle, horses, dogs, cats, you name it, everywhere. The cleanup will be long-term and very expensive."

The phone rang at *The Divide*, and Abe answered.

"Abe, this is Chad."

"Hey Chadbo. Are you in Atlanta?" Abe was at the restaurant cleaning up, and his spirits lifted. He really liked Chad Myers, NEO expert extraordinaire.

Restaurants were some of the few places that would remain open, at least until the comet either hit or missed, or the world ended, whichever came first. Abe was beginning to have his own doubts, even though a comet-strike didn't really seem to be in the biblical picture that he remembered. All those scientists couldn't be wrong, could they? Other than essential businesses, grocery stores, hospitals, gas stations and pharmacies, most all other businesses had been closed by order of the federal government. The National Guard and local police were maintaining the peace in most large American cities and many of the more rural areas.

"No, I'm at Goddard Space Center but will be leaving soon for JPL in Pasadena. Have you heard anything from Jeff and Melissa; or their friends?"

"We haven't heard anything at all. The Caymans, Cuba and Puerto Rico seem to be the hardest hit in the northern Caribbean. Haiti and Jamaica heeded the warnings, and most managed to evacuate low-lying areas. Grand Cayman was without power and had no warning. I guess communicat . . ." Abe stopped in his tracks.

"Abe, are you there? Hello?"

"Wait a minute. I'm going to turn up the news. I'll put you on speaker, so you can hear. Hold on."

"*. . . and have not found the missing woman, Melissa Ross-Jeremias from Sandy Springs, Georgia; just north of Atlanta. The few available ships in the area, since most boats around Cayman were thrown on land or sank, are searching and aiding in the rescue effort.*

"*The three people rescued by a Cayman Navy ship have been identified as Jeffrey Ross, Gray Dorey and Andi Dorey. Andi was the first to spot Mr. Ross floating in the ocean about a mile from Rum Point on Grand Cayman Island. He was semi-conscious when rescued and hallucinating about a bright light or UFO.*

"*Mr. Ross was flown by the U.S. Navy to Atlanta, Georgia, where he is at an undisclosed hospital for treatment. All indications are, his injuries are miraculously minor, considering all he has been through. Both of the Doreys, not sure what their relationship is, were uninjured because they were on jet skis about a mile away from the island when the tsunami hit.*

"*Rich, did you know that? I had no idea that a forty-foot tsunami only measured about a foot a mile out in the ocean. That's amazing.*"

Abe turned the TV sound to mute before Rich Badey could let Condi know if he knew or not.

"Did you hear all that?"

"That's good news, I guess. Please keep me posted about Melissa, about everything. I'm sure they will find her. As soon as you find out where Jeff is, let me know. I have to talk to him about the comet."

"What's going on with the comet?"

"Can't tell ya Abe. If I did, I'd have to kill ya." Chad laughed, a giant emotional turnaround from a few minutes earlier. "Actually, I *can't* tell you; but you will hear something on the news in the next few days. Ever heard of the National Ignition Facility in Livermore, California?"

"Can't say that I have. What is it?"

"Too much to explain. I have to get to Andrews Air Force Base so I don't miss my flight. Google it. Gotta go. Call me as soon as you know something." The line went dead.

"*Folks are cleaning up from the four-foot waves along the Atlantic Coast from Florida to New Jersey. The tsunami had minimal effect along the Gulf*

Coast, but many Caribbean Islands and the Bahamas have been devastated. We are still awaiting reports from Central and South America.

"Speaking of Central America, we have reports, though these have not been verified, of some kind of explosion near the Panama Canal.

"And finally this: The Captain of a cruise ship leaving Ft. Lauderdale for Bermuda reported seeing a pair of small, mid-air explosions over the Atlantic between Cape Canaveral and Jacksonville, just after midnight January 1st. There has been no verification from the FAA, NASA, Homeland Security or the military."

CHAPTER SIX

Korengal Valley, Afghanistan

Muhammed, Mehdi and several other jihadists were gathered at Muhammed's home, a cave-home mostly set into the hillside like so many of the others in the *Valley of Death* along the Afghanistan-Pakistan border. Aludra, Muhammed's sister, was having misgivings about her Muslim faith as she swept the dirt floor with a broom made of corn shoots. She didn't associate with the men, a custom that she dared not break; but she listened intently, picking up bits-and-pieces of their rapid and animated conversations. She was sure she heard "nuclear" but unsure of the meaning or context. The five men seemed worried, except for Ahmed. Even the disgusting Mehdi seemed worried.

Aludra thought about Mehdi and his life. He was the son of an Iranian father, a Shi'ite Muslim, and a Saudi mother, a Sunni. Mehdi's name was a derivative of Midha, meaning "praise," and Mehdi, meaning *Mahdi*, a name for the soon-to-come Twelfth Imam, the Islamic Savior. She couldn't help but laugh, silently. *If the Twelfth Imam is Mehdi, the infidels have nothing to worry about*, she thought. And he certainly wasn't praise-worthy. He would sell his mother for a chance at seventy-two virgins in paradise. Even Muhammed seemed to be tiring of his long friendship with Mehdi.

"What do you think the Americans will do Muhammed?" Mehdi chewed a piece of lamb jerky. He wiped his runny nose on his sleeve and spit on the recently swept floor.

Though Aludra found Mehdi totally repulsive, so were most of Muhammed's friends. All they talked about was killing and bombings, and their hatred of the Jews and Christians, always discussing ways to bring more carnage to the world. All in the name of Allah. Aludra was tired of the Valley and often wished she had never returned from Paris, but she was an Afghani. Plus her brother needed her. Muhammed didn't deserve to be alone without family. Both of their parents were dead, killed by a U.S. drone attack the previous year.

When she paused to serve the men tea, she saw the *New Testament* and couldn't believe she had not hidden it. Even her brother would probably beat her if he saw it, maybe worse. Mehdi would kill her for sure. Of course, she was sure he would have his way with her first. She had noticed Mehdi's suggestive glances. Mehdi already had three wives, and she would not be his fourth. She would die first. She set the teapot down by the fire, walked to her area and nonchalantly picked the book up and hid it in her bedding.

"Where's the tea Aludra?" Mehdi shouted as though she were across the soccer field. *You want hot tea, you got hot tea*, she thought to herself, a slight smirk adorning her olive face.

"They don't know who did it, so who can they bomb? No big deal." Ahmed wasn't worried. He only wanted to get on with the war against the infidels. Aludra set Ahmed's hot tea in front of him on the small, dingy table. He thanked her. The table was wobbly.

"Ahmed, we don't know *what* they know," Muhammed scolded. "Their technology doesn't miss much, so we must not become complacent."

Aludra moved around the table slowly, trying to stay out-of-sight, out-of-mind, like most Muslim women did. She served the other men, waiting last for Mehdi.

"Hurry Aludra. I'm thirsty," Mehdi demanded. *What a pig.* She moved toward Mehdi and stumbled, the rest of the hot tea landing squarely in Mehdi's lap, the scalding tea assuring that Mehdi wouldn't need a fourth wife in the near future.

Mehdi jumped out of his seat like the Jack in the Box that she had seen in a Parisian toy store and slapped Aludra hard across the face. She fell backwards, stumbling over the home-made broom and hit the dirt floor with a *thud*.

Muhammed stood, grabbed Mehdi's arm and forced him into his seat. He did not assist his sister but would later. Aludra did not cry from the pain or from the humiliation. She picked herself up and moved unsteadily toward the back, her nose and mouth bleeding.

Muhammed had spoken with some of his Chechen allies to the north. He planned to send Aludra to Chechnya, anything to save his dear sister, if necessary. He would arrange it with his cousin, now known as Yousef since he changed his name and became a "Christian." Muhammed smiled at that thought. Except for Allah and Muhammad, may peace be upon him, Aludra was his only love. He knew the Americans could not be taken for granted. Or the Israelis. *Especially* the Israelis.

"Ahh, we shall not become complacent," answered Ahmed. "But the time is good. The American President is nearly dead from the flu, and much of Washington is shut down. The White House, Senate and Congress are in quarantine." The thought crossed Ahmed's mind that Allah might take care of the infidels for them. There were plagues, droughts, flu and comets. Allah was helping his true servants.

Muhammed didn't think the West would resort to retaliation by *nuclear* weapons. Ahmed was correct, they really didn't know where to bomb. But then, a decade earlier they had never figured on President George Bush's response either. They knew there would be a response, just hoped not *that* response. It had caught much of the jihadist world by surprise. Muhammed knew that Saddam Hussein would still be alive had he not underestimated the will of Bush. Bush had been a warrior, but the next president had not. Soon there would be another. Muhammed wished the Americans wouldn't change presidents so often, though it was a gift from Allah that Bush was gone.

The meeting finally ended, and the men stood to leave. The dusty floor negated Aludra's previous sweeping efforts; and the men shuffled down the path, their sandals filling with dust.

"Mehdi, you stay here. We need to talk about Aboud's future plans in the United States. Do you mind?"

"No Muhammed; I like Vinny."

After the others left, Muhammed walked to the icebox and grabbed two of the *Cristal* bottled waters. The bottled water was the first ever bottled by an Afghani company, and a case had been stolen in a recent raid. The water was like none other and was revered in the Valley.

He wiped the water off the outside of the polystyrene bottle and returned to the table. He heard Aludra stirring in her quarters. She did not weep, but Muhammed's blood was boiling.

"Do you like the new bottled water, Mehdi?"

"Yes Muhammed. A gift from Allah?" He laughed.

As Muhammed placed Mehdi's water on the rickety table, the table tilted; and the bottle of water flew into the air. Mehdi's instincts were quick as a cat, and he caught the bottle in midair. With a single quick motion, Mehdi's throat was cut with the knife Aludra had used earlier to cut up the lamb for the stew; and his head dropped back over the edge of the chair, nearly severed.

"That's good," Muhammed said. "Have a drink," and he poured the bottle of water directly down Mehdi's throat, blood spilling to, and being absorbed by, the ground.

"You will never slap my sister again you dirty, filthy son-of-a-dog. May the wild dogs eat your flesh."

Muhammed pulled the body outside the cave, down the trail and into the garbage dumping grounds, referred to locally as Gehenna. There, Mehdi would burn with the rest of the garbage. In Gehenna, Mehdi would join the numerous other bodies that were disposed of there on a daily basis. Life in the Korengal Valley was rough.

CHAPTER SEVEN

The Admiral and Sheryl were called back to Washington, meetings galore. Sheryl left on an early flight out of Hartsfield-Jackson; and The Admiral would follow later, after a meeting at Georgia Tech.

Sheryl's flight was non-eventful, other than the unusual turbulence as they approached Ronald Reagan International. The plane landed safely, and Sheryl pulled the navy-blue carry-on behind her, the small plastic wheels "clacking" over the seams in the porcelain, tile floor. The airport was remarkably quiet, almost empty.

Exiting the airport, her chauffeured government car waited by the curb in the VIP area. The driver exited the black Cadillac, walked to the back and placed the carry-on into the trunk.

"Hey Sal, how ya doin'?" He opened the heavy, back door and Sheryl entered the two year old Cadillac. She had always liked Sal. He was funny and personable, and he knew all the shortcuts in the D.C. traffic network. As they traveled toward Sheryl's Georgetown townhome, Washington appeared almost ghostly, at least for a weekday. Nearly every business was closed. There was hardly any traffic. The few people walking the streets were wearing surgical facemasks, thinking that the mask would somehow protect them from the flu. Sheryl knew the virus would go through the mask as though it wasn't there; but if that made the populous more comfortable, so be it.

The chauffeur turned left onto Wisconsin Avenue, only to be blocked by the Washington, D.C. police. There were several fire trucks, armored personnel carriers and ambulances parked along the street, apparently on standby. Blue light reflections danced from police car to police car, up and down the street.

Sheryl lowered the electric window, showed the police woman her ID and asked what was going on.

"Bomb scare, we think. At least we hope it's a scare. We've been kept pretty much in the dark, ma'am. If you will turn around and take a right on M Street, you should be able to make it to Georgetown Row."

Sheryl thanked the young lady, told her to keep her chin up and that she was doing a great job for the nation, not just Washington. Sal made a U-turn, headed down Wisconsin toward M Street and made the right turn just as the explosion occurred; and it was a big one. Out the passenger side window, Sheryl saw the violent ball of orange and angry red, lifting skyward, another bombing. Bombings were becoming routine. Her iPhone chirped. It was The Admiral.

"Sheryl, I just arrived at Andrews Air Force Base. Have you been to the Capitol yet?"

"Hi Justin. No, I'm on my way home. I'll be heading in shortly."

"Don't bother. Just talked to Dan Brumfield, the President's spokesman. Appears Dan is one of the few in D.C. who seems to have an immunity to the Spanish Flu. The Capitol, White House and surrounding areas are under quarantine; and the CDC has set up a base of operations. Dan suggested we return to Atlanta and conduct meetings via secure video conferencing. The White House staff is relocating to Warner Robbins."

"Well, it would've been nice if they had told us in advance." Sheryl huffed. "They had to know."

Dan said they made attempts; but the solar activity is so elevated, communications wouldn't go through. Want me to wait for you?"

Sheryl did want Justin to wait and felt a certain . . . *tingle.* However, duty first. She knew time was wasting. Darn. *Finally*, a man she was truly becoming interested in; and a comet was getting ready to destroy the known world. What luck.

"You go ahead Justin. I'll catch a plane out of Ronald Reagan. Dulles has been closed until further notice, and Ronald Reagan is likely to close soon. I will call as soon as I arrive back in Atlanta. I'll meet you at Jeff's house, and we'll stay there."

The phones disconnected, but the background static had been annoying. *Solar flares* she figured.

"Make a U-turn, Sal."

"What's wrong Ms. Lasseter?"

"Back to Ron Reagan, Sal. Meetings have been cancelled. Washington has been cancelled." Now she knew why there was so little traffic.

Returning to Wisconsin Avenue, Sheryl grabbed the remote and turned on C-Span. The halls of congress were nearly deserted too. The young, handsome congressman from Florida was speaking.

"*Today we have learned that while Spanish Flu has virtually made Washington a ghost town, the smallpox outbreak in Europe appears to be worse. There have been nearly 12,000 deaths out of 30,000 cases the last year, this from a disease that was supposedly eradicated in 1979. There is no vaccine to speak of because of recent decisions to do away with the smallpox virus inventory located at CDC in Atlanta and the Russian State Research Center of Virology and Biotechnology in Koltsovo.*

"*To the members of Congress, I ask this question: Where do we get the necessary vaccines to cure our great nation? The foremost immunologist in the country is getting ready to go on trial in Atlanta for unleashing this plague, yet Samarra Russell is our best bet for survival.*

"*I am calling on the U.S. Congress to take necessary, vital action at this time. We need to quarantine the nation. We have had thirteen outbreaks of smallpox in New Jersey. It is time to take action.*"

The Congressman from Florida finished his speech to the applause of the three congressmen and one congresswoman in attendance, then had a sneezing attack. Grabbing a tissue from his trouser pocket, the congressman wiped his mouth and nose. There was blood discharge from his mouth and both nostrils. The other congressmen looked on in horror as he spasmed and collapsed to the floor.

CHAPTER EIGHT

"**A**be, do you think God causes earthquakes?"

Jeff's spirits were fairly good, considering. He had made little conversation since returning to his Sugarloaf home from the hospital and had not talked about the loss of Melissa. Every time the subject was broached, Jeff would give the time-out sign with his hands, saying he wasn't ready. Then his eyes would moisten.

"That's funny. I had another friend ask me that a few weeks ago. What do you mean?" Abe the Bartender knew that God could do or cause pretty much anything but didn't believe that he caused everything bad.

This was Jeff's first visit to Duluth's newest night spot since returning from Grand Cayman via Navy medical helicopter. *The Divide* was empty, except for Abe, Jeff and Pam, who was in the manager's office with Scott. It would probably remain empty until the comet hit, or missed. Abe hoped, for Jeff's sake, that his mourning period would not last too long; but then, if the dark comet did hit Earth, the mourning period would be brief, most likely. Melissa had been his life; and even after his divorce, he always thought she would come back. Even when she married Rob Jeremias, he still never lost the hope that one day she would return.

"What I mean is, do you think the God *you* believe in causes earthquakes, disease and plagues, hail storms, whatever? Like all the disasters throughout the history of mankind. Do you believe that God, or *some* supernatural force, actually causes that, intentionally? That's a hard thing to believe. Like the Indonesia tsunami of 2004?"

"Or the tsunami in the Caymans last week?" Abe asked.

"Exactly." Jeff's mood was in a downswing. Why wouldn't it be?

Abe thought about the question for a few seconds before responding.

"I believe in the God of the Old and New Testaments, not some new age, feel-good religion type god. I believe in the God who said he would love us unconditionally and guide us through discipline. We now call the discipline thing, karma. But think about it Jeff. If Audry ran into traffic when she was three because you lost sight of her for a second, would you talk to her calmly or scare her?"

"I'd scare the you-know-what out of her!"

Jeff had neglected Audry, at least he felt he had; and she would surely need him now. She had spent much of the last year in Raleigh with her cousin Sherri, was supposed to fly to Grand Cayman to join him and Melissa, but . . . She would be back in Atlanta tomorrow, and he looked forward to picking her up at the airport.

"*Exactly.* Sometimes God does that to us. There is a different line of thought among some Christians and Jews, that God does not 'punish,' because he is a 'loving God' and would not dare do that. To them, all I can say is, read *Proverbs*. Discipline *is* love. Just look at all the undisciplined children running around, especially in single-parent homes; because so many parents want to be 'friends' with their children rather than discipline them. I see God as the *ultimate* parent, the *Parent* of all parents. He's unwaveringly patient, tolerant, forgiving, loving, just and authoritarian. That's what I believe. He said it many times, *spare the rod, spoil the child.* Or something like that . . ."

"He *never* said that!" Jeff made the comment as though he was proud of himself in some sort of way, a gotcha moment. He learned that the comment wasn't really in the *Bible* as so often quoted. He couldn't remember where he read that but knew it was true.

"You're right. In *Proverbs*, those exact words are not mentioned, though *Proverbs* is often given credit. However, it did allude to the 'rod' numerous times when it came to love and discipline. At the time it was written, rods were used in shepherding to control the sheep. In a lot of ways, I think God considers us to be his sheep. Sometimes some really bad stuff happens to us, but some really worse stuff could happen to us were it not for the rod . . . or karma. Just think about it."

"You didn't answer my question." Jeff was determined.

"I believe that God created the Universe, that it wasn't here, and then it was. Like magic. That's what I believe, just like it said in *Genesis*. Because of that, I believe that God can do anything he wants to do, as fast as he wants to do it, as often as he wants to and his time frame is not our time frame. I don't have a clue why he is there, except the *Bible* indicates that he made us for his entertainment, at least that's the way some interpret it. That's good enough for me. I'm glad I'm here."

"So you believe that God actually created everything in seven days?" Jeff was always amazed that some people believed such nonsense.

"How long is seven days to God? That's the question. It got light and then dark. That might have been twenty-four hours, but it could just as easily have been much longer. I do not think that every earthquake, hurricane, tornado or mudslide is God's doing if that's what you're asking. Also, it's confusing that you didn't ask if the devil could be causing it. The devil is described as the ruler of *this* world, so why does God get all the blame?"

"I'll tell you."

Jeff turned toward the gravelly voice but didn't recognize the stranger who made the comment. He was tall, thin, dressed in black pants, black sweater, ivory ascot and a black leather Ivy League cap. He appeared very debonair, or *suavé bollo* as Diana Hendricks, the head waitress, would say.

"I'm sorry. I don't mean to intrude but heard parts of your conversation. I'm Michael." Michael extended his hand, and the three met.

Abe seemed miffed. He had not seen the man come through the french-doored entrance, nor had he heard him. The man was tall, hard to have missed.

"The devil is slick. He's *so* slick that he's convinced most people that he doesn't even exist, even some churches. But he does. He is not red, doesn't have any horns or a tail, can appear human and very likeable. He is the best salesman in this world. He creates all sorts of havoc and then manipulates the populous into thinking God did it. He's great with the media and the Hollywood set and manipulates them regularly.

"Have you not read that the devil is the god of this age and has blinded the minds of unbelievers, so that they cannot see the light of the gospel?"

"Where does it say that?" Jeff asked the stranger. "Plus, isn't there only one God?"

"I'll not tell you. Google it and you will remember better, Jeff Ross. Start with the first of the ten."

"First of the ten what?" Jeff asked. Jeff had not told the stranger his last name. Nor had Abe. He hadn't even told him his first name.

"The first commandment! It specifically says, 'You shall have no other gods before me.' That would indicate that God is numero uno, but there are other *lesser gods* out there, at least that's the way I read it. Or He would've said, 'There are no gods but me.'

"The light you saw in the sky, did it comfort you or scare you?"

"What light?" Jeff wondered if the stranger was talking about *blip*, the light that seemed to be haunting him for over a year. Plus, how would Michael know about *that*?

Michael looked Jeff in the eyes, penetrating to the depths of his soul and said softly, almost lyrically, "You know the light. You've seen it. You saw it last week in Grand Cayman. That light is no accident Jeff. You are being called."

Jeff turned around momentarily, and asked Abe to get him another Duckhorn. Abe walked to the wine display, chose a fresh bottle of merlot and returned to the bar.

"Where did Michael go?" he asked.

Jeff turned quickly, but the stranger was nowhere to be seen. Jeff was sure he hadn't gone to the men's room, or he would've seen him walk around the bar.

"I don't have a clue. That's very, very odd." And Jeff wondered how this total stranger knew about *blip*. Hardly anyone had seen the light, because there had never been any other reports. It seemed that only Jeff and Abe had seen the *blip*, at least until last week when Gray and Andi were guided by it to Jeff's rescue. And now this stranger.

Life was getting interesting; and Jeff thought back to his rescue, a *Gideon Bible* lying on his chest, wrapped in a baggie. The mystery deepened.

CHAPTER NINE

The Admiral and Sheryl approached the temporary *Oval Office*, a little trepidation in their step, and saw the new Chief of Homeland Security, Abu Hassan, in the lobby. They greeted with handshakes all around, but The Admiral had mixed feelings about Hassan. It just didn't seem quite right to have a Muslim-American as the new head of HS, but he contained his thoughts. Otherwise, he would be painted as a bigot. They were soon joined by the Secretary of Defense and the head of the CIA.

Now seated with coffee and cokes served, the serving staff exited. The Vice President called the meeting to order.

"Thanks to all of you for coming to Warner Robins Air Force Base to attend this meeting on such short notice. I understand the holidays are just getting over, but we have a lot to discuss. My spokesman, Dr. Brumfield, will bring everyone up to date. Dan?"

Dan Brumfield; tall, dark, handsome and single, approached the podium. He had become a hit with the ladies in the area, and he was rapidly becoming fond of Southern ladies.

"Thank you Mr. Vice President. All information you hear today in this meeting is classified.

"We have a hell of a mess to say the least, not just here in the United States but virtually every other country in existence. I will not paint a rosy picture, since there is nothing rosy about any of the possible scenarios.

"The near destruction of Buford Dam north of Atlanta has been described in the media as our 'first' nuclear attack. That's not true. It is the first *successful* nuclear attack against the United States on U.S. soil.

"At midnight December 31, there were a total of five other nuclear attacks, only three of which were successful; the one that hit Panama Canal, the one that hit Diego Garcia and Buford Dam in Georgia. Diego has been rendered *not habitable*. Any aircraft and facilities that weren't destroyed on the main base are too hot to approach. Radiation levels are sky-high.

"The Canal is now shut to all seafaring traffic and will be for months to come. The ongoing construction of the second canal has also been stopped. We do not know for sure, at least *absolutely* sure, who fired the cruise-type missile; but it was tracked by military logistics satellites. The missile was fired off the Caribbean coast of Panama at midnight. The missile proceeded several hundred miles to the Pedro Miguel Locks and detonated approximately one-quarter mile above ground. The locks have been fused in the positions they were in at the time of the detonation. So far we have no accurate casualty reports, but the area is not highly populated. The yield of the explosion appears to be 15-20 kilotons, about the size of the bomb dropped on Hiroshima.

"The other attacks, which have not been reported, thankfully, occurred on U.S. military targets, also precisely at midnight. One missile was fired just north of Diego Garcia. The missile launched from below the surface of the water and was of the MIRV variety, Multiple Independently Targetable Reentry Vehicles. The semi-ballistic missile contained two warheads, and the estimated deliverable load was 4-5 megatons. Four *million* tons of TNT.

"Fortunately for Diego Garcia, the U.S.-Israeli joint missile defense system was operational. Unfortunately, the defense system was half successful and eliminated only one of the warheads. The other successfully detonated right over the B-1B bomber facilities. Runways are damaged, radiation levels remain high. Most of the airmen have been killed or maimed. U.S. Naval forces have responded and are stationed around the islands. First reports are sketchy.

"Just after midnight December 31, a missile similar to the one launched in the Indian Ocean was detected by military satellites off the Atlantic Coast, about 200 miles east of West Palm Beach. Again, there were two independent warheads detected; and it appears that one was targeting St. Mary's Submarine Base in Georgia. The other was probably headed to Norfolk.

"The Aegis rail-gun defense system worked flawlessly in this case, and both warheads were destroyed well above Earth. If they had hit with the same mega-tonnage as the Indian Ocean missiles, St. Marys would have been history. Needless to say, President Reagan's vision of the so-called 'Star Wars' defense system worked flawlessly.

"Then there are the disappearances. Last year almost 150,000 people vanished off the face of the Earth. Every country has experienced some losses, and no one seems to have a clue as to what happened to these people. At first, the churches were proclaiming it was the rapture; but they have cooled on that assessment. Apparently the thinking is, had the rapture occurred, why are all the Christians still here? I know nothing about this *rapture* event, but the disappearance is a complete mystery. There have been no other reports of mass disappearances since last fall.

"All this, however, becomes irrelevant in the whole scheme of things. The dark comet . . . does anyone know where that name came from? . . . is expected to hit Earth in a few days. The impact zone is thought to be the North Atlantic. Should that happen, the impact should cause tsunamis world-wide, or worse. The eastern coasts of Canada, the U.S., Central and South America, as well as the western coasts of Europe and Africa can expect tidal waves that could be three thousand feet high. That's more than a half mile folks.

"Because of this anticipated impact, all aggressive military activity will be on hold until February 1. Should a miracle happen and the comet misses Earth, the first primary objective will be to rout Korengal Valley along the Pakistan-Afghanistan border."

"Dr. Brumfield," Sheryl interrupted, "What do you mean by 'rout?'"

"There is a general consensus in Europe and the U.S. that the Valley of Death needs to be cleansed. That's all I can say at this time. Whatever needs to be done, will be done.

"Mr. Vice President?" Dan returned the podium to the Vice President.

"Thanks again for coming. I know it's not convenient but is necessary. For the next few weeks, my staff and I will work out of secure bunkers here at Warner Robins where our medical conditions will be constantly monitored. Congress is calling for a total quarantine, but that is not in the picture at the moment."

"What about martial law? There's been a lot of looting and arson." The question *had* to be asked, and The Admiral asked it.

"That has not been discussed. Keep all your lines of communication open. Within a few more hours, we will either be here, or we won't. I know you would like to spend, possibly the last hours of your lives, with family. Your calling is the country first. Please remain accessible. Things are changing by the minute.

"Have a safe trip back to Atlanta. May God be with you. May He be with us all."

Chapter Ten

The night was dark, and the alleyway was darker. The amber-colored, high-pressure sodium streetlights had long ago burned out, victims of the economy. The odor from the overflowing dumpster was pungent, acrid. As he lay alongside the brick outcropping, using a half-gallon milk jug as a pillow, Ed tried to sleep. The alleyway was wet, and Ed wasn't sure if it was from rain or from bladder relief of the many homeless that dwelled in this area of Atlanta. The smell of ammonia answered the question. His stomach spoke to him, growling with hunger.

Ed again eyed the dead rat lying by the dumpster, not with hunger in mind, but curiosity. He had seen three different cats approach the mouse, take a few subtle, cat-like whiffs and walk away looking for other prey. Not many cats turn down a dead mouse, unless . . .

Trained in the U.S. Army, Ed served in Special Ops during both Iraq wars. He'd finally seen too much for him to bear; and he returned from the war, turning to alcohol and meth to blur his wounded memories. He slept in abandoned cars, houses or alleyways, as was the case tonight. Maybe he would go to the shelter, stop by *Dine for Dollars* and grab something to eat. Did he have a dollar?

Reaching into the right pocket of his dingy, gray trousers, he felt something, maybe two dollars. Withdrawing his hand, there was a single dollar and a business card from Gray Dorey. Mr. Dorey had given him the business card the last time he went to *Dine for Dollars* and had bought Ed's lunch, depositing a dollar into the common bank they all shared, a five-gallon plastic jug sitting at the far side of the chow line. Gray threw in a few extra, just to cover someone who may not have a dollar. There were plenty of those walking the streets.

The dead rat troubled him as he watched another cat, this one solid black with matted hair. He too sniffed the carcass and then moved on, letting out a *meow* of frustration.

Ed managed to get up off the damp alleyway and made his way over to the dead rat. During his Special Ops studies, he remembered reading about some of the methods the CIA had used in the past to convey messages during the Cold War. One plan included dead rats or other vermin. They would catch the animal, euthanize it, slit the belly open and hide microfilm inside the animal. Then they would stitch it up and deposit the creature in an alleyway or roadway by a garbage can, or dumpster. The idea had some initial problems, with cats often carting the microfilm away. Then they discovered Tabasco Sauce. Dash a little Tabasco on the carcass, and the cats would take a quick sniff and high-tail it. Just like what was happening with *this* rat carcass.

Leaning over, Ed picked up the rat by its long, gray tail, the carcass stiff with rigor mortis. He held the rat in his palm and parted the creature's legs. At first he couldn't believe what he was seeing; but there it was, a sutured belly just like he had seen in the graphics he studied.

Ed had few possessions, but he did have a small knife. A man never knew when he might need a knife, or a lighter; and Ed always kept both. He cut the sutures and pried the incision open with the sharp knife blade. The blood had long ago coagulated. He prodded the abdomen with his knife, when suddenly he felt something, something *non*-animal. He removed the small but easily discernible microchip and examined it under the neon sign just outside *Joe's Bar*. He wasn't sure what it was; but it was *something*, he *was* sure of that.

He mentally debated on what he should do next; go to the police maybe, or the FBI? They would never believe him, probably arrest him and throw him in jail. That had happened too many times already. He put the chip in his pocket and removed the business card. Maybe he would go see Mr. Dorey. Hadn't he mentioned that he knew some military intelligence people?

Ed walked back across the damp alley and briefly stopped under the *Joe's Bar* neon sign. Bending over he grabbed his small bag of personal items and again fondled the small chip in his pants pocket, just to make sure it was still there. He never saw the white business card fall from his shirt pocket, actually a *personal* card with his name. As night gave way to dawn, he walked out of the alley, turned right on 5th Street and headed to *Dine for Dollars*. Maybe Mr. Dorey would be there early.

CHAPTER ELEVEN

"Gray, get up! We have to get downtown and serve breakfast. It's late!"

It was 5:30, and Andi knew the sun would be rising before they made it to the diner. She also knew that Gray was tired. He had been since the Cayman trip that didn't exactly turn out to be relaxing. They had planned on staying in the Islands until the comet either hit or missed, but that was before the tsunami. All resorts were now closed until further notice.

"Nooooo, honey. Can we just miss one day? Just one day, that's all I ask. Please?"

"No Gray, we can't. Several people are not coming to work because of this God-forsaken comet. You know, the comet may not hit! I'll make some coffee. And besides, the *Bible* didn't say anything about a comet destroying civilization."

Or did it? She was certainly not a *Bible* scholar, but her grandmother had been; and Granny Kirby had never mentioned a comet or anything wiping out the Earth. She had mentioned something about fire though. Her thoughts drifted.

She hit the ON button, and the morning news alert appeared on the flat screen, as usual. Since 9/11 there had been an abundance of "news alerts," most not alerts at all; unless one considered a fire in a record warehouse or a bear falling out of a tree, a *news alert*. Andi twirled out of the bedroom and into the kitchen, her white, silk robe making the sounds that silk robes make, a *silky* sound.

"For decades, what several U.S. Presidents and world leaders could not do, the dark comet has done; rid the world of nuclear weapons, or at least many.

At this moment, there are approximately 1500 ballistic missiles, the number is classified for whatever reason, headed toward the mysterious dark object."

Erica Robbins paused her report and reminisced about her days as a war correspondent, almost longingly. This was far more stressful. In a war zone, you could always find a place to hide. How does one hide from a one hundred-mile-wide comet?

Andi's phone rang. Perplexed about such an early call, 5:30 AM calls were usually not bearers of good news, Andi answered, holding her breath. There had been way too much bad news lately. The caller ID showed a call from Jeff. Jeff was an early riser, but usually not this early.

"Jeff, what's wrong?" The worry in her voice was noticeable.

"Nothing's wrong," Jeff stated, almost laughing at his own comment. A comet was about to destroy the world, Melissa's memorial service would be in two days and a bright light in the sky had spoken to him. "I couldn't sleep. Are you guys working at the diner today, what's the name of it?"

"*Dine for Dollars*, and yes, why?"

"*Some of the missiles have multiple nuclear warheads, as many as ten independently guided and programmed. These Multiple Targeted Reentry Vehicles, known as MIRV missiles, increase the total number of warheads possibly to as many as 5,000 total nuclear devices. These will not be making any reentries however.*" Erica continued reporting the latest news.

"Well, since I can't sleep, I thought I would join you guys if you need help."

Andi pondered the request. Jeff was a contributor to good causes, sort of; at least for someone who thought God was a myth. Maybe this was a good sign. Or maybe he was looking for a way to keep his mind off the loss of Melissa. When they were married, they had been much more than lovers and were almost inseparable, at least until . . . things started going wrong. The divorce had taken its toll; and Jeff had been especially distraught when Melissa married the missionary, Rob Jeremias. And then Rob died in a plane crash. His body was never found.

"Jeffrey, we always need help. You would be most welcome. Want us to pick you up?" Andi heard the shower running and figured they would be ready to leave in about fifteen minutes. Gray didn't lollygag.

Jeff thought a minute, wondering if his GTR would be safe in the forlorn neighborhood and quickly decided it wouldn't be.

"Do you guys drive your new Lexus when you go?" Andi knew where this was headed, Jeff and his toys. Would he ever change?

"No, we don't. But it's not because we're worried about anyone breaking into the car or stealing it. We just don't think it would make the diners comfortable. We don't want them to think we are flaunting. We always take the Jeep."

"The first wave of missiles, about five hundred we believe, should detonate the day after tomorrow, about one hundred miles from the comet."

Jeff overheard the news in the background and felt there was a certain irony involved. Melissa's burial . . . strike that . . . there would be no burial since her body had never been found and was probably at the bottom of the Cayman Trench; her *memorial* would be the same day as the first wave of missiles detonated. His heart ached at the thought, the thought that they would not be together in the end; and he truly felt that Melissa had been wrong. The end really was coming, thanks to the comet express headed their way. She had been so sure that the comet would not hit, because *God* didn't mention it in the *Bible*. But Jeff was a scientist, not a mythologist; and he knew already that the missiles would not be able to alter the path of the monster comet.

"Sure, if you don't mind. What time will you pick me up?"

Jeff's home in Sugarloaf was only a few minutes away from Gray and Andi's townhome overlooking Duluth's Towne Green. The home had originally been purchased as a rental property but never rented after the economy hit rock-bottom. Now Gray and Andi were staying there, since their gorgeous and very large home in Sweet Bottom Plantation was no more.

The Buford Dam was heavily damaged in the nuclear attack, and the midnight deluge headed downstream, overflowing the banks of the Chattahoochee River from the get-go. It didn't take long to sweep through Sugar Hill and Suwanee before flooding one of Duluth's premiere neighborhoods. The *gated* Sweet Bottom Plantation neighborhood had been located on the banks of Georgia's most famous river. The "Old South" plantation replicas never stood a chance. Sweet Bottom Plantation was no more, though the water had now receded. Forty-seven perished in the flood and probably never knew what hit them. Jeff was glad that Gray and Andi had been in *The Islands* and not at home at the time.

"The second wave, several thousand miles from the first, should detonate a few minutes later. Ten minutes after the second wave, the third and final wave will detonate."

"Erica, do we know why the missiles will detonate so far away from the comet instead of actually exploding at the surface?"

"*Condi, the information we've received so far from the Department of Defense and Goddard Space Flight Center indicates that a blast wave some distance from the comet may 'nudge' the comet off course without creating unwanted debris. An explosion at or near the surface may be ineffective at nudging the comet off course, while possibly creating a large debris field that would continue toward Earth. The fear would be, instead of one comet, we may have several hundred objects headed to Earth.*"

"We'll pick you up in twenty minutes. And thanks Jeff. We can always use more help."

"*Condi, the expectation is, maybe I should say the* hope *is, that the combined effort of the three shock waves will slightly deflect the object. I say 'object' because most scientists do not believe this is a comet. That namesake was first used by a gentleman from Raleigh, N.C., Chuck Hutz, I think that's correct. He has no scientific background and is an ex-used car salesman in Research Triangle Park. In a television interview last month, he stated that this object was a 'dark comet.'*"

"*Yes Erica, I saw that interview. He mentioned a 'dark comet' from the Kuiper belt. This Mr. Hutz is quite an interesting character. Many scientists and theologians refer to him as Hutz the Putz. I had never heard of the Kuiper belt, but apparently astronomers have discovered at least 70,000 objects with diameters greater than 62 miles. That's scary.*"

Andi poured a little of the chocolate macadamia creamer into two Styrofoam cups, followed by Gray's favorite Jamaica Blue Mountain blend. She grabbed her iPhone off the rose granite countertop, pulled up the Jeep app and started the Grand Cherokee III remotely. It wouldn't take the car long to warm up. The weather was unseasonably warm for January. She headed through the townhome just as another *Breaking News Alert* interrupted the commentator who was already doing a News Alert.

"*This just in from Reuters: Homeland Security has confirmed that an explosion that occurred high in the sky over a Carnival Cruise liner late New Year's Eve was a missile intercept. An Aegis Missile Cruiser equipped with the Navy's new 'Rail Gun Combat System' destroyed incoming missiles from a source 'unknown,' whatever that means. They did not mention how many incoming there were.*"

"*Passengers aboard the cruise liner, just off the coast of Florida, reported seeing two small explosions in the sky to the north, just after midnight New Year's Eve. Reuters does not mention what type of missiles were 'incoming' or what type of warhead the missiles may have carried. Passengers initially thought it was the last of the ship's fireworks display.*"

The sound faded in the background as Andi continued down the hallway toward the bedroom. She glanced out the casement-style window of their Towne Green home, the sun still several minutes away from the eastern horizon. The comet, or whatever it was, was clearly visible now and getting brighter with each day. Andi found it hard to believe how *big* it appeared. She shivered as she crossed the threshold of the master suite. She wasn't sure if she shivered because of fear or because of the way Gray looked standing in the bedroom, wearing nothing but his bath towel. She found herself wishing they weren't in a hurry.

CHAPTER TWELVE

E d Poe took a left on Peachtree Court, subconsciously checking that the computer chip was still secure in his pocket. He walked with a purpose in his step, the first time in a long time.

He reminisced of the time that Peachtree Court had been as nice as its name. Not the case anymore, as he stepped around discarded trash littering the crumbling sidewalk and gutter, and the three men passed out by the lone Pin oak tree lining the cracked, dark sidewalk. Two blocks later he arrived at the double-glass door and entered *Dine for Dollars*. The two chow lines were especially long today, and Ed noticed there was a shortage of helpers. The comet had changed everything. Businesses were closed, people heading to the mountains, or somewhere safe. "*For what?*" he thought to himself. There was nowhere safe.

Ed spotted Mr. Dorey, his very beautiful wife at his side serving the less fortunate children of God, one plate stacked with food after another. The helpings were never small at the *Diner*. With stomach singing an opera by now, he grabbed a tray and went to the back of the line. He heard the crash behind him and crouched to the floor, ready for hand-to-hand combat. He sometimes seemed to lose his mind. Fortunately for the stranger, Ed retained his composure.

"What the hell's wrong with you man? That kinda crap'll get you killed." Ed was riled.

"I'm sorry. I dropped the silverware. It's my first day, and I'm kind of clumsy I guess."

"What's your name?" Ed demanded from the stranger, beginning to feel guilty about chiding the old fart. Probably a veteran himself. He leaned over to help the man pick up the silverware, finding that fact rather funny. Why would they use real silverware when they could use plastic forks?

"To make the folk happy. My name is Jeff Ross." Jeff stuck out his hand. Ed shook it and said, "Ed Poe."

"Ed Poe? As in *Edgar Allen Poe*?" He noted Ed's short, military style haircut. "Are you a veteran, Mr. Poe?"

"Yep and yep, just like Edgar Allen Poe. And yep, I'm a veteran. Special Ops. Army." He laughed, guardedly. "My folks had a hell of a sense of humor. To make *what* folk happy?"

"Pardon moi?" Jeff had lost his line of thought.

"You said just before you introduced yourself, 'to make the folk happy.' Right after you picked up the silverware."

"Oh. That's why they use silverware instead of plastic. They think it shows more respect."

Ed cocked his left eye, pursed his lip, looked Jeff straight in the eye and asked, "How did you know what I was thinkin'?"

It sure had been an odd day so far, and it was really early. Passing the collection jar, Ed put in his dollar. Jeff smiled and headed to the kitchen.

"See you later Mr. Poe, and nice to meet you. I'm a veteran too."

The man was stooped, wearing a dark hat with brim, the kind *Dick Tracy* used to wear, only droopier. His overcoat was worn and dirty, and way too much coat for the unusually warm, January night. He shuffled more than walked and approached the dumpster slowly, scanning the ground with his dark-brown eyes. Seeing nothing, he shuffled to the back of the dumpster, nearly slipping in the slime that was drooling from the bottom of the refuse, a liquidy, dark-green ooze. For a moment, Vinny thought he would throw up. *Where was the rat?*

Vinny glanced up the street, scoping out the street sign that read *Peachtree Court*, so this had to be the dumpster. His heart skipped a beat, maybe a couple. He shuffled around the green-gray dumpster again, one of the doors on the top, open and warped, as usual. *Maybe American dumpsters came from the factory with warped doors.* He was startled by the sound but turned slowly.

"Got any dope, skank-head?"

The man was tall, maybe a boy, and skinny. His stained baseball cap was on sideways, and Vinny almost laughed at the sight.

"You better have some dope dude, or you gonna find Jesus tonight." The tall, skinny guy's friend walked in from the shadows.

This is just great, Vinny thought; and he quickly scanned the alleyway. No one else was around to witness.

"Are you asking me if I have drugs?" Vinny asked the question with a slight, French accent.

"Yeah, pea-brain. Mon-sewer." The thief laughed at the joke.

The friend of the thief, the *associate* thief, also with way-to-floppy hair, was even shorter than Vinny, and fat. Vinny saw the reflection of the moon flash from the blade that the Pillsbury doughboy-looking guy had pulled from beneath his belt, about seven inches long.

"We don't do dope in my country."

Vinny made the comment as he thrust his Egyptian stiletto deep into the short, squatty man's throat and jerked the blade sideways until the jugular was completely severed. *Tall-skinny dude* looked on in shock, the smirk no longer on his face, his friend's blood now spraying on his already-stained and ragged jeans. Before he could run, he was as dead as his buddy. There wasn't much that Vinny enjoyed more than killing infidels.

He pulled the two bodies to the dumpster and heaved them over the side, careful to avoid the blood.

Calmly, Vinny took one more tour around the dumpster; and this time he didn't shuffle. *Where was the rat?* His rage was building. The chip was vital. He looked up, just to make sure no one was on the roofs of the adjacent buildings; and to glimpse the smudge in the sky, directly overhead. It was getting bigger and brighter.

Glancing across the alley, the neon sign for *Joe's Bar* provided royal blue and red light, just enough to see the concrete sidewalk below. Something was lying on the ground beneath the sign.

Spotting the grimy business card on the ground, Vinny bent over and picked it up. He held the card up to the neon light, and read: Ed Poe, Homeless Veteran.

Maybe this was a clue, maybe it wasn't. He dropped the card into his shirt pocket and headed to the little diner he passed down the street. He had not eaten in several hours, and he could use a dollar breakfast. Killing people always made Vinny hungry.

Chapter Thirteen

J eff picked up his smart phone on the second ring.

"Hey Chadbo!" Jeff's spirits were lifted like they always were when Chadbo called.

"Hey Dude, I got some news."

Jeff hated that term, *dude*; and none of his friends ever used it, except Chad. It was more of a younger-generation thing, except Chad wasn't *younger*.

"I hope it's good." Jeff didn't mention *dude* and felt that almost any news at this point would have to be better than the recent news.

"Not really. Maybe. How did you weather the flood?"

Jeff briefly explained the damage and the protection offered to Duluth by the Eastern Continental Divide. The death toll in the Greater Atlanta area now exceeded 2,660 with another 3,400 unaccounted for, so far. The intentional breach of Buford Dam was now America's greatest terrorist attack, and the death toll would far exceed that of September 11, 2001.

"Dude, that's freakin' awful. Is the Rexall still there?"

Jeff had known Chad for so long, he was like family; and he thought Chad might have been smoking a little juicy-fruit before *this* call. "Yep, the Rexall made it. Why? Are you hungry?"

"I'm *always* hungry. Have you ever heard of the National Ignition Facility?"

"I have. Don't know much about it. Some kind of laser facility, isn't it?"

"Yeah. It's the bad Mamma Jamma of lasers, *supposedly* for energy research. *Supposedly*. You can check out their web site when you get a chance. Livermore, California. Or call Wild Willy. He can tell you all you wanna know."

"OK, so what? Is this a geography lesson?"

Chad Myers, Jeff and The Admiral were all ex-Navy buddies; and Chadbo ignored Jeff's sarcasm.

"It's the world's most powerful laser facility. It was designed to research the production of energy through *fusion*. That's how the sun does it. Fusion has been elusive. It's like trying to go faster than light. Seems impossible, but we know fusion happens in stars. If we can make it happen at an affordable cost, the world could have free energy. It's like a perpetual motion machine. Once it starts, it will keep on going. Until stopped."

"*Hopefully* we could stop it."

"Well, that is a possibility. It would take tremendous pressure to control it."

"So what does this have to do with the price of tea in China?" Jeff interrupted.

"It has to do with the comet. I can't tell you the details on an unsecure phone, but watch the news. Well, you *always* watch the news; but just pay attention if anyone mentions *laser*. When the nukes fail to deter the comet, which they will, don't despair. Just look west for the dark-blue beam leaving Lawrence Livermore Labs. Get my drift?"

"Sorta. Can't you tell me more than that?"

"Nope. Too many meetings and too many ears. It's a joint project between Israel and the United States; and if it's successful, Melissa would have been right." Chad immediately regretted the comment, bringing up Melissa's name at a time like this.

"I'm sorry Jeff. I was trying to avoid that, but you know what I mean. She *never* believed the comet would hit. I don't think it will either."

"Melissa didn't think the comet, or *whatever* as she used to say, would hit. It wasn't *biblical*." Jeff's mood changed, and melancholy set in for just a moment; but then he was again in control.

"Yeah, she always said it wasn't a part of God's plan, at least if the *Bible* was correct."

"Will you be coming to the memorial?" Jeff doubted Chad would make it. Too much *stuff* going on.

Chad hated to tell Jeff he would miss Melissa's service, but there was nothing he could do about it. He had to stay at Goddard.

"Jeff, I love you buddy, you and Melissa both. I have to stay here because of the . . . you know." Chad paused. He sounded a little more serious for a change.

"I understand. I'm surprised The Admiral and Sheryl were able to get a delay. They're supposed to be in Bethesda for a meeting at *National Institutes of Health*. It came from the President himself. One thing before you go. How's the wind looking?"

Jeff had once thought that no one could actually *see* wind, but Chad had a gift.

"*I can see the wind if the wind-speed is over about fifty miles an hour. Lawn blowers drive me crazy. I still see things normally, except the wind is translucent, like a film. The darker the color; the higher the wind-speed. It's kind of like looking through a tinted window. Covers the entire spectrum.*"

Jeff had only seen that trait one time before, last year at the Denver airport.

"Different. It's looking more different than usual."

"What do you mean?"

"The high-altitude winds have been darker than normal for the last month or so, almost indigo. I have *never* seen indigo before and would guess the wind speeds are in excess of three hundred."

"Anything to do with the dark comet?" Jeff asked. "Maybe some effects of the magnetic field? I read that a strong magnetic field in the comet has been detected. That's kind of strange in itself."

"It is strange; but this whole baby's been strange, right from the start. I hadn't thought about that actually. I wonder if the Earth's magnetic field could be reacting with the comet's? You *know* the geographical magnetic field of the Earth is moving eastward, about 400 miles in the last five years? Of course the North Pole is in the same place, but the north magnetic pole is shifting." Chad knew a *lot* about astronomy and physics.

"I thought the magnetic poles were always shifting."

"They are, but never at this speed; at least not in recorded history. The poles have reversed in the past, not wham-bam, thank-you-ma'am fast, but fast. However, this is not a pole reversal, thank goodness.

"Jeff, I gotta go. My plane's boarding. I'm sorry I can't make the service. If there was any way . . ."

"I know. Don't start feeling guilty about it." And Jeff really did understand.

He hung up the phone and went to the kitchen where he poured a glass of merlot. It was still morning, but who cared? He would celebrate the possible *near miss*; and if the near miss didn't happen, what difference would it make? He would just get drunk.

He turned on the TV, now tuned to the *latest* "all news" satellite channel, *APN*, and sat in the dark-gray, leather recliner. Three glasses later, Jeff passed out to dreams about Melissa, dreams where a tsunami never happened and they were still lying in the Honduran hammock on Seven Mile Beach, entwined. She kissed him like he'd never been kissed before.

"Thank you for watching the new <u>Apocalypse News Channel</u>, where we bring you the latest news of catastrophic events that are occurring all over the globe. 'Nothing but Nature.'

"This just in: A major earthquake has once again hit Japan. Every nuclear power plant has been shut down, either by man or by Mother Nature, who has been showing her bad side lately.

"Hailstorms have again battered Europe with the largest hailstones in recent memory; and three small villages have been wiped out, pummeled into the ground by hailstones weighing as much as twenty to thirty pounds each, about the size of a volley ball or small beach ball.

"In Turkey, hail accumulated to depths of sixty feet at the bottom of the eastern flank of Mt. Ararat, and some reports state that the entire eastern flank has eroded by several feet, resulting in a massive landslide.

"Thousands of villagers are reported dead or missing, with more than a million domestic animals and other wildlife killed. Many cattle farms have simply disappeared.

"Now for the latest on the comet, scheduled to hit Earth in less than ten days." Condi Zimmerman was the new anchor. Beautiful Condi. But Jeff never heard a word she said. Nor did he hear the glass break at the rear of his home. Jeff was in merlot-land.

CHAPTER FOURTEEN

Vinny cursed at himself. How could he have been so careless? The carefully cut glass wasn't supposed to crash to the floor, and now Jeffrey Ross' ten-month old Great Dane puppy went tearing through the Sugarloaf home, galloping like a kangaroo, more lope than gallop, toward the sound of the glass. Vinny wasn't quite sure he had ever heard a bark like that, one that rattled the window panes. He squatted low to the ground and backed away, using little caution, and fell backwards over the hibiscus bush, still blooming because of the warm, winter temperatures. His intent had been to steal Jeff's laptop.

While visiting *Dine for Dollars* the day before to pick up a quick breakfast, Vinny overheard one of the volunteers ask Jeff if he had his laptop.

He couldn't hear Jeff's answer, but Vinny thought it a bit odd that anyone would carry a laptop to a volunteer diner in a low-rent neighborhood. Jeff must be an "important" guy, couldn't leave home without it. The chow line progressed, and Vinny slowly worked his way forward toward the biscuits and gravy, the smell of sausage tantalizing but forbidden by Vinny's religious beliefs. He salivated anyway.

"Sir, what can I get you?" The guy called "Jeff" asked the man in front of Vinny, then recognized him. "Mr. Poe, I presume?" Jeff had met Ed earlier.

Vinny did not miss the name and fished in his pocket for the business card. He glanced down, and there it was. *Ed Poe, Homeless Veteran.* Pay dirt. Allah is great. He took it as a sign.

"Hey Mr. Jeff. I need to talk with you about something. Very important."

"What is it?" Jeff answered while ladling a large portion of sausage gravy into a bowl and passing it forward. The smell of the country sausage made Vinny hungrier, and he felt guilty for succumbing to the smell of the pig. "Can it wait for fifteen minutes? I have a break then."

"Sure, I'll hang out. Do you have your laptop? I heard someone ask." Ed was generously served sausage, gravy, a biscuit and three eggs, over easy. Jeff answered the laptop question in the affirmative.

Vinny was sure he knew why the veteran needed a computer. He was next in line; and when Jeff asked him what he needed, Vinny asked for sausage gravy and biscuits, a scrambled egg and a slice of cantaloupe. He knew Allah would forgive him for dirtying his plate with pork. Vinny needed to "blend in" and look as *American* as possible.

"You have a French accent," and Jeff seemed surprised.

"Oui monsieur." Vinny answered and stuck out his right hand. "My name is Jean Philippe. Born and raised in Sucy-en-Brie, the home of Fort de Sucy. My parents moved here when I was 16. They were killed two years later."

"Jeff Ross," Jeff shook Jean Philippe's hand, and proceeded to generously fill the plate. He handed it to the Frenchman.

"Merci, Mr. Ross. Are you from Atlanta? I have been here for the last few months, hoping to find work."

"Actually, I live in a north Atlanta suburb." Jeff was hesitant to give the stranger too much info. You just never knew, and his military training had conditioned him to never give too much info.

Jean Philippe thanked Jeff again, and took a seat at the long, community table. He had an excellent view of Army veteran Poe. He could kill Poe right now and escape in the panic and turmoil; but he didn't know where the microchip was hidden.

Finishing the eggs and cantaloupe, he saw Jeff sit down across from Poe ... *was his name really Edgar Allen Poe?* Poe talked too quietly for Vinny to hear. He had a directional recorder, shaped like a felt-tip marker; but the din of the crowd was too great. Maybe he could pick up something.

After a few minutes, the two men stood. Poe placed the silverware in the wash container and carried the plate over to the small conveyor belt. Then they entered the room behind the serving line, probably the kitchen; and an opportunity was lost. He would take care of Mr. Poe later. He wiped his mouth and left the diner, leaving his dirty dishes on the table. A couple of the "regulars" gave him a dirty look, and Jean Philippe, aka

Vinny, aka Aboud Rehza in his homeland, could not wait until the infidels were wiped from the face of the Earth. Vinny returned to the moment.

Scurrying to his feet, a pink hibiscus blossom clinging to his rear pocket, Vinny didn't hang around to play with the puppy. He wasn't afraid of many things, but a hundred-twenty pound dog was one of them. The computer would have to wait. Securing the hoodie around his head, he ran around the western-most side of the house, around the multi-car garage and collided with Jeff's' dark-gray GTR, still parked in the driveway. Getting back to his feet for the second time that evening, Vinny couldn't believe his luck as he spotted the laptop in the passenger seat. Using the metal handle of his hunting knife, Vinny made quick work of the passenger side window, paying little respect to Jeff's $90,000 sports car. He reached in the now-shattered window to grab the laptop, but not before the car's horn started blaring and the headlights flashing. Vinny searched in his pocket for the homeless veteran's card he had secured yesterday, found it and dropped it by the door of the GTR. Dressed in dark clothing, Vinny ran across the front yard and was thankful that the house occupied a large, well landscaped lot. It offered protection from prying eyes.

There were no prying eyes this night though, as Jeff slept right through the breaking glass, the barking Dane, the crashing hibiscus plant and blaring GTR horn as he lay in his merlot stupor. A drunken sleep was not the norm for Jeff Ross, but nothing seemed the norm these days.

Chief Belker, the Chief of Police, wasn't on duty as his cruiser passed Jeff's Sugarloaf Country Club home. It had been a long day, and the Chief would be glad to get home. He was relieved that the charges filed by the American Civil Liberties group had been dismissed. The wannabe jihadist who shot up the American Legion Post finally confessed that he was not water-boarded by the Duluth Police, broke down crying for his mother and was admitted into a local mental hospital for treatment until trial.

The Chief glanced out the windshield of the black cruiser and up into the northern sky. The comet was plainly visible above all the light pollution. Almost all businesses in the area were keeping outside lights ON because of reports of roving street gangs taking advantage of the situation caused by the impending doom. Chief Belker supposed the fake jihadist's trial would never come to fruition.

Suddenly, the Chief heard the blaring horn in the distance and pulled to the side of the road to get a better bearing on the sound. It wasn't unusual to hear automobile alarms going off, but . . . Glancing around, he finally spotted the flashing lights off to the right, down the long driveway to the Ross home. The Chief did a U-turn and made a right into the driveway, cautious as he slowly progressed toward the sound. The gated drive was not secure, and the Chief called for backup, just in case. From the periphery, he was sure he saw movement among some of the bushes and aimed his remotely powered spot light. Nothing. He eased the cruiser through the open gate, and the hair stood up on the back of his neck. Something wasn't *right*.

Driving slowly toward the flashing lights of Jeff's car, three other Duluth Police cars entered the driveway and raced toward their boss. Randy Belker knew Jeff Ross, and his concern grew when he didn't see Jeff checking on his car. It was common knowledge in the area that Jeff liked his cars.

Prepared and cautious, the Chief did a complete 360 degree scan with the high-powered spot light. Seeing nothing, he turned his attention to the passenger window that was clearly smashed and immediately noticed the small blood stain on the ground, and a hibiscus bloom. The veteran's "business" card, carried by an earlier breeze, lay a few feet away, unseen.

The car alarm went silent as Jeff, also smashed, finally awakened from merlot-land, grabbed the car's remote and switched the alarm to silent. Rubbing his eyes from the glare of police lights, Jeff regained his senses and exited his home.

Vinny shed his dark clothing and walked down Meadow Church Road. There weren't many people out because of the comet. Most businesses remained closed. He spotted headlights coming his way and moved behind some large camellia bushes, pink blooms covering the ground. The car passed, and he was relieved to see the young girl drive slowly by. It wasn't the police, praise Allah.

The red Volkswagen Beetle with red wheel covers turned into the parking lot of the deserted office building a half-block away, and he saw his chance. Vinny creeped through the lush landscaping; and he watched the young girl texting the night away as she sat in the driver's seat, motor idling. She giggled. Vinny withdrew his Egyptian hunting knife, most recently used on Jeff's GTR window, and walked from behind the pampas grass. Jenni Ross never saw him coming.

CHAPTER FIFTEEN

The dark comet continued unabated, speed still just under 100,000 miles per hour, an encounter only a couple of days away that would end Earth as man knows it.

The first wave of nuclear missiles had simultaneously exploded just as scientists predicted but with no noticeable impact, even though the explosions were *directed*. The nuclear force was focused *toward* the comet, eliminating most back-blast that might affect the next two waves of missiles.

The dark, graphite cover hid the ice core from view. As the comet hurtled toward planet Earth, it also hurtled closer to the sun. The dark cover, estimated to be several miles thick by people in-the-know, absorbed the heat of the sun until it began to dissolve, gradually exposing the ice core and developing tail.

The second wave of nuclear deterrent, though having no effect on the comet's direction, was given credit for exposing the ice core. Dark Comet was now the brightest object in the night sky and was clearly visible throughout the day. Great herds of animals on every continent began to get antsy, as though the herds actually knew what was going on.

"*The third and final wave of nuclear warheads has once again failed to deter the course of Dark Comet, the name now inappropriate for this bright, mysterious object.*

"*Just a few months ago, no one knew of this gigantic comet. Geologists now say that the comet remained invisible to even the Hubble Space Telescope because it is composed, at least the surface is composed, of graphite which absorbs radar like a sponge, as well as light.*

"According to Dr. Chad Myers, an astrophysicist with Goddard Space Flight Center in Maryland, had it not been for all the amateur astronomers trying to find a 'very bright blip of light' that briefly appeared last year . . ."

"Get your window fixed yet?" Abe asked Jeff, referring to the break-in of his car and theft of a computer, as though that was somehow important.

"Yeah. Suwanee Glass was out the same day, one of the few businesses that survived the flood. Did you hear what Condi just said? Abe, do you think that's *our* blip?"

Jeff had now seen the light several times, and his thoughts drifted back to that night at Grand Cayman, floating in the sea after the tsunami. The light actually spoke that time. But how *was* that possible? It wasn't.

"Could be," Abe replied. "I've been seeing more on the Internet about a brief, bright light that astronomers keep getting a glimpse of. There's even a *Blip in the Night* fan page on Facebook with 22,000 fans. Most people seem to think it has something to do with the comet.

"By the way," Abe continued, "Has Chief Belker said anything about the break-in? Good thing you had that great, big puppy!" Abe had been surprised that Jeff drank himself into a stupor the night of the break-in. Ever since Melissa's memorial service, Jeff seemed to be in a downward spiral. Getting drunk was unusual, but maybe warranted to kill his pain. Abe was sympathetic.

"There wasn't much evidence, no finger prints. I'm not sure why anyone would want that laptop so bad. Didn't even have the hard drive. You know, Chief Belker surprises me."

"Why?"

"Just that he's even interested in this, or *any* case. When this comet hits, even if it's in China, that's it. Break-ins won't matter. Nothing will matter except staying alive. It will be survival of the fittest. Yet the chief keeps doing his work, helping the people." Jeff's voice trailed.

"Boy! Aren't we dismal today?"

Abe knew Jeff was right though. He walked from around the bar, out the front, french-doored entrance and onto the Towne Green. Looking up, the night sky had few clouds and the moon peeked over the eastern horizon. Even if the moon had been full, the dark comet was no longer dark. It shown brightly, directly overhead, but appeared to be stationary.

Are you gonna hit here big boy? Abe knew the comet wouldn't answer, and it probably would make no difference where it hit. Doing a one-eighty, he reentered *The Divide* and found Jeff glued to the TV.

"*The red Volkswagen was discovered just a little while ago in a creek outside Dalton, Georgia. The police have divulged little information so far; but according to a cell phone photo of the license plate, the VW is registered to Jenni Ross. We located an address for a Jenni Ross who lives in Virginia Highlands, but no one came to the door of the Atlanta home. We have learned that Jenni Ross is the twin daughter of Jeffrey and the late Melissa Ross, also from the Atlanta area. Melissa Ross was recently killed in the Soufriére Hills tsunami that hit Grand Cayman while she was vacationing with friends.*

"*In other news, the missing Louisiana highway patrolman, patrol woman, has been found in her submerged car . . .*"

Jeff's heart pounded in his chest as he wondered what else could possibly go wrong in his life. Jenni hadn't called since the memorial service, and he knew in his heart the VW was hers.

CHAPTER SIXTEEN

"He will be a wild donkey of a man; his hand will be against everyone and everyone's hand against him, and he will live in hostility toward all his brothers." Genesis 16:12 NIV

Korengal Valley, Pakistan (Valley of Death)

"**M**uhammed, Mehdi's body has been discovered. Did you kill him Muhammed?" Aludra loved her brother but knew he could be ruthless. Mehdi should never have slapped her that night. *Would they ever stop killing their brothers?*

"No. Why would I do that? Mehdi was a good friend."

Muhammed thought the discovery quite unusual. No one ever talked about the bodies that were dumped in the burning fields, for fear they might be in the fields next, awaiting resurrection from the dead on Judgment Day. The Hebrews sometimes referred to these places of the dead as Gehenna, and sometimes She'ol. Bodies were *never* discovered in She'ol.

"Dogs dragged his body from the fields and were eating him when some Bedouins discovered his head and an arm."

"That's too bad," was Muhammed's only comment.

"Muhmi?" Aludra addressed her brother by the name she had always used since she was little. "Do you think this comet will actually hit? I'm so fearful."

"The comet will not hit, insha'Allah. It cannot hit before the Twelfth Imam is here. The Mahdi has to come first. Then, who knows?"

"I have heard the Twelfth Imam is in Iran. She's supposed to be very pretty." Aludra smiled, and her brother threw a towel at her. The Islamic messiah would *not* be a woman. She had heard the rumors about al-Mahdi from other Afghan women down by the river where they washed their clothes in the dark-brown water.

Muhammed spat into the arid dust. He was a Sunni and the Persians were Shi'a. The split between the two began at Muhammad's death, peace be upon him, in 632 AD, and led to an eternal love-hate relationship, with brothers killing brothers on a regular basis, just like the angel had told Ishmael's mother 4,000 years before.

The descendants of Ishmael will always fight, even brother against brother. The prophecy had certainly come true.

"The Mahdi is not here Aludra. These rumors come up from time to time. The whole world must be at war when he comes."

Of course, a lot of the world was at war, he thought.

The entire Middle East seemed in an uproar and had been; and now Asian countries had joined the fray, at least those with large Muslim populations. Islamic clashes within Russia and China were at unprecedented levels. The floods and fires were consuming vast parts of countries. *Could the Mahdi be upon them?* Muhammed wondered, and worried. *Would this be a good thing or a bad thing?*

Aludra took the *Bible* from under her bedding, approaching her dear brother cautiously. Having the book was cause of instant execution in this part of the Muslim world, a world that proclaimed Jesus as a great prophet, just slightly inferior to Muhammad himself; just don't mention him. That had not made sense to her for many years, probably since her trip to Paris where she had an opportunity to read about this man, Y'shua in Hebrew, when a stranger handed her a *New Testament* in Arabic. She found the story of the healings, the miracles and the extraordinary teachings to be compelling; and she began that day to question some of her Islamic beliefs, just a little. She *especially* liked the part about living in God's Kingdom when all the fighting and destruction was finally over, and she knew that the Kingdom would be what the Garden of Eden was supposed to be. She had read that story too.

"Muhammed, I am giving you my most precious possession."

She handed the *Bible* to Muhammed and held her breath.

Twenty-five hundred feet below the Atlantic, the hijacked nuclear powered Nerpa submarine proceeded quietly toward the Mediterranean Sea.

The Chechnyan commander was disobeying the orders from the Japanese *consortium* that paid for the hijacking and their final supplies. Their beef was with the Americans, not the Jews. The consortium, he had heard, was composed of wealthy Japanese who were still pissed at the U.S. for nuking Hiroshima. The Nerpa commander had no intention of using his missiles on the United States as long as Israel still existed. And besides, some of the sub's intercontinental ballistic missiles were programmed for key cities in the U.S. and Europe, and the hated Russia. With each ICBM came ten nuclear warheads. There would be plenty of death and destruction.

The commander was oblivious to activities occurring on the surface of the world and had no clue that the nuclear missile pods, earlier deployed, had been virtually ineffective, except for one, thanks to what had started several decades earlier under Ronald Reagan. Everyone thought his missile defense ideas were crazy, like they thought Jules Verne's *Nautilus* was, so long ago. The commander had heard of Reagan but knew little of the U.S. king.

Reagan's *Strategic Defense Initiative* was ridiculed in the press when first proposed and was dubbed the *Star Wars Program* by the derisionists du jour. Ten years later the name of the program and the emphasis was changed as defense and intelligence budgets were slashed in order to balance the budget.

Unfortunately for the Nerpa submarine commander, a joint U.S. and Israeli team developed the Arrow anti-missile system, more accurate than the Patriot system used to protect Israel against Saddam Hussein's attacks during the *first* Iraq war.

New Year's Eve on Diego Garcia had been hot and muggy, as usual. Just before the stroke of midnight, the missile pods resting on the surface of the sea had become active. A military recon satellite located *23,000* miles above Earth detected the two missile launches in the Indian Ocean, just 300 miles north of the island of Diego Garcia, home to a fleet of B-1B bombers, B-52 Stratofortress bombers and other "secret" hardware.

The launch coordinates were relayed at the speed of light from the Department of Defense recon satellite to the Arrow launch command center on Diego Garcia. Within two minutes of the launch detection, six Arrow 3 intercept missiles were fired. At an altitude of 60 miles, the intercept had been halfway successful. One missile was destroyed, saving the western part of the military base from annihilation. The news was not so good for the east, as the Arrows missed their target because of the zigzag nature of the warhead's flight.

Sixty miles below, the *Enlisted Men's Club* was bustling with some of the 1500 soldiers stationed on the island, joined by several dozen sailors stationed on ships guarding the archipelago.

U.S.A.F. Staff Sargent Jimmy Newhouse left the club, hand-in-hand with Navy Corpsman Misti Taggarts. She was *gorgeous*; dark hair, black-slinky dress, curves in all the right places. Love was in the air *this* New Year's Eve; and Jimmy and Misti would be saying their vows as soon as they got back to the States, a July 4th wedding.

They made their way across the base to the beach, never far away from any part of the narrow island. The night was clear and the sky was covered in stars like diamonds in the sky. Jimmy and Misti grabbed a chaise lounge, they didn't need two, and joined one another in a moment of passion. Misti usually kissed with her eyes closed, like most people; but in the distance she thought she heard a slight sound. Opening her dark brown eyes, she separated from Jimmy and looked skyward.

"Jim, look at those shooting stars! They're so close!"

Jim wasn't interested in shooting stars, he was interested in getting naked; but apparently that would have to wait. What rotten luck.

Suddenly, a great noise erupted from the far side of the base, over by the anti-missile defense system, followed by the launch of several Arrow missiles. They both had friends who worked closely with the Israelis stationed at the compound and knew that Arrow missiles going off in the night was not a good thing. As they watched, they were spellbound, like a deer in the headlights on a lonely, rural road at midnight.

Rocketing skyward, Jimmy and Misti quickly became aware that the shooting stars were not meteors at all. In a split second, or so it seemed, there was a terrific explosion in the night sky, followed by hundreds of fiery shards falling toward Earth, and them. They were too mesmerized to run; and besides, where would they run?

One of the *shooting stars* continued its journey, seemingly closer to their beach paradise with each passing second. Jimmy grabbed Misti's left hand and pulled her back into reality.

"We gotta go honey," and they ran with all their might.

A half mile above the runways filled with U.S. Air Force bombers, the two-megaton warhead ignited, becoming the first-ever successful nuclear strike against U.S. and British territory. Jimmy and Misti would not be getting married July 4ᵗʰ after all, as most of the 2000 soldiers and 1200 private contractors on the island would not need funerals. In a world of budget cuts, there would be no headstones to buy. There would be nothing to bury. Most vanished in a cloud of bloody evaporation, never to be found again.

Briefly, for just an instant, Misti glanced over her shoulder and out to sea as the equivalent of two million tons of TNT came to fruition. In less than a second, Misti was blinded and her deep-brown eyes turned to ash as her eyeballs evaporated, then her skin, and then . . . there was nothing. Jimmy and Misti, all the soldiers and contractors, disappeared in the blink of an eye; but this was not the rapture. The death was painless but noisy. Jimmy and Misti would never sit in a tree, KISSING . . .

Chapter Seventeen

"Any word from Jenni? I just heard the police found her car in a river or something."

Chad and Jeff went back a long time; had served in Viet Nam together. Jeff was glad to get Chad's call. His concern for Jenni was genuine, and appreciated.

"Hey man. Yeah, she called shortly after the news broke about her car. It could've been much worse. The Chief thinks it might be related to the break-in at my house. She was coming to visit, but I just thought she changed her mind. She's like that, girlish." He was in control, as usual.

Jeff had to face the facts, he knew. He had been neglectful of the twins since Melissa's . . . he still couldn't force himself to say the word . . . departure. Hell, he'd been neglectful the last five years, since they were divorced. Between mourning his loss to trying to be a playboy to escape his loneliness, he had neglected a lot of fatherly necessities. He would do better. Life had to go on, maybe. They would all know if life was going on in less than forty-eight hours, that was for sure.

"She pulled off the road to text her sister, Jami. She's good about doing that. Next thing she knows, some guy walks up to her car and that's the last thing she remembered. When she came to, she was gagged and tied-up and had been left in some woods along I-75, near Dalton. Other than a big knot on her head where he hit her, assuming it was a *he*, she's fine, just traumatized a little.

"So what's up with you? Think I will ever see you again? Looks like the comet is a definite."

"Not necessarily." Chad was cool.

"What do you mean?" Jeff was hearing things, he was sure.

79

"You said you were familiar with the National Ignition Facility," Chad stated.

"Laser research. Lawrence Livermore Labs in California. What about it? I heard some pilot's report yesterday that they were shooting lasers into the sky 24/7."

"Exactly. They're aiming 192 high-intensity lasers at the comet. These are the most powerful lasers ever developed. Laboratory physicists believe the continuous bombardment will alter the comet's course. Only a miniscule change in trajectory would easily spare Earth."

"And?" Jeff asked.

"Good news; bad news. It appears that the comet is responding positively, though the angle of trajectory has only changed about a thousandth of a degree. That means it should miss Earth; and if it does not, it won't be a direct hit."

"What do you mean by that?" Jeff asked his friend.

"It could just skim the Earth, like a glancing blow so to speak. That would be tragic but not devastation. It will be close. Here's another possibility. The waves of nuclear missiles apparently slowed the speed to less than 100,000 miles per hour. Based on the moon's orbit and speed, the direct hit could be the moon."

"That would be good." Had to be, Jeff thought.

"Not necessarily."

"I hate it when you do that Chadbo. Get to the point!"

"The point is this: We know that the nukes have probably fractured part of the comet's surface. That means there are now numerous small NEO's headed toward us. Secondly, a direct collision with the moon will cause a tremendous loss of mass that will be ejected thousands of miles into space. Many of those newly created near-Earth objects could, will definitely, hit the Earth's atmosphere. Could take the space station with it, which is being abandoned as we speak."

"Well that's just super. So glad you called, Chadbo."

"Sorry big guy. Just thought you would want to know the latest. We will soon know, one way or the other."

"What are you going to do the next two days?" What a thing to be thinking about, Jeff thought. Two days 'til Doomsday.

"Think I'm gonna practice kissing my ass goodbye."

They laughed.

"Well, since the streets are basically deserted and street gangs are nowhere to be found . . . not a creature is stirring, not even a mouse . . . I think I'm heading to Long Beach where they're having a "Hutz the Putz Comet Welcoming Party."

"Who? A *what?*"

"You know. That guy who first said it was a comet, has been on TV a lot lately, was on Discovery Channel last week and Oprah the week before? The guy who suddenly started speaking fluent Hebrew. Capiche?"

"You're partying?" Jeff knew Chadbo wasn't kidding. He would probably be partying the day he died, which could be Tuesday. The thought was sickly humorous. If there were ladies, Chad would be there.

"Not kidding. Supposed to be a lot of babes there."

"Hey man, I feel sorry for *those* babes. Are you sending any kind of warning?"

"Very funny, J-hole."

After a promise to be in touch as soon as *whatever* happened, if communication would be possible, the conversation ended. Chad's last comments were troubling, and puzzling.

"The winds are strengthening, the high altitude winds. I've never seen darker, and the jet stream is all over the place. Something's going on with Momma Nature."

Jeff first learned about Chad's ability to see wind when they were stationed in Japan, forty some years earlier. He, Chad and Wild Willy Briggs were leaving Tommy's Bar & Grill and heading back to base when Chad stopped in his tracks. He scanned the night sky that night like he was some kind of scanning machine. Then he said to run like hell, a windstorm was coming. And had it ever. He would never forget that night, as long as he lived. Then a couple of years ago, he saw a kid at the Denver International Airport with the same gift. Chad considered it more a curse than gift.

The gate alarm sounded.

Vinny, aka Jean Philippe, dumped the red VW soon after stashing the girl in the woods, the girl *Jenni*. Nothing had ever happened to him like *that* in his life.

The young girl had been alone in her car, he could plainly see. She stopped directly under the metal halide security lamp, a *smart* thing to do, making his approach *less* than secret. He would do what he always did. Vinny hated guns, too noisy. The stiletto was his friend.

No sooner had his feet hit the pavement of the parking lot when he heard it. *Aboud.* He heard his Arabic name, coming from the left, or maybe the right. The voice seemed to come from all directions. He glanced at the driver, now busily texting away. *Why can't they just talk* he asked himself, silently. She apparently had not heard the voice, though she should have. Her window was open, the night unusually warm, again. He continued across the parking lot, edging toward the rear of the red Volkswagen.

Jesus is watching you Aboud, I promise. There will be no virgins, like you think.

He turned to the left and there she was, a little girl, couldn't be more than nine or ten years old, standing less than twenty feet away wearing a red dress, white socks and black patent-leather shoes that reflected the metal halide lamp. The red dress was good, he thought; and was suddenly aroused. He would have her before he slit her throat.

Vinny had always liked young girls, *little* girls. He found himself more-and-more often checking the nambla.com web site. In some ways, he was beginning to like the freedoms in the United States. Those Christians never drew a line in the sand. There sure wouldn't be a nambla.com web site in Saudi, or any Islamic country for that matter. They loved freedom as much as anyone, but some things were surely a slap in the face to Allah. And the Americans wonder why the Muslims hate them. They slap God right in the face, that's why. He wet his lips with his tongue and was looking forward to two girls in one night.

"Who are you?" He whispered.

My name is Audry, and you are an evil man Aboud. Mr. Hutz told me all about you. I hope you find Jesus so you can be happy too.

Now within ten feet of the girl, Vinny showed the young Audry his stiletto, putting his left index finger across his lips indicating silence.

You've been warned, she said; and in a tremendous flash of light, she was gone, vanished. Blinded, Vinny regained his sight in a few seconds, checked *Jenni* and questioned what just happened, *really* happened. He turned and continued toward the car unabated. *Jenni* apparently had not seen the light, but he knew it was no hallucination.

Thinking about what the young girl said, Vinny decided not to tempt the gods tonight. He surely didn't want to suffer the consequences of never-ending fire and thirst. He thought about the name. *Audry.*

Jenni slid the phone into the console just as Vinny's left fist slammed into the side of her head, tearing her ear. Out like a light. Vinny smiled.

He wasn't a big man, but he was one tough brownie. He had trouble with sayings.

He quickly placed Jenni into the trunk and quietly drove away. There was absolutely no traffic. No witnesses. Just blood flowing from Jenni's ear, staining her new Volkswagen's dark, gray trunk.

Driving north, Vinny was troubled by the girl-*Audry*. How did she know his name? *No one* knew his name on this continent. His superstition overcame his being; and he decided he would not kill the girl, nor would he have his way with her. He had a bad feeling. *How did Audry just disappear?*

He glanced into the night sky, and the comet was even brighter than the previous night. He could almost see it moving.

Vinny was aroused by thoughts of Audry. Muhammad, may peace be upon him, had married a seven year old girl. A'isha had been The Prophet's favorite wife. He might have to rethink the consequences of raping the young girl in the trunk. It had been awhile.

CHAPTER EIGHTEEN

"The third angel sounded his trumpet, and a great star, blazing like a torch, fell from the sky on a third of the rivers and on the springs of water—the name of the star is Wormwood. A third of the waters turned bitter, and many people died from the waters that had become bitter." Revelation 8:10-11 NIV

Fadila held her young child in her arms, like any loving mother would do. Emira had been born into this God-forsaken world just five years earlier. Life in Bosnia was hard, even under the best circumstances. Muslim life was hard; always had been. Fadila probed that thought, why Muslim life always seemed so much more difficult than the lives of her Christian friends, her *few* Christian friends. Her husband did not allow Christian friends, but she had secrets.

Fadila rubbed olive oil on the young girl's sores, hoping to soothe the agony; but there was no soothing the agony and anguish suffered by Emira. Fadila lost her other child just a month before to the same terrifying disease.

"Majka." Emira called her mother. "Majka, I'm hurting so bad. Please Majka."

Fadila noted the weakness in her child's voice and knew it wouldn't be long now. Momentarily she stopped rubbing the oil on Emira's pustules to attend to her own. The small bumps had appeared yesterday and were now spreading to her chest and abdomen, not yet oozing the malodorous drainage that covered Emira's limp body. That would come soon.

Sitting on the grassy knoll outside their small shelter, Fadila cried as she looked into the night sky. She had not heard of the comet headed her way, there were no radios or TVs in her village, so she feared silently that

Allah was throwing another tragedy in her direction. How much could He dish out? She had asked herself that question many times during the past year. The comet was bright; and a small, wispy tail had appeared since the previous night. The child was silent.

Changing her position, Fadila tried to pull young Emira to her when the young child's flesh fell into her lap, leaving the bones of her lower arm and hand exposed to the elements. The child let out one scream, and then it was over.

Fadila didn't scream this time. She had seen it before, with her other daughter. Black pox had claimed another. She would be next.

Bosnia seemed to always be in a state of turmoil, Fadila thought; but since the smallpox outbreak, everything had changed. People avoided one another like the ancients avoided the lepers. There was little crime anymore in her small village. Priorities were different, and survival was the key word.

Just twelve months earlier, Fadila had never heard of the black pox; but a visit to an Internet café changed all that. Linking to Wikipedia, she quickly learned what the darkening, smooth skin meant. A symptom of smallpox, black pox was 99% fatal because the sloughing off of the skin, sometimes all the skin, caused immediate death.

Once the skin turned a dark, almost black color, the hemorrhaging dissolved the lining that held the skin to the bones, a painful process. Skin would often fall off in large slabs, causing excruciating pain. Then death would come knocking, mercifully.

Fadila studied the space object. It was much closer. *What are you doing Allah?*

She laid her daughter to rest on the ground outside her small shelter. What else could she do? She took one more glance at the comet, subconsciously scratching the spreading pustules. Fadila would not lose her skin as her two children had. She had the *other* kind of black pox, the hemorrhagic form. This particular form attacked the mucous membranes of the body, eating away the linings of the throat, stomach, bowels and reproductive system. Her symptoms would include massive bleeding from all body orifices.

Fadila wiped her runny nose on the sleeve of her burqa but did not notice the blood. She cried, tears of red.

Aludra hated the Korengal Valley. It truly was a Valley of Death, and depression. Muhammed had said nothing when she slipped her brother the *Bible,* and she was glad about that. The thought of an honor killing crossed her mind; but she didn't believe her brother would be that radical, but maybe.

She pulled her curtain to, affording a little visual privacy, and went to bed. She was asleep in minutes, a comfortable sleep like she had not experienced in a while. She did not hear Muhammed sharpening his knives, and her sleep deepened.

Muhammed was deeply troubled. He must do what he must do. It was his duty to uphold the Holy *Quran,* at any cost. *Why* had she done this? Aludra knew the cost of her misguidance in the hills of Pakistan, that death was swift for anyone carrying a *Bible.* As surely as Nero killed the Christians, he would kill Aludra, tomorrow, if the comet missed Earth; and he knew it would. He would wait until after Friday prayers, and he would pray that Allah would forgive Aludra for her blasphemy. He agonized over his decision, but it wasn't really *his* decision. It was Allah's Law. She had brought this curse upon herself. If only she hadn't gone to Paris.

Muhammed placed the sharpened knives in his quarters and walked out into the night air, cool and crisp. The sky was clear and the moon was full. Even so, the comet was as bright and visible as the moon. Soon, if the comet didn't hit, the sweet smell of poppy plants would fill the spring air, heroin in wait. Leaning against a tree, Muhammed yawned and his heart ached for the action he must take. *My dear sister*, he thought; and the thought lingered. Two yawns later, Muhammed fell into a deep sleep of his own but not before taking one more long look at the comet. In a strange and ironic way, it was a thing of beauty. It looked like it would hit the moon.

Aludra!
Aludra stirred in her sleep. Was someone calling her name? She rolled to her left side and pulled the single quilt over her long legs, cold from the night air.

Aludra!

The dream seemed real, and her eyes did not open. She loved to dream, and the voice she heard could not be real. She pulled the covers up, blanketing her head from the cold.

Aludra. You must go!

The voice was the voice of her deceased mother.

Aludra. You must get up and flee the valley. I will help you. Muhammed is going to kill you tomorrow. You must go.

Aludra woke from her dream with a start, sitting straight up on her sleeping mat. There was no one there, no one who had spoken to her. The night was dark, except for the light from the moon, and the *thing*. Just a dream, and Aludra once again closed her eyes; but the sleep didn't come as easy this time. The dream had been troubling, or was she just paranoid? Before she could drift from consciousness and back to the world of dreams, she was startled by the voice, and the light in her quarters. The light was so bright, she could not stare at it.

Aludra, do not be afraid. You will be protected because of your grace. You must dress in your brother's clothes. He is asleep under the banyan tree. Hurry.

Aludra *was* afraid however, and her heart raced. She had never spoken with a light before but recalled stories in the *Bible* about talking lights. They were usually angels, and usually quite fearsome.

"Are you an angel?" Aludra asked the question, timidly.

You must hurry Aludra. Muhammed is stirring. I will protect you. You must go now.

"But where do I go? How do I go?"

Walk down the path toward the watering hole. There you will find a gray donkey, draped with four bags of food and water. The donkey will let you ride, but you must let him lead the way. He will know.

The light disappeared and the night was once again quiet, and the moonlight now appeared dim. Aludra donned Muhammed's pants, grabbed the warm lamb-skin coat and put his qarakul on her head. The hat, lined with lamb's wool, would not only keep her head warm but would also aid her disguise. She was sure to see some of the tribal elders, they seemed to never sleep, *nessun dorma*.

Cautiously, Aludra exited the dwelling, hoping, praying that Muhammed would not awaken before making her escape. She scolded herself and wondered about her naiveté, a donkey that knows directions? She chuckled.

Walking down the dusty path, the two bright lights in the sky highlighted her way. Surprisingly, there were no elders *or* tribesmen to be seen. *Unusual* she thought.

She approached the watering hole, her gait a walk of trepidation. Surely she would be caught, unless . . . . unless she really *had* encountered an angel. What else could it be, though she remembered that the angel had not acknowledged her question. *Are you an angel?*

There it was! A gray donkey with four saddle-bags, and no one was around. *How could this be?* There were always some men around the watering hole, watering their beasts of burden.

She mounted the gray beast, and the animal uttered not a sound. As soon as she was stable, the animal turned south, walking slowly as donkeys do. Aludra wiped the tears from her face, tears of sadness but also, joy. She *felt* protected. Praise Allah, she thought, or *Yahweh*.

Four hours later, Aludra and the donkey continued their way. Finally, they came upon a woman walking with children and singing songs. The donkey suddenly stopped beside the old woman, and Aludra nearly fell over the donkey's head.

"Are you Aludra?"

This was just too weird, but Aludra acknowledged her birth name. "I am."

"You are to join us on our walk. We will take you to safety." The villager was an old woman, her wrinkled and weathered olive skin revealed a hard life. All lives were hard in this part of the world.

"Are you a Muslim?" Aludra asked the woman after noting the small cross in her hand.

"No. I am a Jew. I am to save your life. The angel has spoken."

"Then why do you have the cross in your hand." Mysterious, she thought.

"Christians are safer in this God-forsaken land than Jews. Also, the Cross will save us. The angel told me, "Moses saved you from the Egyptians; the Cross will save you from eternal death.""

"Only if you believe Jesus was who he said."

"Exactly. Come."

"But, you said you were Jewish."

"Come."

Aludra had never lived a night like this night. She glanced skyward. The comet's tail was growing. It looked like it would hit the moon.

CHAPTER NINETEEN

"Men will faint from terror, apprehensive of what is coming on the world, for the heavenly bodies will be shaken." Luke 21:26 NIV

Jeff entered *The Divide* on the Duluth Towne Green and was surprised at the size of the crowd. The late afternoon sun was making the daily journey over the western horizon, and night crawled across the land. All flat screens showed the same story. T minus 3 hours until impact, and it surely looked like it would be making a direct hit. The comet was now the size of the nearly full moon, at least it appeared so from the glowing coma. The comet's tail had grown but could not really be appreciated, as most of the tail was hidden by the comet as it hurtled directly toward Earth. The flat screens flickered, the Earth's magnetic field now feeling the effect of the comet's magnetism. Beneath the comet's dark, graphite surface laid a core of iron.

"Big crowd."

"Hey Jeff. Good to see you, man." Abe the Bartender was now Abe the Manager; but to Jeff, he would always be Abe the Bartender.

Jeff looked better than Abe thought he would. Maybe the day's memorial service was a burden lifted. Though Jeff had been stoic at the service, a strong soldier, he knew Jeff well and knew it would be a long time before he dealt with the loss of Melissa. Unfortunately, it appeared from the night sky that Jeff wouldn't have a long time to mourn. The televisions flickered again, and the digital signal was iffy as the screens pixilated.

"How're you doing?"

"I'm doing. What else is there to do?" Jeff smiled.

"I guess. Want a Duckhorn?"

"Nope, think I'll forgo the merlot tonight." He looked across the room to the other side of the mahogany bar and spotted Samarra Russell. He hadn't seen her since her release from the Atlanta Federal Prison, awaiting the trial from hell. The usually smiling, beautiful Samarra wasn't smiling tonight.

"Think I'll go say hello to Samarra. Where's Jack?"

"Jack's been in Israel, didn't you hear?"

Jeff had been good friends with Jack and Samarra Russell for several years. Jack was a U.S. Senator, was active in the defense community and an expert in nanotechnology. Much of his time was spent in Israel, where Mossad was continuing research into microscopic, mechanical insects that could fly like a summer gnat in South Georgia. Jack had been fortunate to win the affections of the beautiful Samarra, twenty-some years his junior.

"I didn't hear." Normally a news junkie, Jeff had been in a semi-stupor for the last few weeks.

"Then you won't believe *this* story!"

The full moon edged beyond the tops of the pin oak trees, leaves from the last season still clinging to the branches in a continual struggle of "I'm never gonna let you go."

Half a world away, Dmitry Ustinov glanced up and shivered; but not from the cold. It hadn't been cold for months. A fear came upon him like he had never felt, as he marveled at the increasing size and brightness of the dark comet. *Why did they name it that?* It was the brightest light he had ever seen, at least in the sky. He shivered again, a heavy shiver, the kind that shakes the body from head to toe.

Dmitry thought about the destruction caused by the nuclear submarine, a destruction that could not have happened but for him. He found himself sympathizing with all the innocent Panamanians who had been killed from the nuclear strike on the canal. Sympathy had never been one of Dmitry's attributes, and he wondered about that too. He had no sympathy for those who were incinerated at the U.S. base in Diego Garcia. They deserved what they got, they were only arrogant Americans.

The hijacking plan that Dmitry and Yousef had devised was a work of art, and the takeover had been even easier than he had expected. The crew had been specifically assigned to the Indian nuclear submarine, part of the plan; and most were members of the *Special Purpose Islamic Regiment* (SPIR), a Chechnyan terrorist cell loosely associated with al-Qaeda and a few other groups, or the *diminished* al-Qaeda, he thought. After the Americans killed Osama bin Laden, the rumored demise of al-Qaeda had not happened. Dmitry was *sure* Osama wasn't dead, probably in a torture camp somewhere. No one had seen a body, and Dmitry was well aware of the cosmetic abilities of *Photoshop*. He had used it himself to doctor photos.

Dmitry was certain he could feel a rumble in the atmosphere, very low in frequency but noticeable. The moon and the comet seemed to merge as one, and Dmitry felt like he would wet his pants. He began to pray for the first time in his life.

CHAPTER TWENTY

The Admiral and Sheryl had been out of touch with Washington since the early evening when communications became negligible. Relaxing as best they could in the chaise lounges by Jeff's pool, the TV had totally pixilated. The magnetic interference from the comet's approach had been unexpected.

They lay silently on the separate lounges, staring at the nearly-full moon and the comet side-by-side, holding hands, their fingers entwined. Sheryl gave a little squeeze.

"Let's go to *The Divide*. Why not? Might as well get creamed there as anywhere."

Sheryl was frustrated with the *on-again off-again* news coverage of the coming doom. She and Justin had decided to await their fates at Jeff's Sugarloaf estate, alone. She was anxious. According to Chad, there was nothing to worry about; but according to the night sky, there was.

"Are you sure?" The Admiral wasn't sure they would even make it as the comet's glow ever increased in size. Maybe it would hit earlier than projected.

"Sure, it's ten minutes away, maybe less since there's no traffic. Let's go see how many of our friends are there."

The Admiral stood but decided otherwise. His arms slid around Sheryl and he kissed her softly on the lips as they stood merged as one. "I only want to be with you Sheryl. I have found myself smitten and don't want to share." He kissed her again, and Sheryl's head spun in a bliss she had never felt.

I've been waiting so long for this, she thought; and now it's going to last only a moment. She closed her eyes as the kiss lingered. She was either in love or in lust; but either way, she liked it.

Johnson Propulsion Laboratory

The moon and comet merged closer and closer as Chad Myers watched the monitor. The concentrated beam of lasers that had been aimed at the comet for several days may or may not have worked. The comet's path had deviated from the bombardment, but only the slightest of deviations. *Would it be enough?*

"How's it lookin'?" The question came from the JPL NEO Project Manager. The small staff seemed certain a collision with the moon was inevitable.

"It's looking iffy-but-maybe at this point. We'll know in about 30 seconds," and a mental countdown began in everyone's head. *Twenty-nine, twenty-eight, twenty-seven* . . . . The moon continued its painfully slow journey across the night sky, toward the comet's path. *Ten, nine, eight* . . . It was 8:08 Eastern Standard Time.

In the mid-Atlantic, the Nerpa nuclear submarine crew, totally oblivious to the comet above, continued slowly and quietly. Commander Kadyrov ran a tight ship with no dissent.

"Do you think they are looking for us Ismail?" the sailor used Julio's middle name. It was Islamic.

"Of course." The commander's comment was brief. He was a man of few words. He knew every available attack submarine from the U.S., Britain and other western countries, maybe even Israel, would be scouring the ocean depths in hot pursuit. Why wouldn't they be?

Unaware of the comet's approach and the deadly plagues haunting Europe and the Americas, Kadyrov was also unaware that many attack sub schedules had been modified. More than a third of the U.S. submarine contingency staffs and crews were either dead or in quarantine from the spreading flu; and most of the land based militaries were even harder hit. England, France, Spain and Italy had suffered similar losses, mostly from the smallpox. In many ways, Asia had been spared from disease and their navies and militaries were mostly intact. Every day, China's military became stronger by default as the militaries of the world dwindled from disease.

The sub moved slowly toward the Mediterranean as the paths of the moon and the dark comet began to intersect 237,000 miles above Earth.

"If we somehow make it through this night Sheryl . . ." the Admiral's words drifted as he contemplated his next, "I think we should go steady." They both laughed at the term. "Do they still say that?"

"You betcha," Sheryl replied. "I don't know if they still use it; but I know what you mean. And I accept. They kissed again, a brief kiss, held hands, looked skyward and began to pray out loud.

The small crowd gathered on the Duluth Towne Green outside *The Divide* stood in silence, silence except for a few whimpers here and there, and a cry from nearby. West of Duluth, many roads were still underwater with bridges washed out. Several water trucks idled nearby, waiting for *the end*. Again, the cry from nearby.

"Oh Jesus, Jeeessussss. Please save us. PLEEEEASE SAVE US!"

The cry came from one of the expensive townhomes adjacent to the Green. No one was drinking at this moment as all were mesmerized from the *signs in the sky*, nor were they paying attention to the screaming lady.

"Looks like it's going to hit the moon." The man shouted from across the Green as the moon and comet became one. They all held their breath as the clock approached 8:08, two hours from the predicted time of impact.

Chad continued to watch the JPL monitors and scour the data as the time approached, *six, five, four . . .*

"Looks like we're gonna make it!" Chad held his breath. *Three, two, one . . .* nothing. A small cloud of lunar and comet dust, like a white fog, appeared on the left side of the Moon; and Chad knew the Earth had been spared, at least for the time being. There would be much debris, and part of that debris was sure to hit earth eventually; but that was far better than a direct hit by the comet. The debris cloud grew; and the night sky became brighter, as did the mood at the Johnson Propulsion Lab. The cometary-lunar dust mixture made the Moon appear to swell.

Jeff and Abe watched almost straight overhead, intently focused as the comet seemed to just disappear. As 8:08 PM crept into the past, the crowd began to stir, the din growing into a crescendo of jubilation. *Where had it gone?* Had it collided with the moon?

As reality of their salvation set in, strangers hugged each other, men kissed women they didn't know, like the sailor kissing the nurse in Times Square after World War II; and the world sighed in disbelief. For a brief moment, the entire world was united in fear; but now the world was united in gratitude to God that *something* had happened, a *miracle* had happened.

The large dust plume continued to grow above the moon.

"Bar's open!" Pam MacLott shouted from the front entrance of *The Divide*, "And it's on the house."

Abe the Bartender/Manager hugged Jeff, a mutual bear-hug. They had made it. As forlorn as Jeff had found himself earlier, he suddenly was euphoric. He was just glad to be alive; and he acknowledged silently to himself that yes, he had prayed they would be spared.

And they were.

CHAPTER TWENTY-ONE

The crowd at *The Divide* finally began to dwindle about two in the morning, and there were plenty who shouldn't be driving. The police offered free rides home for anyone who needed one; and suddenly the night was almost like any other, the massive, Earth-shattering annihilation that was sure to happen, now an event of the past that never did.

"Well, we escaped the big one it looks like."

Abe was glad to be alive; and even though he knew a comet collision had not been spelled out in the Scriptures, he was sure it would happen eventually. Had the dark comet missed the Moon, most of the world would surely be deceased at this point. *Most of the world would surely be deceased at this moment.* Abe recalled a quote from Jesus, Matthew something.

"If those days had not been cut short, <u>no one</u> would survive, but for the sake of the elect those days will be shortened."

The thought crossed Abe's mind, were *they* the *elect*, the survivors? But that would be everyone. They had all survived. That made no sense.

"Yep, we did," Jeff answered, and he was as relaxed as he had been since Melissa . . . went missing. He still couldn't force himself to say *dead.* "I think I'm heading back to Sugarloaf. I *never* stay up this late."

"What are you going to do tomorrow? You know everyone will be celebrating through the weekend." Abe figured biz would be good at *The Divide* for the next few days.

"I'm going to plan my trip to California; gonna buy me a Cadillac."

"So you're buying that car, what is it?" Abe couldn't remember.

"It's one of a kind; and she's a beauty, a 1954 Cadillac Cabriolet Pininfarina."

"Are you flying to LA?" Abe asked, already missing his friend who had not yet left.

"La Jolla, my friend; near San Diego. New jetport just opened."

"When will you be back?"

"I don't know Abe. Not really sure when I'm leaving. First I'm going to Jamaica to check on the SCUBA business, what's left after the *wave*. If it's salvageable, I may be there for a few weeks. Then I'll go to La Jolla."

"OK. So how long before you're back here?"

"Maybe a couple of months, maybe three. I don't know. I just need to get away, get my head straight. I'm going to drive the new Caddy cross-country, take my time. The kids said they would feed the dog and stay at the house."

Jeff said goodbye, shook Abe's hand, walked to the front entry and turned back to Abe. "Why do you think God chose the Jews?"

"Pardon moi?"

"Why do you think that God picked the Jews to be his *chosen*?"

"I'll tell you when you get back."

Jeff walked out into the warm night, now early morning. The Moon was much larger and glowing from the growing dust cloud.

He started the dark-gray GTR, and savored the sound of the throaty exhaust. He headed north on Buford Highway, past Woody's Nursery and the Duluth Historical Museum and turned right onto Sugarloaf Parkway. Glancing at the moon again, he was sure it had a pinkish tint. Maybe the moon's iron core was closer to the surface than thought by the experts; but if that was the case, it wouldn't appear with a red hue. Ferrous oxide would surely produce a reddish color, but there was no oxygen on the moon to react with the iron. *Strange.*

Everything had been strange for a year.

CHAPTER TWENTY-TWO

Jeff awoke to the smell of Chocolate Perks' famous Duluth Blend, chocolate-truffle coffee. It was 7:30, a "sleep in" for Jeff, who was always an early riser. He rolled out of bed and accepted the pain only arthritis sufferers can describe and massaged the back of his neck, stiff from star-gazing just a few hours earlier. Then it hit him. *They were saved.* Glory Halleluiah! He ran out on the deck off his master suite to see if he could still see the Moon. Gone. He would see it on FOX, CNN, MSNBC, *Entertainment Tonight*; it would be everywhere.

Jeff brushed his teeth, washed his face and gargled in less than two minutes, donned his seersucker Bermuda shorts and walked out to the pool. The morning air smelled magnificent, but it was warm for a January morning. He hoped the coming summer wouldn't be as hot as the last.

"Hey sleepy head. He finally arises, Admiral."

Sheryl had a cup of coffee waiting. "Went to City Hall last time I was here and stopped by Chocolate Perks to get your favorite blend. How's that for service?"

"Good morning, Ms. Lasseter. The smell woke me up, or I might've made it to 7:40." He gave her a hug and cheek-kiss and told her he loved her.

Sheryl noted Jeff's good mood, first she had seen it since he returned from Grand Cayman. Maybe there had been a silver lining in the comet's dark cloud. He was finally thinking of something other than Melissa.

"You know Sheryl, I've been thinking a lot about Melissa."

Sheryl rolled her eyes, to herself only. *Go figger.*

"Jeff, you were always thinking a lot about Melissa. I imagine you will be thinking about her for a long time to come."

"You're right, and that's why I'm going shopping. Cal-i-forn-i-a, here I come."

Jeff thought about the growing world-wide mortality from the plagues, and now AIDS from mosquitos. Duluth hadn't experienced even a single case of Spanish Flu, and the infections seemed to be concentrated in specific areas of the nation. *What if he caught the flu in California?*

"And besides, shopping is good for down-in-the-dumpsness."

"You mean depression?" Sheryl spoke before thinking.

"What are you going to buy?" The Admiral exited the kitchen, swatted a mosquito and joined the group. The water falls along the back edge of the pool reminded him briefly of days long ago when he and his friends would play in caves behind waterfalls along the creek. His mom and dad never knew about *that*!

"Like your jam-jams there, Admiral. *Chartreuse*. Very, very Admirally!"

"It's all I could find in your closet big-guy."

"I'm going to buy a car, well, not exactly a car. At least, not just any car."

"The Cadillac?" The Admiral knew that one day Jeff would track down the Cadillac. He had talked about it for years, the only one ever produced.

"Yep. Going to book a flight today to see what's left of *The Dive Shop Next To Rick's Café.*" They all laughed at the name of Jeff's dive business in Jamaica.

"I remember when you chose that name. We all thought you were nuts. Which of course you were." The Admiral put just a dab of the Perks Truffle Creamer into his cup. "And still are as far as we know." He winked at Jeff and noticed he seemed a *little* happier.

Jeff had chosen the name several years earlier when he opened the dive shops, one on Grand Cayman and the other in Jamaica, next to Rick's Café. It had been a marketing coup, at least in terms of Jamaica. Every American and European tourist knew about *Rick's,* and the intoxicated, testosterone-driven tourists who would make the twenty-five foot jump from the cliffs to the crystal clear water below. Jeff had done that himself a few times, after a few adult beverages.

As the tourists flocked to Rick's, Jeff offered discount-diving packages to any patron bringing in a Rick's receipt. It had worked like a charm. A half-day dive package came with dinner for two at Rick's. The relationship between the two businesses grew, symbiotically.

"Oh, speaking of Jamaica, Wild Willy called. He's back from Israel. Remember the Lear Business Jet he repo'd in Grand Cayman?" Sheryl immediately wished she hadn't brought up Grand Cayman, thinking the tragic memories may stir in Jeff's head. "Now he's flying it to the new owner in Puerto Rico. He wanted to know if you might want to go along."

Jeff contemplated that sudden turn of fate. A private jet to Jamaica wouldn't be bad.

"Wonder if he would drop me off in Negril or Montego Bay. I don't think Negril's small airport can handle a Lear." He knew it couldn't handle a jet of any kind. It was downright frightening to fly in on a prop plane. The last trip, he recalled, the plane barely stopped before running into the palm grove at the end of the short, bumpy runway.

"I'm sure he would. He's landing at Briscoe Field in Lawrenceville. Said it would be just before lunch."

"Great. He always does that. Now I will have to buy him lunch!"

"Yeah, and Wild Willy can put down the food!" The Admiral laughed. Everyone's mood seemed almost jubilant. The Moon had saved the day, or maybe God saved the day. He was a believer.

"He said if you want to go, be at Briscoe by noon. He doesn't want to *dally*."

At 11:30, after kissing and hugging everybody goodbye, Jeff packed the carryall into the small trunk of the GTR, cranked the engine, savored the sound and headed up Duluth Highway 120, careful not to break the speed limit. Passing Bill Head Funeral Home, he noted the large crowd at *Wally's Shack* on the left. It wasn't unusual to see a crowd at Wally's. Wally had built the screened-in enclosure just to host large crowds and charitable functions. The crowd didn't look happy, as several gathered around someone lying on the ground. In the distance he could hear the approaching sirens.

Wild Willy saw Jeff's GTR pulling into Briscoe Field and called him on the iPhone.

"Mr. Ross, please proceed to Jetport 4 and leave all your money and jewelry with the handsome guy at the door." Will was always a joker, like their friend Chad, speaking of. He hadn't heard from Chad and thought for sure he would've called from JPL. The lab was on top of all the events of the previous evening. Maybe he was partying. That would be Chad.

Jeff and Will greeted each other, handshakes and hugs.

"You ready?"

"Only if you can drop me by Montego Bay. I have to get to Negril."

"Say what??"

"Have to go to Negril and check the shop. When will you be coming back?"

"I wasn't planning on coming back to Jamaica. I wasn't planning on stopping in Jamaica." Will didn't seem annoyed and continued his checkout.

"Just fly low over Negril, and I'll bail out. Try to put me close to Charela Inn." Jeff loved Charela Inn, his favorite place in Jamaica if he wasn't staying at Bluefields Bay. "Just don't drop me in the middle of Norman Manly Boulevard. Those Jamaicans get a little crazy when they get in a car."

The carryall now loaded on board, the Executive Jet taxied down the 9,000 foot taxiway, made the U-turn, gunned the engines and the jet accelerated with gusto, roaring into the warmer than normal January air.

"Wow. This thing'll haul ass."

"Yes it will." And Jeff knew Wild Willy loved his high-end, vehicle repossession business.

At 10,000 feet, Will began the task of getting clearance over Cuba's airspace. Due to a recent warming trend between the governments of the United States and Cuba, he didn't think he would have trouble; and he didn't. Only 1,100 miles away, they would be in MoBay in less than three hours.

CHAPTER TWENTY-THREE

"I watched as he opened the sixth seal. There was a great earthquake. The sun turned black like sackcloth made of goat hair, the whole moon turned blood red . . ." Revelation 6:12

Jeff checked in at the Charela Inn, surprised that Negril and the north side of the island had escaped most of the tsunami damage. The taxi ride along the north shore from Montego Bay to Negril was uneventful. The driver was smoking *ganja-mon*, as they always did in Jamaica.

"Hey Mon," the taxi driver said, turning around to face the back seat, "Want a hit?"

"No thanks. Watch the road *mon*." He hated the drive from MoBay to Negril for this very reason. Curvy roads and stoned drivers.

"Irie mon, irie. Everythin' is gonna be all right."

There was no porter, so Jeff rolled the overnighter to Charela's nicest suite, *The Ross Suite,* overlooking Negril's famous beach, seven miles of the most beautiful sand and palms that anyone could ever imagine. He was always mesmerized by Jamaica's beauty; and the suite was named such because of the many visits that Jeff and Melissa, and now just Jeff, had made over the years.

Unloading the overnight bag, Jeff carefully placed the Italian, marble-framed photo of Melissa on the dresser. It was his most favorite, and he would always have it with him. *Would he ever get over her?* He pondered the possibility and knew the answer. Time heals all hurts, but this is some *bad* hurt.

Leaving the Inn his driver headed west down Norman Manly Boulevard toward *The Dive Shop Next To Rick's Café*, about a five minute drive. Jeff had never seen heavily armed soldiers on the city's streets, but they were everywhere.

"Why all the soldiers?" Jeff asked his driver, George.

"Looters mon. Looters evrywhere mon. Since de wave come, tings have changed. Refuhgees from de east and de south uh de island make dere way here, mon; dey be lookin' for de work, food, anythin'. Lass week de lady was caught eatin' de baby."

"What?"

"No problem mon, de baby had die de day befo. She told de police she had eat de baby or she an' de udder kids would die. It's vedy sad mon. Dere ain't no money, and dere ain't no food. You be careful mon. Dey might eat you." The driver laughed, uneasily. "Dey did dat at Masada mon, you know?"

"They did what at Masada?"

Jeff had never visited Israel but knew the stories about Roman soldiers surrounding the ancient, plateaued city in Israel, nearly 2,000 years before. Starved the Jews to death. The remaining Jews committed suicide rather than be taken by the Romans.

"De Israeli women ate dere dead babies mon, boiled de babies in de goat's milk. It was de fulfillment uh de *Bible* prophecy mon. Don't you know your *Bible* mon?"

"I guess not, *mon*." Jeff had the Gideon Bible with him, sitting on *de* dresser next to Melissa's photograph. Maybe he would start reading some of the books Abe recommended months before. He had the books in his bag.

"You can read it yuhself mon. *Jerrymiah 19:9*. I always liked dat prophet mon."

Jeff made a mental note and would look it up later. *Surely* that wasn't a prediction. *What kind of god would do something like that?* He kept his thoughts to himself.

"George, you say 'mon' a lot man."

"*God* didn't *do* it mon. Nope, you cain't blame de Lawd suh." George interrupted. "He jist said dat would happen 'cause uh dere rebellion. De Israelis, don't ya see, dey always rebelled against dere God, even since de days uh Moses. Dey do it again, right now mon. Dey have de gay p'rade evuh year mon, you know? Right dere'n Israel, dey do. Dat's not whut God say de do mon. Dey ev'n raise de swine, ya know?"

The driver lit up another cigarette, what he called *de spleef mon*, the smell wafting to the rear and dropped Jeff off at the dive shop pathway down to the beach.

"I'll call you George. I have to check damage, then will have dinner at *Rick's*. I want to turn in early."

"No problem mon. Yuh call me on de phone mon." George was proud of his new cell phone, which of course wasn't new at all, just new to George, vintage 1996, sixteen years earlier, in a satchel.

Walking down the path, Jeff thought about the driver, and how George could've known what he was thinking about God, or god. The din from the afternoon crowd at *Rick's* was loud and joyous, full of "comet tourists" who had visited the beautiful island to watch *the end*. No one seemed to believe it would happen in the touristy crowd; but in the hills of Jamaica, along the Black River, the natives sang Voodoo chants, praying to the gods that they would be spared. The animals were prepared for sacrifice.

Rosalie, a native from Kingston, Jamaica's capital, entered *The Ross Suite*, closed the door and immediately began checking the room to make sure everything was *just right* for Mr. Ross. Her bright blue dress and yellow hat added needed color to the room, now not quite as nice as it used to be. The staff knew of the recent tragedy and the loss of Mr. Ross' wife. They were not aware that the Ross' had been divorced for several years. Rosalie had never met Melissa but had met Jeffrey on his previous trip. He was very handsome she thought, for an *elderly*-type of man.

She spotted the twenty dollar bill on the dresser, but the thought of stealing it never crossed her mind. She noticed the photograph in the emerald frame, also on the dresser, then the note: *Rosalie, thanks for always doing a great job. Take the twenty dollar bill and buy something for your kids.* The note was signed by *Mr. Ross*. She stared at the photograph.

Walking onto the Roman-tiled deck, Rosalie was always stunned at the beauty of Negril's famous beach and the crystal-clear, azure water. *How nice it must be to live like this*, she daydreamed. She loved her Island but would like to leave the poverty and downtrodden life behind. Not likely now, she knew. Since the plagues in Europe and America, the tourism had almost stopped, at least until the asteroid or whatever became the latest *thing*.

This part of Negril had escaped the ferocity of *the wave*, at least mostly, unlike Kingston, where she was raised; and her family still lived in the hills. Many were killed in the wave, with Kingston being hit especially hard.

Making her final check, she glanced around the suite, did a three-sixty and walked toward the door.

She smiled, put the twenty in the pocket of her hibiscus-print apron, and turned to the photograph. It must be his wife she thought, or at least used to be. She *was* beautiful in the photograph, and Rosalie thought the woman looked vaguely familiar. *Maybe from a fashion magazine?*

The damage, if there was any, had not been apparent as Jeff walked up the steps to *The Dive Shop Next To Rick's Café*. The worn but sturdy, bamboo stairs led from the sandy beach to the elevated shop above. There had been a surge of sorts as the sand had accumulated under the shop. He was totally amazed at the lack of damage. The shop was open for business, and a few guests from Rick's were ready to give SCUBA a try. They got like that after a few Margaritas or Piña Coladas. They would have to wait.

Jeff applauded his small staff, worked on the books and chatted it up with the three employees and customers. He repeatedly pointed to the sign, *Drinkee Drinkee, No Divee Divee.*

As the sun passed and set into the western sea, the crowd at Rick's oohed and ahhed at the scene, a scene made famous by the setting sun and Hollywood. There was not a more beautiful sunset, at least none that he had seen; and he had been a lot of places. The sun was so . . . . *reddish.*

Jeff bid his staff goodbye and walked to Rick's to have his favorite dish, *Jamaican Shrimp and Sweet Potato Stir Fry.* The night was warm and the ocean breeze was unusually calm. He wiped a bead of sweat from his brow, as the red sun disappeared beneath the water and the solar pathway on the sea surface passed away, just like it did most every afternoon.

After dinner and a couple of martinis, Jeff was ready to call George as the din from the deck grew. Looking toward the sea, he saw everyone pointing at the sky. He was too beat to take much notice and walked out the front entrance and up the steps to Norman Manly Boulevard.

George answered on the first ring.

"George, can you come pick me up?"

"No probleem mon. Be right dere. Mr. Ross, did yuh see de Moon?"

"Nope, why?" Did he slur a little? He hadn't had *that* much to drink?

"Just look mon."

Turning around and again facing seaward, Jeff looked toward the eastern sky and couldn't believe what he saw. The moon was *pink*. The craters that were normally visible were not, but the moon had taken on a definite pink tint. Maybe it was all the lunar dust that had been stirred up the night before. Along the perimeters of the lunar dust cloud, there were some clearly visible objects. He would call Chad at JPL when he got to his room. Chad would know the latest status.

When George dropped Jeff off at the front of Charela Inn, he looked up toward the Moon again, a further analysis. The objects along the perimeter had moved across the surface of the dust cloud, just a little. *The Moon has moons.*

Jeff's knowledge of astronomy and his interest in near-Earth objects told him the bad news. There would surely be some kind of debris from the collision, and some of it would be heading Earth's way. *What if all that lunar dust is poisonous?* The thought was troubling.

Crossing the tiled entrance and stepping over the calico kitty sleeping by the door, Jeff entered his room, feeling no pain. He would sleep well tonight. His bed was turned down, a dark Godiva on both pillows; and the TV was still on FOX News. After brushing his teeth, Jeff did a hundred pushups, turned off the table lamp and looked forward to *Dreamland*. He liked to dream, at least most of the time. Maybe he could visit Melissa tonight, like he had the night before. As he drifted toward sleep, he first dreamt of his Mom and her constant preaching; and this sermon was something about the Moon turning red. *You just wait Mr. Smarty Pants. When you see that Moon turn red, you'll know. Yes sir, you will. It's in the Book!*

Jeff missed the *News Alert*.

"*The International Space Station has been evacuated, I repeat; the ISS has been evacuated.*"

CHAPTER TWENTY-FOUR

Four months later

Jeffrey Ross landed at La Jolla Regional Jetport at 1:05, California time, just an hour away from his latest acquisition. Departing the Learjet, the Becker JetVan was waiting to transport him to *Thomas White Exotics,* the driver a most gorgeous California blonde with long legs, blue eyes, and more. His intended arrival was months earlier, but *stuff happens.*

San Diego was known for its almost perfect climate, 75 and sunny; but today was an exception, especially for Mother's Day. The early afternoon sun beat down through the haze, a gift from the injured Moon; and the temperature was already in the nineties. The ocean breeze that always blew in from the Pacific brought high humidity and steamy conditions. The blonde was a bombshell, as so many California girls are. She keyed the remote and the side panel slid open, quietly and smoothly and a step unfolded.

"Welcome Mr. Ross. It is my pleasure to be your hostess today. Please watch your step."

Jeff entered the van, not exactly a *van,* and was in awe. He had never heard of the Mercedes JetVan but knew he needed one. The perfect means of land transportation to better entertain his good friends when they came to Atlanta. Plush leather would be a misnomer, three flat screens and surround sound, roving Wi-Fi, and complete bar setup. The hostess made sure Jeff was comfy and prepared his Diet Coke with peanuts as he had requested. Georgia peanuts.

"If you need anything Mr. Ross," the young lady pointed to the audio controls on the sides of the leather chairs, "just push that button; or you can say 'speak to hostess,' and that will open communications between the cockpit and the lounge." She smiled.

Jeff noted her name badge. It only said *HOSTESS*.

"I like your name. I've never met anyone named *Hostess*." He winked.

"Yes, my parents had quite the sense of humor." She pressed the remote and the side panel door slid silently shut.

As the JetVan made its way onto Torrey Pines Road and merged into the unusually heavy traffic, Jeff heard something loud in the distance, even over the surround-sound. It almost sounded like an aircraft flying really low, and his first thoughts were 9/11. *Hostess* looked around nervously, scanning the skies to the left. The sound grew; and Jeff knew this was no aircraft, at least none known to him.

Though the JetVan's windows were darkly tinted and the sun was bright in the cloudless sky, the image to the south was only recognizable as an angry, fiery, orange glow approaching rapidly from the horizon. Whatever it was, it was coming extraordinarily fast; and Jeff's heart raced in a fear he hadn't experienced before, even the tsunami of a few months . . . he quashed the thought. The sound grew exponentially by the millisecond; and then it was over, a loud explosion now to the north of the JetVan. Whatever had just flown overhead was as bright as bright could be, and Jeff felt the blast of heat inside the air conditioned carrier. He held his hand over his eyes as the Soledad Towers disappeared in fire and destruction, now 37 stories of nothingness, an *upscale* retirement community no more.

"Speak to Hostess." Jeff spoke the three words, and *Hostess* responded immediately but was out of breath it seemed, as no words came through the JBL speakers mounted in the ceiling above Jeff's head. He could hear her heavy breathing. The van rocked as the blast wave made its arrival, and *Hostess* steered the heavy vehicle under an overpass and stopped. Burning debris was raining down all around, but the JetVan had escaped unharmed but for a bit of shaking. Briefly, everything turned dark.

"Stay in the van *Hostess*. It's the safest place. I'll be right back." Jeff pushed the remote opener and the side panel again slid open. He exited with caution, glass and concrete falling from the sky like hailstones. "By the way *Hostess*, what's your real name?"

"Taci. Taci Edwards."

Jet Propulsion Laboratory

Pasadena, California

"Take a look-see at this!" The young grad student handed the data to Chad, a degree of excitement in his voice, or fear.

Chad knew as much as anyone about NEOs, and the dangers they posed to mankind. He had written numerous papers on the subject of near-Earth Objects for some of the finest schools in the country; Harvard, MIT, Georgia Tech. Glancing at the data, a dread clung to him like a San Diego fog.

"Does Sheryl know about this yet? Has anyone in Washington been notified?" Chad felt faint.

"There's no one in Washington, sir. At least no powers-that-be. Spanish Flu has most quarantined, and the hospitals are over capacity. Command Center is temporarily at Warner Robins Air Force Base in Georgia. Sheryl is in Atlanta. Should I notify her?"

"No. I'll call her." Chad first wanted to talk to The Admiral. Autodialing Jeff's home, Admiral McLemore picked the phone up on the first ring. He always did.

"Hey Chad. Looks like we made it." The Admiral referred to the comet's demise.

"Bad news, my man. Several small asteroid-like objects are expected to hit Southern California and parts of Arizona, leftovers from the comet's collision on the *dark side* of the moon."

Chad was puzzled that so many people didn't know that we only see one side of the moon, that the dark side is always on the *other* side and is only *dark* some of the time. The moon did rotate of course, but that was the really strange part. It rotated at exactly the speed that keeps the same side facing Earth, twenty-four seven, year after year, an oddity for certain.

"Sandouping has been wiped off the face of the earth, along with all 35,000 Chinese inhabitants. They are only finding small pieces of charred remains." The student continued his update.

"Admiral, please standby just a minute." Chad listened to the update and a frown crossed his face. This was *not* good.

"Sandouping?"

"China, along the Yangtze River; home of the Three Gorges Dam, the world's largest power supplier."

"What about the dam?" Chad was familiar with the world-renown structure. He also knew that if *that* dam was breached, hundreds of thousands could die, maybe millions, a disaster far greater that the Buford Dam fiasco.

"No word yet sir. The area is still too hot to visit, or even send in remote operating vehicles. The Chinese sent in a heat-resistant drone this morning, and it melted before it got within fifteen miles. So far there is no word on the dam, but it seems to be holding. Will concrete melt?"

"It's not holding, believe me." Chad was matter-of-fact.

"I'm not sure sir. There has been no flooding downstream of the dam," the student continued.

"There's no flooding because all the water is evaporating. Concrete melts at about 1,800 degrees."

Chad's temper was unusually short, as he thought about Interns and the stupid questions they ask. Why couldn't he have that cute little Debra as his trainee? *Everything melts.*

"Depending on the size of the impact, temperatures could be in the millions. There will be flooding, you can bet on it. There will be a lot more than 35,000 dead. Admiral, you hearing all this?"

"Yeah Chadbo. I assume this is from the Moon?"

"Yeah, or maybe the comet. We won the battle, but will we win the war?" Chad did not know that answer.

"So tell me about the debris headed to Southern Cal. How many objects, how large, do you know?"

"There appear to be several hundred, but most should burn up in the atmosphere. However, some are larger than a football stadium and *will* hit somewhere. I am sure that we will get our share in the northern hemisphere and better pray to God it's not near a city."

"Or dam," The Admiral replied, "or nuclear power plant."

"Is Sheryl with you?"

"Not at the moment. She's at Warner Robins. Since the military is on high alert, she's spending a lot of time in the secure bunker."

Chad wasn't surprised of the change in status. After all, the U.S. had sustained five nuclear attacks, three in U.S. territory, the evening of December 31. There had been two missiles shot down over the territorial waters off Florida and the one that destroyed Buford Dam, probably *not* a missile. The military readiness status had gone from DEFCON 4 to

DEFCON 1 in less than a day with troops on a "war is imminent" status. But who was war imminent with? That was the question. *Who fired the missiles?*

"How many nukes do you think are left, I mean after we sent them all to the comet?" Chad knew there were still plenty of nuclear bombs; but with the B-1B bomber fleet nearly destroyed, at least those on Diego Garcia, the antiquated B-52 would again be the delivery vector in this unidentifiable war.

"Well, you can bet your bippy that we did *not* send all our missiles, and neither did the Ruskies or the Chinese. There are still plenty to go around, and the briefcase nukes are who knows where. Even with tritium degradation, the BC nukes will make a statement, apparently already have." Admiral McLemore referred again to the destruction of the Buford Dam just north of Hotlanta, which was hotter than ever now that the drinking supply had virtually disappeared. The temperatures were record-setting.

"One more thing."

The Admiral listened.

"You know I can see wind don't you?" Chad was sure The Admiral had heard that oddity.

"I've heard."

"The jet stream is doing some things I've never seen before. It hasn't been reported in the news, but some weather bloggers are talking about it."

"What's different?"

"Admiral, some of the winds have to be 500 to 600 miles an hour. I know because of the color. That's what I see; it's a shade of color but almost transparent. The darker the shade, the higher the wind speed."

"What's the darkest shade you've seen?" The Admiral queried.

"Until this point in my life, a dark, royal blue. Yesterday it was indigo, almost black."

The conversation ended and another one started when Chad's iPhone chirped, the obnoxious sound indicating an incoming call. It was Jeff.

"Hey! What's up? I thought you were shopping." When one is depressed, one goes shopping. Chad had experienced the remedy in his own life.

"I was hoping you could tell me." Chad heard sirens in the background and a lot of honking horns. "I'm in San Diego, La Jolla actually; and all hell's broken loose. Thought it was another terrorist attack but think it was a meteorite. It couldn't have been very massive, because it only took out about a city block. Do you know anything?"

Chad explained the debris field that was traveling from the Moon to Earth and that several had probably hit by now in the Southern California and Tucson areas.

"Yes-by-God they've hit! That's for sure."

Chad had known Jeffrey Ross for many years. This was the first time he ever sounded scared; and though Jeff was an unbeliever, he never used the Lord's name in vain, out of respect for others. This was not good.

"Well, there're more headed your way. It's a meteor storm."

The line went dead.

CHAPTER TWENTY-FIVE

Vinny headed west along I-10. The late afternoon sun slipped over the Arizona mountaintops as the sun slowly began its daily descent, and Vinny's sunglasses hardly did the trick. Vinny wondered what *did the trick* really mean, and he recounted the day of the red Volkswagen.

He had dumped the Volkswagen, stolen earlier from the young girl in Atlanta; and Vinny thought again of the strangeness of the little girl, *Audry* he thought she said. The Volkswagen had been too obvious, plus it was very *girly*. Not to worry, as the VW now rested on the bottom of Lake Dalton, submerged in a deep water cove. Audry the Apparition.

Attaining another vehicle proved easy enough. After ditching the VW, Vinny walked back to the highway and stuck out his thumb. He had hitch-hiked many times in Europe and the United States, but the people in the U.S. were much more gullible than their European counterparts, especially in the South. Christians were trusting, and that was fine with Vinny. Muslims trusted no one! The morning was exceptionally warm, and a couple stopped within ten minutes to offer assistance. *Americans were so stupid.*

"Good morning young man. Are you stranded?" The old lady with the blue-gray hair looked to be straight out of an AARP commercial. "Ted and I would be glad to give you a lift honey. It's much too warm for you to be standing by the highway."

"God bless you ma'am." Vinny used his best drawl. "You must be an angel from heaven."

"Well, people have called us that before." The old lady laughed. "Our children are always telling us to be careful with strangers, but the *Good Book* tells us to be *kind* to strangers."

Vinny opened the back door, slid across the gray-vinyl bench seat and removed the knife from his backpack, now in the floorboard, as he slid. Miss AARP handed him a bottled water and a pack of peanut butter crackers.

Twenty minutes later, the elderly man and his "wife of 55 years" lay snug-as-a-bug-in-a-rug at the bottom of a steep gorge, the victims of a tragic accident. It had been so easy, and Vinny smirked. He loved killing infidels. Actually, Vinny just loved killing; and it always aroused him sexually.

The blue Impala, now newly painted, had pulled off the shoulder and headed north, jerked left and ran into the median, as Vinny began his *art*. When he grabbed Miss AARP's head, yanked it straight back and held the knife to the woman's throat, grandpa had a heart attack and died in the driver seat. With a swift jerk, Vinny broke the old lady's fragile neck; and the *crack* of the cervical vertebrae brought a smile to Vinny's handsome, tanned face. He loved the sound of breaking bones, but he *especially* loved the sight of someone else's blood. Today sadly, there was no blood. No blood to be detected in his new car, and Vinny caressed the plastic steering wheel.

Now in Arizona, the evening had been long but beautiful. The clear Arizona sky was filled with shooting stars, hundreds if not thousands. It had to be a sign from Allah; and Vinny made his way toward Lukeville and the J. Blanton Concrete Company, just north of the Mexican border. There he would meet with Ahmed and 200 other martyrs in the secretive *Brotherhood*, 200 highly fluent and intelligent *home grown* martyrs. There were many more than the 200 though, centered at various points across the U.S. and Europe.

The martyrs waited, patiently. At the previous meeting in January, Ahmed insisted on keeping a *low profile* for a while, just to let things calm down. Vinny didn't know it then, but Ahmed was beginning to think the comet would solve the infidel problem *without* the help of the martyrs. He knew *absolutely* that Allah sent the comet to signify the arrival of the Twelfth Imam, and plague had invaded the perverted world.

Watching the sky, intrigued with the numerous meteorites, Vinny knew that only ten to fifteen percent of the world's Muslims really adhered to the *Holy Quran*; and they were the true followers of Muhammad, *may Allah bless him*. The *true* Muslim was the chosen now, not the Jews; and certainly not the Christians. The *true* Muslims would lead the world to

Allah's promised Holy Land. And it sure as hell wouldn't be Israel or Jerusalem. The land of Mecca was the land of Allah.

Now driving southwest along Arizona Highway 86, Tucson gradually faded in the rearview mirror. Vinny continued toward Lukeville. He rolled down the Impala's windows to let in the cooler night air when, from the periphery to his left, he caught a glimpse of a light of some kind. Before he could ponder the object and its origins, it passed overhead, clearly visible in the rearview mirror now; and explosions lit up the dark sky in the distance. *Whatever it was, it was sure going fast.* Faster than anything ever observed by Vinny's dark eyes.

Vinny loved explosions.

CHAPTER TWENTY-SIX

"There will be signs in the sun, moon and stars. On the earth, nations will be in anguish and perplexity at the roaring and tossing of the sea." Matthew 21:25 NIV

"Are you OK Taci?"

Jeff remotely opened the JetVan's sliding door. The young driver appeared ashen and frightened. Who wouldn't be? He had been scared to death himself; but Chad's words had calmed him a bit, at least to the fact that this was *not* another terrorist attack. She opened the door, stepped out and sneezed loudly just as she managed to cover her mouth; and dust swirled about.

"I . . . I guess. What *was* that?" Her gait was *not* steady. She wiped her hands with a tissue from the peach-scented Kleenex box in the front seat. Young Taci looked distraught.

Jeff explained to the best of his knowledge and hugged the young lady, visibly shaken to the core. He knew there was more to come and worried. He suddenly felt light-headed, and his mind drifted.

Ten minutes later they were headed once again to Thomas White Exotics, a little dustier. Distant sirens could be heard. Soon he would have the treasure he had relished for months since seeing the Cadillac on the *History Channel*, or one of the satellite channels. This of course was no ordinary Cadillac. The one million dollar cashier's check in his briefcase could attest to that, and he hoped a meteorite didn't land on him and his new car. The JetVan began to slow, finally stopping in the emergency lane. When the door didn't budge, he grabbed the remote and the door was soon sliding open. Jeff exited and looked in the driver's window. Taci seemed to be in a daze. He opened the door and began to help the young woman exit the van. He held her.

"Are you alright?" He asked the question again, noting that her nose was bleeding; and Taci fainted in his arms. Life suddenly felt like a dream.

Jeff rode to the emergency room with the young lady, hoping a stranger would do the same for his daughters. The siren wailed but was lost in the continuous din of sirens from all sorts of rescue and police vehicles. Taci went into cardiac arrest before reaching emergency room doctors, but the paramedics responded immediately and professionally, defibrillating her back into the realm of the living. The troubling aspect was the nose bleed, now profuse.

Leaving the hospital, Jeff walked across the street to a Starbucks, grabbed a frozen mocha latté and thought about his day so far, hoping it wasn't some kind of omen. He phoned JetVan Services, and explained where the other van was parked. Another was sent his way, and within 20 minutes a new chauffeur girl picked him up. She wasn't nearly as pretty as Taci, but not many were. He climbed in the back; and the chauffeur filled his request, handing him a diet soda before closing the door. Just the perfect beverage to wash down the mocha latté and forget the near miss.

Two minutes later, he was once again headed to Thomas White Exotics where his 1954 Cadillac Pininfarina Cabriolet waited patiently. He could hardly wait to pick that blue beauty up and head cross-country to Atlanta. Newly serviced and with only 3,000 and a few miles on the odometer, Jeff felt confident that the car would have no problems.

The JetVan pulled through the massive marble-stone, gated entry into the Thomas White Estate; and a quarter mile later the chauffeur pulled into the rotunda and up to the entrance. Thom White was waiting, dressed in tan slacks, white tee-shirt and navy blue blazer. The gold braid on his captain's hat matched the gold buttons that adorned the blazer, 24 carat Jeff was sure.

The sliding door opened, and Jeff exited like his previous chauffeur . . . with a sneeze.

While the world was experiencing the warmest weather in recorded history, Aludra and the Jewish woman with the cross were freezing as they made their way toward Chechnya via the secretive Khorugh passage on the mountainous southern border of Tajikistan. The area was once known as the Samanid Empire.

It was snowing, the wind was harsh and Aludra was wondering if she made the right decision. Her heart still ached for Muhammed, her dear brother; but the angel had instructed her to leave *that* night. At first she thought she was dreaming; but the angel insisted she leave on a gray donkey that would be found along the way, and she did.

"Do you think your brother would have killed you Aludra?"

Aludra thought about the question and wondered about that herself. It was the "rule" of the land in many Islamic countries, especially Middle Eastern. Anyone caught with a *Bible* would be stoned to death, hung or *cut into pieces*. Would Muhammed have cut her to pieces? She knew the answer.

Aludra pulled the quilt tightly around her, thinking about Muhammed; and the strange weather. Why was it snowing in the summer?

"Probably so. It's our way for some reason, a sick reason. I just don't understand the harshness and rigidity of the *Quran* when some of it truly is peaceful and caring.

"How can you kill people because they don't convert to your religion?" Aludra asked the question more to herself than Naomi.

"It is the only religion with such a mandate," the Jewish woman replied. And women are treated like . . ." The old lady hesitated.

"Like camel-doo! That's the way we're treated. Did you know when we have an election, which is seldom, women only get half a vote? The male gets a whole vote, and a woman gets only half. And these burqas we have to wear, it's like wearing a tent. That's not even in the *Quran*."

The old woman, a glint in her eye, looked at Aludra with a motherly affection. *Camel-doo?* Her rough, cracked lips turned up slightly, a smile.

"I think it started with Paul."

"Who?" Aludra questioned.

"Paul, you know, Paul and the road to Damascus in the *New Testament*? You've read it."

Aludra remembered Paul, the road and the blindness that followed. *How did the old woman know she had read the New Testament in the first place?*

"Oh, *that* Paul. What do you mean 'it started with Paul'?"

"Paul, if you remember, was one of the Jews who absolutely hated Jesus, even though he had heard but seen none of the miracles. We are all like that sometimes I think. Paul was a Roman Jew, and like the Pharisees, *the* rabbis of the time, he knew that Jesus was not the awaited savior. The first Christians were all Jews you understand, before they were even called Christians?"

Aludra had not thought about it but guessed it must be true. Naomi seemed a fitting name for the old woman, who seemed to know a lot about a lot. She had known Jewish people before, but none knew anything about the *New Testament* and the *Quran*. Naomi was an odd one, indeed she was.

"Paul chased down the Jews who thought Jesus was the Messiah, persecuting every chance he could for their blasphemy, at least blasphemy in *his* mind. Others in Israel chased down and killed their brethren as well, even though many had seen the miracles that Jesus performed and knew who he was. It was predicted and had to happen that way.

"Then Paul, he was called Saul in those days, saw the light, so to speak, on the road back to Damascus in Syria. The light had been so bright, it blinded him instantly."

The old woman thought of some of the exploding stars she had seen lately.

"Remarkably, that incident led him to believe that Jesus *was* the Christ who had been foretold; and he ended up giving his life, literally. Did you know the *Bible* says that the Jews of the *final* generation, the generation that will see the end of things, will *mourn* the day we see the Messiah come; because we will know we were wrong for two thousand years? We may know soon." Naomi rubbed the cross between her fingers.

"So what does all that have to do with a burqa? Are you a Christian, Naomi?" Aludra had assumed the old woman was Jewish and carried the small cross for safety. She *said* she was Jewish.

"Oh no, I'm Jewish. But I'm too old to be *narrow-minded*. I listen and think for myself. I always have. Sometimes the teachers are not truthful, either with a purpose or because they don't know the truth. Intentional omission of detail is deceptive.

"Paul said that women should be covered, their *head* should be covered, when going to temple. When Islam came along, that symbol of piety was misconstrued and expounded upon. You know, Islam apparently took a lot of information from the *Old Testament*, put its own spin on it and came out with a different book. I do not mean to offend you Aludra, but that's the way it was. The *Quran* is a re-write of the *Bible,* a manipulation of the word of God."

Aludra liked the way the old woman talked in everyday slang, putting her *spin* on it. She smiled for the first time in days. But she was offended at the old woman's criticism of the *Quran*, and her cheeks warmed a little from the sudden rush of blood in the cold, night air.

Following the path, the two ladies and the donkey were several miles into Tajikistan. The night was getting colder, but the clear sky was bright. The Moon, for some reason, was far brighter and larger than it had been a few months earlier; and the familiar craters could no longer be seen, hidden under a mist of pinkness. The women stared at the moon and wondered what had happened. The old woman considered the ancient prophecies; and she thought this *new* Moon might be one of the "signs in the sky" that was predicted to come . . . in the last days. Surely the God of Abraham would show us all mercy.

"No Aludra, I am not a Christian; but in my old age I have learned, the things we are told are sometimes not the truth. For *whatever* reason." The old woman was less than emphatic.

"Why are the Jews considered God's chosen, Naomi?"

The three Tajik men came out of the woods along the path the women and the donkey were taking and began walking toward them. All the men had machetes in their hands. The women held their collective breaths; but the men walked by, ignoring them.

"That's a good question, Aludra. I'm not sure I have the answer; but in the beginning, we weren't."

To the east, the horizon turned white, and then orange, as another meteorite crashed into a small Tajik village.

CHAPTER TWENTY-SEVEN

"But mark this: There will be terrible times in the last days. People will be lovers of themselves, lovers of money, boastful, proud, abusive, disobedient to their parents, ungrateful, unholy, without love, unforgiving, slanderous, without self-control, brutal, not lovers of the good, treacherous, rash, conceited, lovers of pleasure rather than lovers of God—having a form of godliness but denying its power. Have nothing to do with such people." 2Timothy 3:1-5 NIV

J eff loved his new toy, but he especially liked the admiring glances the automobile evoked. The blue Cadillac Cabriolet was an attention getter, and he liked that.

Thom White had been a gentleman indeed, a raspberry farmer with farms in Eastern Europe and rose farms for the perfume industry. *Was that correct?* Jeff found his memory suddenly *fuzzy*.

After leaving La Jolla, Jeff headed toward the eastern horizon, the gleaming, royal-blue beauty a little stiff compared to his GTR. He planned to stop by Surprise, Arizona, to visit one of Abe the Bartender's friends from high school, Rod Smith, now a research archeologist specializing in Middle Eastern Biblical Archeology. Jeff had some questions about Biblical archeology, like: *Where's the beef?* Maybe Rod could answer.

Six hours later, the air pleasantly *crisp* for a change, the Cadillac continued eastward along Interstate 8. The early-evening sky resembled a continuous fireworks display, remnants of the collision between the dark comet and the Moon, burning up as they traveled through Earth's atmosphere. It was fear-provoking, but also an exquisite beauty that Jeff had never seen before. He tuned the radio to an all-news channel, the Sirius satellite option the only real change to the original Cadillac's specifications.

"*The weather continues to be stranger with each passing day, not just the global warming phenomenon but also these massive hailstones that have wiped out several hundred villages in China, Africa and Bangladesh.*"

It wasn't Condi the news-babe, and the NPR broadcaster's voice was British. It seemed that British accents were *the* thing these days with news channels.

"*Let's first start with an interesting tidbit from Mt. Ararat, Turkey. A few days ago, the area was hit by the mother of all hailstorms with tens of thousands of livestock killed. As reported at the time here on NPR, the entire eastern slope of the mountain collapsed, displacing more than a billion tons of mountainside. Environmentalists on this show yesterday stated that these kinds of catastrophes are inevitable, a result of man-kind's attack on the environment.*

"*As a result of the collapse of the eastern slope of Mt. Ararat, satellite photography picked up what looked like a large, ancient, wooden ship lying on the mountainside. University of Arizona archeologist Rod Smith has visited the site, and he described the large ship as more rectangular than later ships, and very massive. The ship is reported to be in remarkable shape, probably preserved in the ice on the mountain's top. It is said to measure about 450 feet long and 75 feet wide. The top of the large ship has eroded but appears to have been about 40—50 feet in height.*

"*Carbon dating on a small piece of wood dates the ship to somewhere between six and eight thousand years ago.*

"*We have as our guest today, Dr. Rod Smith, a biblical archeology professor at University of Arizona. Dr. Smith, what do you think of this discovery?*"

Jeff wondered if this was Abe's Rod Smith? Had to be.

"*Thank you for having me on Ms. Barwick. This is quite an incredible find and both churches and synagogues from around the world, as well as the Israeli Antiquity Society, are planning tours.*"

"*Why exactly would churches and synagogues be planning tours Dr. Smith? Do they give these reports credence?*"

Pat Barwick was a long-time employee with NPR and could recall only a few occasions that religious scholars had been on the network. That had to be minimized because of the church-state separation clause, only Pat knew there was no such clause. There never had been, but the Supreme Court had reinterpreted the 1st Amendment numerous times, based on an 1802 letter from Thomas Jefferson to the Baptists. Jefferson was informing the Baptists that the government would not establish a state religion, like the Church of England, so they needn't worry. Jefferson had fears that the Quakers would become the Church of the United States.

Pat had thoroughly researched constitutional law; and one thing she had learned was; while the words *Separation of Church and State* appeared nowhere in the U.S. Constitution, it was clearly stated in the constitution of the former communist Soviet Union.

She glanced at the iPad on her desk and re-read the quote from Chief Justice William Rehnquist of the U.S. Supreme Court:

"The metaphor of a wall of separation is bad history and worse law. It has made a positive chaos out of court rulings. It should be explicitly abandoned."

Dr. Smith continued.

"Obviously Ms. Barwick, there is much speculation that this could be the remains of the Biblical ark as described in Genesis."

"What do you think, Dr. Smith?"

"Pat, this appears to be a most remarkable find . . ."

"But do you think it's the Biblical ark?" she interrupted.

"Well, according to the <u>Genesis</u> story, the ark's physical attributes are well described. The outer dimensions of the ark were 300 cubits long, 50 cubits wide and 30 cubits high. That is nearly the exact dimensions of this ship."

"How long is a 'cubit' Dr. Warner?" Patricia asked the other guest.

Dru Warner, an associate and fellow archeologist, spoke for the first time.

"Pat, a cubit is an ancient unit of measure and varied among cultures. For example, an Egyptian cubit was considered 17.6 inches long, and a Hebrew cubit was considered 17.5 inches. A cubit was the distance in an adult from the finger tips to the elbow and is commonly considered to be 18 inches."

Pat punched in the numbers on her iPad and had the answer immediately.

"This information <u>is</u> stunning to say the least, Dr. Warner. That would make the ancient, legendary ark 450 feet long, 75 feet wide and 45 feet in height, almost the exact dimensions. My-o-my, this will set the world on its ear!"

"You're correct, Ms. Barwick; and it may prove that the ark wasn't a legend after all. And besides that, DNA sampling from the flooring of the ship indicates several different animal species. One sample appears to be the DNA of a giant, woolly mammoth, thought to have been extinct at the time of the Biblical flood and usually located in the far northern areas of the globe,

certainly not in ancient Biblical lands. They preferred the frigid Siberian and Arctic climates, so this is an interesting find."

Jeff couldn't believe his ears as Drs. Smith and Warner continued to define some of the DNA findings from the relic. The night was cool as Jeff traveled along Interstate 8 at a smooth 75 miles per hour. He suddenly felt dizzy and grabbed a Snickers from the console. Blood sugar.

"He's in cardiac arrest. Hand me the defibs."

What?? Had Dr. Smith said that? *Who's* in cardiac arrest?

Jeff must not have properly heard the good doctor, because they certainly weren't discussing heart attacks on Noah's ark; and he knew it would turn out to be something different. There had been many "discoveries" of Noah's ark over the years, and this would be just another fluke. No one *way back then* could've built a 450 foot long ship. Ridiculous.

The Arizona countryside was desolate, a mixture of desert cactus, intermingled with a dose of flowering bougainvillea, the pink and white leaves offering color to an otherwise drab landscape. Bufflegrass ran along the interstate and up into the distant mountains. Bufflegrass, a dense, invasive and rapidly growing, native species provided the necessary fuel for the annual, Arizona wildfires that sometimes seemed to burn all year. The smell of smoke wafted through the Cadillac interior, and Jeff knew the fires were nearby. Bufflegrass fires.

Just east of Theba, Arizona, Jeff made a right turn and aimed the Cadillac Cabriolet south on Highway 85. He was supposed to head north toward Phoenix to meet Rod at *Mitzi's,* an all—night diner. Only Rod was talking archeology on the radio with Pat Barwick. It didn't matter though; because Jeff was having a great time, cruising down the highway like the boys from *Route 66,* and he was in no hurry.

"In other news, the missing nuclear attack submarine is still missing, the Panama Canal remains closed and it will be for months to come, if not years. The submarine seems to have disappeared, and an oil slick has been spotted in the Gulf of Mexico. Of course, oil slicks are common in the Gulf.

"The U.S. Coast Guard, the U.S. Navy and the European Navies are on the lookout. The sub was believed to be in the Atlantic, destination unknown. Boston, Washington and New York City are on high alert under a Code Red, and the new U.S. Navy Rail Gun Defense System is standing guard.

"Israel's on-again-off-again peace treaty is off again as Hamas continues to launch missiles into southern Israel.

"In California, the 9th Circuit Court today threw out the suit over the controversial 'Marry My Pet' law. This suit was filed, if you remember, after a

northern California farmer suffered a severe financial loss after the deportation of California's illegal-immigrant communities. The farmer has now married two cows and is claiming them as dependents. The ruling also provides for free, indigent veterinary care. Not sure if this ruling applies to transgender cows."

Pat Barwick couldn't believe her teleprompter, and tried to stifle her laugh. The two archeologists laughed out loud.

Glancing to the left, Jeff was surprised to see the small white church sitting a hundred feet off Highway 85 in the middle of a field of bright-yellow daffodils. He had never seen so many daffodils in his life. There was nothing around *except* for the small church in the daffodil-laden field, a parking lot to the rear. He wasn't sure if he had ever seen a whiter church, it seemed almost to glow in a reflective yellow. The illuminated message sign by the highway is what really captured his attention:

Welcome to Ephesus
Today's Sermon
WHY ARE THE JEWS GOD'S CHOSEN?

That was the *same* question Jeff had asked Abe before leaving for California. *I'll tell you when you get back,* Abe's reply.

"We're losing him doc. Blood pressure has dropped to 96 over 56."

There it was again, the strange voice with a strange message. This time it definitely didn't come from the Sirius broadcast. Late afternoon advanced toward darkness.

Continuing his southward journey along Highway 85, Jeff had traveled twenty-five miles from the small white church in a field of yellow daffodils when he saw another, identical to the first, illuminated sign by the highway:

Welcome to Smyrna
Today's Sermon
A FETUS IS NOT A ROCK

How odd was his only thought. The church appeared empty like the other. Again, it was immaculately maintained and appeared freshly painted, white as snow, the yellow flowers offering a slight tint. The streaming meteorites continued to light the night sky, and the small church glowed in the emanating light. The parking lot across the field was large for a small church, but not a car was to be seen.

Pressing the accelerator, Jeff let the Cadillac perform and perform it did. In no time it seemed, he was cruising down Highway 85 at 105 miles per hour, journeying farther-and-farther away from Surprise, Arizona, which had been his destination. Twenty-four miles later, a white glow appeared about a mile in front of him. He slowed. Cresting the slight hill, there it was, on the left like the others, another church identical to the first two.

The illuminated sign by the road read:

<u>**Welcome to Pergamos**</u>
Today's Sermon
IS GOD A HOMOPHOBE??

Jeff did a double-take on that one, not sure if the message board was real. By the time he saw another weather-beaten, green road sign indicating 32 miles to Lukeville, he was at the next little white church. They were all identical, the parking lots were empty and in the distance, the asphalt looked newly painted, the white parking stripes illuminated by the night sky full of blazing meteorites. The glorious field of yellow daffodils spread out as far as the eye could see, the green leaves offering the only green to be seen in this god-forsaken land. The illuminated sign displayed subtle lettering, like the others:

<u>**Welcome to Thyatira**</u>
Today's Sermon
ARE YOU GOING THE WRONG DIRECTION IN LIFE?
BETTER SLOW THAT CADILLAC DOWN.

Jeff checked the speedometer, still reading 105, and slowed the sleek Cabriolet down, just like the sign demanded. The church signs weren't just *illuminated*, they actually glowed as though surrounded by a fine mist; but there was no mist, there was no humidity in the arid, desert land. Only the shot-up and weather-blasted road sign on the shoulder ahead:

Lukeville: 32 Miles

Now *this* was getting very strange.

"Doc, blood's coming out of the ears and eyes. We have to stop the hemorrhaging! NOW!"

The voice again. *Am I losing my mind?* Jeff asked out loud, but there was no one to hear. There weren't even crickets to sing their mating songs in the night. The dark indigo sky suddenly changed to a light purple as thousands, maybe millions of dust-sized meteorites, danced across the atmosphere. The newly rising moon in the east, now pink, appeared to have translucent rings in the haze, like a small Saturn.

Jeff felt dizzy and light-headed.

CHAPTER TWENTY-EIGHT

"*A*nd now to some national news. Would you say this is astounding news Ronn?*"

Ronn Aronson worked for the High Point, North Carolina, radio station as a news analyst for years, since the "last century" as he liked to tell with a laugh. He and Cheryll Crouch made up the small weekend anchor team. What they liked most about each other was not media relations or the High Point *social set*, and there was *definitely* a social set, but their Friday night visits to world-renown Kepley's Barbeque on Main Street, there was none better, anywhere. It had been that way for years. Had to be the sauce. Cheryll's love of Kepley's was close to Ronn's heart and his somewhat ample belly. Being an international correspondent had not helped the waist line.

"*I would certainly say so Cheryll! Listeners can email, twitter or facebook us; and let us know what you think.*"

Cheryll was fond of ample bellies, and a romance was born. Maybe they would get married at Kepley's.

"*I'm standing outside the Richard B. Russell Federal Building and Courthouse in Atlanta where Samarra Russell's trial starts today on terrorism charges. She is married, at least at this time, to Senator Jack Russell from Cumming, Georgia.*

"*As has been well-publicized, Samarra Russell is accused of releasing the deadly Spanish Flu toxin to a Christian militant group. That toxin is now devastating America, Mexico, Canada and some parts of Europe, more than 100,000 deaths now attributed to the disease, and climbing. This trial is expected to be brief.*"

Abe the Bartender turned down the volume on the flat-panel TV.

Toxin? Spanish Flu was a *virus* you bunch of dummies, not a toxin. *The Divide* was empty but would be filling soon with the lunch crowd, and Abe waited for the water truck to arrive with bottled water. Since the flooding of the Chattahoochee Valley after the Buford Dam destruction, the Duluth Towne Green was much closer to the river; and the local restaurants couldn't cook enough food. The Rexall Grill and Family Restaurant were more crowded than they had ever been, even during the Runaway Bride *event*; and financially, things seemed to be picking up, at least around Duluth's Towne Green. Neighboring towns to the north and west were still flooded. *Funny how devastation sometimes brought silver-linings,* he spoke silently to himself. Abe was not in a good mood.

"Heard from Jeff?" Pam owned the place, *The Divide,* and this was always her first question of late.

"Not a word." They were both worried. It was not like Jeff to be out of touch for so long. Abe continued.

"Talked to Chadbo. He's back at Goddard Space Center in Greenbelt. He's worried too. He also said some *bad stuff* was getting ready to happen."

"That's just *super.* We need some more bad stuff. What kind of bad stuff?"

"He wouldn't say. Said he'd have to kill me, my family and my dogs if he told me."

"Chad will never change." Pam sighed, and she knew he wouldn't.

Her mood was as sour as Abe's lemonade. She grabbed the remote and turned up the sound as soon as she saw Samarra Russell's photo on the screen. What an absolutely stunning woman, so beautiful and so unpretentious. Pamela had known Samarra a couple of years, introduced by Melissa . . . She missed Melissa a lot, and even more for Jeffrey's sake. Where the hell *was* Jeffrey???

"Ronn, why do you say Samarra Russell is 'married at least at this time?' Are they filing for divorce?" This would be Jack Russell's fifth divorce. Most people didn't know that, but Cheryll's mom had been the third.

"Cheryll, we are the first to report, yes, right here at our little station in High Point, a news scoop if there ever was one. Senator Jack Russell was arrested last night in San Francisco on child porn and molestation charges. A new church-funded Internet safety group called pornagain.com tracks most pedophilic web sites, though as soon as one goes down, another appears."

"Isn't that the group who is being threatened by the ACLU or some legal organization for invasion of privacy?"

"*That's the one Cheryll. The group GPS-tracked Senator Russell after noting some comments he made on the boylove.com web site, and he was arrested tonight with an 11 year old boy at the 'SanFran Shower Stall.'*"

"*You mean there are web sites for pedophiles? Ronn, surely you jest.*"

Cheryll knew he wasn't jesting. The comment was for the audience. Most folk did not know these sites existed, degenerative products of *First Amendment* '*rights*'. You never heard this news on *Entertainment Tonight* or other *progressive* news shows, at least progressive in their program directors' minds. She supposed the Founding Fathers were spinning in their graves and wondered what Thomas Jefferson would've said in his day. *Hey Tom, mind if we start a newspaper in Philly for perverted men looking for little kids to have sex with?* She knew exactly what Thomas Jefferson would have said. It was a different world back then, not nearly as *progressive* as today. The progressives were the enlightened, and God didn't really mean all that stuff he said. Oh, for the good ol' days.

"*No jesting here Cheryll. I think the 'North American Man Boy Love Association' was the first, or one of the first; and their web site, nambla.com, is still up and running. Senator Russell was also traced to the NAMBLA site.*"

"*You know Ronn, this is really ironic. Senator Russell has condemned homosexuality and pedophilia so many times on national television, calling it 'sexually impaired,' and goes to church every Sunday, no matter where he is, even in Israel. You just never know.*"

"*You just never know,*" Ronn repeated.

Pam supported herself with the leather barstool and couldn't believe what she just heard. How much more could Samarra take?

"*The United States, Central America, the European Union and Canada are drawing up contingency plans for the bombing of Korengal Valley, the well-publicized Valley of Death, once-and-for-all. A confidential Interpol connection has leaked to The Jerusalem Post the possibility of the 'nuclear option' since the United States has suffered several nuclear attacks from the rogue submarine. The theory has always been, 'We won't use nuclear weapons unless we are attacked with nuclear weapons.' That has happened.*"

By 11:45, the lunch crowd ruled and the din was heavy, gaining volume as the luncheoniers saw the *latest* local news about the *latest* terrorist-inspired tragedy and Samarra's holier-than-thou-husband, caught with his pants down, so to speak.

The din came to a hush as the Breaking News Banner suddenly interrupted programming on all the restaurant's numerous TVs. The bright red letters let everyone know instantly that this was *REAL* breaking news, color-coded to denote urgency. The Emergency Alert jingle played briefly before Dan Brumfield, the *new* President's spokesman, appeared on screen.

"A U.S. Navy robotic submarine, the SCUBAdrone, has detected what may be the rogue nuclear submarine off the coast of Boston. The SCUBAdrone has now lost contact with the object, but we have reason to believe this submarine is in the Boston-Philly-New York targeting arena.

"As I speak to you, the President is on his way back to Warner Robins Air Force Strategic Center and will speak from the temporary Oval Office this evening. The evacuation of these three metropolitan areas has begun; and all Interstates have been changed to one-direction only, from the coastal areas going westward. This is all I can say at the moment, but any breaking news will be passed on to the media as necessary."

"What? As necessary? That's all they can say?" Larry Joe, a regular and retired baseball player, shouted at the flat-panel TV as though it could hear. "That *'as necessary'* stuff is what's always gettin' us in dad-gone stew. Horse manure."

The din rose once again.

"Haseem, we need to conserve the food unless we can somehow be resupplied. The 36 prisoners haven't been fed in three days. They are sick."

Haseem was well aware that the submarine's supplies were dwindling. He had a contingency plan.

"They are traitors, Mohmad. They are not really people. How many Shi'ites are there?" Haseem was surprised that the Shi'ites had mutinied.

"Only four, Haseem. The rest are Sunni."

"You know what to do Mohmad." Haseem turned and walked down the narrow gray corridor. Mohmad knew *exactly* what he must do. Less than an hour later, the bodies had been disposed of, except the four Shi'ites, via the vacant torpedo tubes, soon to be fish-food. Now there would be food for the valiant and brave, *insha'Allah*.

The Nerpa submarine continued slowly, a hundred fathoms beneath the surface of the mid-Atlantic, edging closer to the Rock of Gibraltar and the Mediterranean Sea. Traveling at six knots, they would enter the Mediterranean, *insha'Allah*, in another week.

The three Tajik men passed Naomi and Aludra without a word, when one stopped and turned around. The air was brisk, and the night sky was alight in color from the meteors.

"Do not speak Aludra. I will handle this."

Aludra couldn't have spoken if she wanted to, at least in an understandable language. She didn't know a word of Tajik, and her heart pounded. A bead of sweat appeared on her brow, even as she shivered from the cool, night air . . . or from the fear.

"What are you doing?" the man asked, demanded. "Don't you know it is dangerous here?" The old man with the weathered skin looked up into the night sky, a look of fear in his eyes. "The sky is falling, you must be careful. Come."

In the distance, flashes of light appeared on the eastern horizon, followed thirty seconds later by thunderous booms. The thunder was the sound of nothing the two ladies had ever heard before, much louder than the mortars Aludra's brother played war with.

"We must hurry to the caves," the grizzled man insisted, a tear appearing in the corner of his eye. "Mountains are falling from the sky. They have been falling for several days, but they are larger now."

The ground shook beneath their feet, more of a sudden *rock* than a shake; and the women fell to their knees. The old Muslim man grabbed the Jewish woman, he didn't know she was a Jew, telling them, "You must hurry; Now!"

Aludra followed, as the thunder continued.

CHAPTER TWENTY-NINE

"To the angel of the church in Sardis write:
These are the words of him who holds the seven spirits of God and the seven
stars. I know your deeds; you have a reputation of being alive, but you are
dead. Wake up! Strengthen what remains and is about to die, for I have
found your deeds unfinished in the sight of my God." Revelation 3: 1-2 NIV

*"M**r. Hutz, does it bother you that so many call you Hutz the*
Putz?"
The PBS host was tall, dark and handsome, resembling
a Hollywood star more than a television host. Abe turned the volume up,
and the early afternoon diners at *The Divide* listened intently. Chuck Hutz
had become quite a phenom during the past year.

"Not really. At first, after the accident and my miraculous recovery . . ."

"Why do you say 'miraculous' Mr. Putz; I mean Mr. Hutz. Sorry about
that."

"Because it was miraculous. I was dead; now I'm not."

Chuck knew a little about the host interviewer. He had conducted a
Google search and learned of his previous interviews with *conservatives.*
The host's distaste for anything right-leaning was well known and very
apparent so far.

"Let me continue, please. At first it bothered me; but as I learned about
my previous life, I . . ."

Another interruption. The host was known for that too.

"Previous life? You had a previous life Mr. Hutz?" The host smirked.

"Yes, actually. I would guess if I lived, died and lived again, I would
have a previous life. Yes. That is the miracle. It wasn't time for me to leave.

As I learned more, it seems I was quite the ass. So no, it doesn't bother me anymore."

"Mr. Hutz, you said in previous interviews that the 'rapture' had occurred. Is that correct? Why did you say that, and do you believe it? You have ticked off quite a few remaining Christians, like <u>most</u> of them."

Jeff yawned; and the night air rushed past the car as he drove his new Cadillac south toward Lukeville, thirty-two miles away. He listened to the PBS broadcast on his Sirius radio and couldn't believe Hutz the Putz was still around. *Thought someone would've killed him by now.* He adjusted the volume.

"I said the first rapture had happened. I don't know how I know that. This stuff comes to me in the trance."

"When you speak Hebrew, a language you claim not to speak."

"That's correct. I know it's weird, but . . . well, it <u>is</u> weird. When I watch the replays of these trances, I can't understand a word. Audry Ross translates for me if Ms. Ophelia isn't around. Ophelia's getting old, so I've been depending on Audry."

"The 'first' rapture?" The host questioned.

"Sir, I'm not saying that what I say in these trances is the absolute truth. That's just what I'm led to say. Not all will make the first rapture."

"Mr. Hutz, you're saying that the 100,000 plus people who have disappeared in the last year have been 'raptured ta Jeeezus?'" The PBS interviewer dropped his latté all over his navy, pin-striped suit; and this time, Chuck smirked.

The host was getting terribly annoying, but Chuck continued the interview. The thought crossed his mind to get up and leave, but he didn't.

"Your words, Sir; not mine. Don't kill the messenger. I am not sure what it means."

"Mr. Hutz, you've also stated in these 'trances' that other things will come from the heavens; meteors, comets, whatever. You mentioned they would come from the Kuiper Belt."

"And solar flares. Don't forget the flares, because their devastation is to be tremendous. Yes, they will come from the Kuiper Belt and the Oort Cloud."

"Could you explain to our viewers about the Kuiper Cloud?"

"It's the Kuiper Belt and the Oort Cloud. Yes, let me explain."

Jeff crested a hill, and there it was on the left.

<u>Welcome to Sardis</u>
Today's Sermon
Why Did Christians Change the 4ᵗʰ Commandment?

Another weird church, but another question Jeff used to ask his mother, rest her soul. How many were there? Jeff rubbed his sleepy eyes. There were no hotels or motels to be seen, he had seen none since Thebes. He was tiring fast. Maybe he should go back and park in the last church's parking lot. He had his two guns for security, of course. *No*, he thought, *I'll press on a little farther.* The Cadillac's fuel gauge indicated a half tank. His iPhone rang, the first time in . . . how long had it been? Seemed like days.

"The patient died. We tried our best, but the hemorrhaging was too much to control. I'm sorry."

The line went dead; The Voice now silent.

Am I in the Twilight Zone? What is going on??

Jeff had a headache and rubbed his temples while steering with his knees, heading south at ninety miles an hour. He turned the radio on; but there was nothing but static, probably out of satellite range. Could be solar flare activity, he reckoned. There had been plenty of that. The night sky had suddenly turned dark, except for the eastern moon, glowing pink above the horizon. Suddenly there were no meteorites to be seen.

The dark gray shadow, it looked like a beast, ran directly in front of Jeff's new car, showing no respect for the fancy Cadillac; and Jeff was certain there would be a collision. He hit the brake, hard; but the Cadillac did not waver and stopped quickly in the southbound lane. Jeff looked to the right and to the left. There was nothing, no beasts or shadows, only the sounds of silence. He again aimed the car south; and suddenly the shadow appeared again, this time running down the middle of the southbound lane.

Follow me.

Jeff *felt* the message more than he *heard* it. What a totally weird night this had turned out to be; and he followed the shadow, like Alice followed the rabbit down the rabbit hole in 1865. *Weird* was no longer an appropriate adjective to describe the night, and Jeff searched his vast memory for a better word. He found none. The Cadillac followed the shadow, seemed to be pulled along by the shadow, like one car drafting another at a Road Atlanta NASCAR event. The Cadillac was going 125, the highest number on the speedometer. The car felt as light snow as he became more-and-more light-headed himself.

He was no longer sleepy as he flew past the road sign, *Lukeville 32 miles.*

CHAPTER THIRTY

"Men will faint from terror, apprehensive of what is coming on the world, for the heavenly bodies will be shaken." Luke 21:26 NIV

Aboud Rehza, aka Vinny, aka Jean Philippe, et al., turned south toward Lukeville. He had been careful to keep the same "look" at the J. Blanton Concrete Distributors after the purchase by an *anonymous* Japanese group, had even tried to hire the previous owner, Judy Blanton, to no avail. *A shame*, Vinny thought, *she's the prettiest American woman I've ever seen.*

Judy did stop by occasionally to have a cup of coffee with Vinny, who she knew as Jean Philippe. He was very articulate, a nice man she thought, and often talked about his late wife in Sucy-en-Brie, France, and the family farm. His wife, a nice Catholic woman, had died in birth, having a stillborn child. He had *more* interesting stories than any man she had ever met and spoke the most *perfect* French and Italian. His French made her feel all giddy inside.

"Mr. Philippe?"

"Oui mademoiselle. My friends call me Jean Philippe."

Vinny smiled the charming smile that Allah had gifted him with; and Judy thought maybe she liked this Frenchman, maybe just a little.

Jean Philippe was a generous sort and made frequent donations to the local Lukeville Girl Scout Troop and the Police Benevolent Fund, though there were only four policemen and a Chief. Vinny especially liked little girls and thought of the *apparition*. He was once the silent sponsor of a home building project for an injured Marine.

Though Jean Philippe was slightly *height impaired*, Judy found him quite attractive. He attended the Lukeville First Baptist Church, sang

Holy Holy Holy with gusto and vigor, and occasionally attended Mass at St. Agatha's in a nearby town, explaining that he did so out of respect for his late wife. Plus he donated the new concrete sidewalks along Puerto Blanco Drive.

Vinny blended in, and the citizens of Lukeville were beginning to love their newest resident of only a few months. He had proven to be a real Christian man, and there weren't many of *them* they knew, a man who walked the walk and talked the talk, even kept the concrete plant closed on Fridays, Saturdays *and* Sundays to accommodate all religions. Vinny only needed four days a week to complete *his* work.

The white Impala slowed, and Vinny turned left into the entrance of J. Blanton Concrete. It was early morning, and the good people of Lukeville were not yet up for church. There was no traffic, as usual, in the small town. Vinny liked Lukeville more than he thought he would. There were no Jews, at least it seemed so. The small but growing Mexican population provided labor for the concrete plant, as well as many residential services for the locals. Only a few thought it odd that the immigrants spoke English almost as well as they spoke Spanish. They did *not* know the immigrants also spoke fluent Farsi and Arabic.

The electric garage door quietly opened upon Vinny's digital command, and soon the Impala was secreted away. No one had seen him, which was a good thing. He was not usually at the plant on Sundays but at the church on Main Street instead.

Making his way down the grungy dark stairs to the basement, he switched breaker number thirteen off and then on; and the wall silently slid open, leading the way to the tunnel below. Riding the fully-charged, electric golf cart through the dimly lit tunnel, Vinny crossed well under the Mexican border, deep enough that ground-penetrating radar or infrared technology could not detect his stealth. The LED lighting made no detectable sound at this depth, unlike fluorescent, and discharged very little heat.

In less than three minutes, Vinny pulled the cart into the storage area of the new beer distribution center, just a few hundred feet south of the Mexican border. The cargo elevator slowly made its way upward to the main level. Vinny exited and remotely activated the hidden doorway, similar to the sliding wall at J. Blanton Concrete, and walked up a flight of seven steps to the first floor. Latif was waiting, as were the dozen jihadist warriors. Each warrior was the leader of a small clan of jihadists, smuggled across the porous border with ease during the past few years.

"Hey! Long time no see-um!" Abe beamed.

It had just been a few days, actually; but time seemed to be flying by. The guy with the *THE END IS NEAR* sign was walking along the edge of the Towne Green. The lanky and well-groomed man had appeared out of nowhere just a few days before, and no one seemed to know who he was. As the man turned toward West Lawrenceville Street, the back of the sign asked a troubling question: *Are you ready?*

Abe the Bartender's smile betrayed his admiration for the duo coming through the open French doors. He was glad to see The Admiral and Sheryl, and he was especially glad to see they were holding hands. There had been some rumors going around about a possible romance in the making. Then all hell broke loose, and the rumors faded.

"You two look happy."

"Well," The Admiral said, "There's nothing like a good comet collision to get a new romance going." The Admiral leaned over and gave Sheryl an affectionate peck-on-the-cheek. Abe grinned as the sight stirred the memory of his Mum's favorite song when he was a small child in Israel,

I love you, a bushel and a peck,
A bushel and a peck and a hug around the neck . . .

And he wished his Mum was still alive, both parents now deceased at the hands of Hezbollah, now the ruling party in Lebanon. A rare and brief moment of anger crossed Abe's mind as he thought about the land that Israel had recently given away, at the urging of the United States and Europe. The U.S. referred to the land as "occupied territory." What a joke, but he didn't laugh.

At one time, the U.S. had been an unconditional ally of Israel but not since the *Arab Spring*. That uprising that so many in the western world heralded, had now turned into Israel's biggest thorn since her rebirth May 14, 1948, the same day the *reborn* Israel was attacked by no less than five Arab, Islamic countries.

Occupied land should be changed to war booty, like happens in other wars. Except in the case of Israel.

Wars and rumors of wars. It was happening like no time before. The Middle East was in flames, oil had sky-rocketed, and people just *wished*

gas was only $8.00 a gallon. That would never happen again. Everything seemed to be in the extreme lately.

"Any word from Jeff?" Sheryl, as cosmopolitan as she was, could not conceal her worry. Her eyes were almost teary with concern.

"Nope, but don't worry. We will hear. He told me not to call unless it was an absolute emergency, said he needs some time to get his head straight; and he may be gone for two or three months. He plans to tour the countryside, even mentioned visiting Yellowstone to see what all the recent rumbling is about."

"I'm still worried. It's just not like him to go underground. Do you know where he was going to pick up that car?"

"California is all I know, Sheryl." Abe replied and began *his* art-form, constructing his frozen Bloody Mary specialty

"Don't worry so much Hon, Jeff's a big boy. There aren't many situations he can't get out of, and he'll call if he needs us. Losing Melissa like he did, I can understand a soldier's need to get away; and Jeff will always be a soldier." The Admiral was worried though.

The Admiral and Sheryl took a seat in the plush, rose-leather booth closest to the restaurant's largest TV; and Abe carried the two Bloody Marys with celery salt lining the rim of the twelve ounce, faux-crystal glasses. Another *urgent* news bulletin streamed across the lower third of the screen, blotting out the hole in one, Tiger's first in a long time. The golf was interrupted.

"The national alert level, once again color-coded, may be lowered from red to orange, a result of not a single terrorist attack since New Year's Eve. As a matter of fact there have been no Islamic . . . excuse me . . . sorry, there have been no terrorist attacks on U.S. or European soil since December 31. Most National Security leaders are opposed to this move, it should be noted. Apparently, the talking-heads believe this easing of security concerns will somehow help the dismal mood of the country and win hearts-and-minds in the world of terrorism. It should also be noted, it was a Christian terrorist group that infiltrated the transportation networks last year and turned all traffic lights to green. What a mess that was."

The lovely and talented Condi Zimmerman, news-babe-extraordinaire, paused as a sudden gust of wind blew a sign off the top of a building on Raleigh's North Carolina State University campus and nearly blew off her dress. Wind gusts had become prevalent in the last month or so, and it could get down-right scary during a live news broadcast. Abe thought about what a nice sight it would be if Condi's tropically-colored sun dress with the yellow mangos went flying across the North Carolina State University campus. *Go Wolfpack!*

"They're in waiting, that's all." The Admiral interrupted and couldn't believe what he had just heard.

Sheryl knew that Justin was correct, fundamentalist Islamism had not faded away. It had never faded away since Muhammad's death in 632 AD. The message had always been the same: convert, enslave or kill. Why in the world would they lower the alert level when the world had just undergone multiple nuclear attacks? It made no sense.

"Windstorms have become rampant in the northern hemisphere in the last month, with Phoenix just surviving it's eleventh major dust storm in four months. Swimming pool companies are making a fortune cleaning the mud out of pools, fountains and landscaped fish ponds, a silver-lining in a large dust cloud.

"In the North Atlantic, five large cargo tankers have disappeared, the result of a series of eighty to one hundred foot, rogue waves. These waves have become more common and are virtually unpredictable. Suddenly a lot of bad things have become 'more common.'

"In the Czech Republic there has been yet another outbreak of the newly accepted phenomenon of megacryometeorites. Previous outbreaks have most often occurred in Spain where the strange occurrence was first reported and documented in the year 2000. There was a report in South America of one of the large chunks of ice falling from the sky and destroying a red Mustang convertible. Locals claimed it weighed more than 400 pounds. Yikes! And these things fall out of a perfectly clear sky?"

The report of four hundred pound chunks of ice falling out of the clear, blue sky got the attention of both The Admiral and Abe the Bartender. They looked at each other in mild astonishment. Just last year, Chadbo gave a speech to the Duluth Civitan Club about this exact subject.

"This is the fifth such storm in less than a month; and fortunately, only eleven people have been killed so far. The ice balls have been confirmed to weigh 30-40 pounds each; and though these storms are brief, whatever they hit is flattened.

"Food riots are continuing to rock Europe where food prices have skyrocketed. Gasoline prices in most parts of Europe now top $15.00 a gallon."

"The fools are lowering the alert level. All the better for us. I'm beginning to love the stupid Americans."

Vinny knew this was Allah's doing and looked each man in the eye as he began to speak after turning the volume down. Condi's speech now faded into nothingness. Noting Latif's stare, Vinny turned the TV off before Latif started salivating at the news woman's beauty.

"Aboud, how much fertilizer do we have."

Vinny started to slap Latif, but then thought better of it. He didn't care much for Latif's style, but there were few more ruthless. Vinny addressed him by his new moniker, *David*.

"David, I will say this again; but only one more time. Don't *ever* call me Aboud, you or anyone else in this room. Call me Vinny or Ricky or Jean Philippe when we meet. Capiche?"

"Sorry Vinny. I understand." Latif's face flushed in anger more than embarrassment. How could anyone keep up with all Vinny's aliases? Vinny, Ricky, Jean Philippe?

"We have more than 80,000 pounds of fertilizer and 5,000 gallons of diesel fuel, but bombs are not always the way, Latif. We are going to cool it for a little while. Mother Nature is at Allah's whim, and she may take care of the American problem. Plus, we will catch them off guard if we wait. Just a few months."

Grabbing the rusted handle of the hydraulic lift, Vinny rolled the large, wooden container away from its concrete enclosure and to the middle of the room. Depressing the green icon on his new iPad, the electronic lock disengaged.

Vinny loved his new iPad. Before coming into his possession, it had adorned the home of the old couple who once owned Vinny's white Impala; but now it was his, kind of a departure gift from the old man and woman. He grinned and opened the lid of the container. He removed an AK-47 assault rifle, a rocket-propelled grenade launcher and three different types of automatic pistols. Then he pulled out his pride and joy, a Tavor CTAR-21 compact assault rifle and grenade launcher. He thought he might feel a little *dirty*, holding an Israeli weapon; but instead he felt a wave of pride. In his hands was Israel's most advanced assault rifle. Vinny spoke to his small but attentive audience in Farsi, a language they all spoke and understood fluently, the language of Iran.

"This weapon is ours, compliments of Israel. The Israel Defense Forces has undergone a series of kidnappings the past few months and as a result, we have accrued quite an armory."

Holding the compact rifle over his head so all could see, Vinny smiled and continued, "With this weapon, we can kill Jews with their own bullets."

The small crowd laughed loudly at the irony, but Vinny didn't laugh. He was heart-attack serious. This weapon would be used at synagogues and any other place the Jew gathered. He would kill them with their own weapons.

"What about the Christians, atheists and other vermin?" one of the men asked.

"Them too," Vinny responded, and the group guffawed again.

"I believe, with the supply of these weapons that we have been gifted, insh'Allah, we can kill many more infidels than we can with car bombs." They weren't, after all, *people.* They were just *cock-a-roaches* as the Rwandan Hutus often said about the Tutsis.

"How many weapons are there Vinny?"

Vinny pointed to the concrete enclosure and motioned for the men to follow. Stepping into the room, the gray walls were lined with other massive wooden chests; and the smell of gun oil permeated the stale air. One wall was lined with large canisters and other containers of who knows what? Only Vinny *did* know: anthrax, compressed air, sarin and VX nerve agents. Plus the two remaining vials of Spanish Flu that he had maintained in dry-ice storage. A chemistry lab was secreted behind the far wall, and the nerve agents were easily manufactured from everyday items, as long as caution was maintained. Nerve gas wasn't a pretty way to die; and Vinny had seen the effects after Iraq's Saddam Hussein gassed the Kurds. Five thousand succumbed in an agonizing dance with death, a death that occurred in just a couple of horrifyingly long moments.

"We have three thousand martyrs and four thousand weapons. Those chests over there," Vinny pointed to the far corner of the dank room, "are filled with ammo. We are ready to start war. Watch the news, because it won't be long. Be patient my friends, and let the Americans continue to drop their guard."

Latif interrupted. "But the bombs Vinny, they put the fear of God in their hearts. And they make great, big noise!"

"Believe me *David*, when the martyrs get these gifts from Allah in their hands, the fear of God will be in the American's hearts. Assault rifles instill fear, believe me. When we walk into children's hospitals, city parks and day care centers, when the Americans see the bodies of their children in pools of blood on the playgrounds, *fear will be in their hearts.* Security is so lax, the martyrs will have no problems getting into the sites we choose. Getting out may be a problem, but they will not be taken alive. The Israeli rifle is so small; it can be carried in a back pack or brief case.

"We will be coordinating clandestine acts with the Christian militia in the north Georgia mountains. We have the snipers armed and in place."

Latif interrupted.

"Why are we doing that Vinny? Anyway, I thought they were all dead from the flu. We should do no business with the Christians."

"The enemy of my enemy is my friend, Latif. Remember that. I was in Atlanta's MARTA train station three times when I was last there. There were a lot of college students with heavy backpacks, some with duffle bags. No security was in sight most of the time. We just have to coordinate these attacks; because once they happen, security will be tripled." *And America will be broker*, Vinny thought. How much more could they take before the entire economic system failed? The European riots had now spread to New York, Chicago and Denver. It wouldn't take much longer, Vinny was sure. A few shootings here and there, some forest fires in the national forests. The USA would be out of money soon.

The meeting continued, and Vinny gave the men their marching orders. They would go back to their homes and wait for the sign from Vinny. He assured Latif that the fertilizer-diesel bombs would be abundant and put to good use.

"The grenade launchers have been distributed in Houston, Atlanta, Charleston, Savannah, New Orleans and Baton Rouge. There are numerous oil and gas storage facilities in those locations. When things appear to be getting better, the Bible-Belt will explode in flames. Wait for my instructions."

CHAPTER THIRTY-ONE

L ight-headed, Jeff's shiny, blue caddy continued southward, following the shadow, getting ever closer to Lukeville. Yet every sign he had seen said Lukeville was 32 miles away.

Topping the next hill, the shadowy beast ahead seemed to point or look to the left; and Jeff saw yet another little white church in a daffodil field.

Welcome to Philadelphia
Today's Sermon
Did Jesus *Really* Walk on Water?

I need to go there and listen to that sermon, he thought, remembering how many times he'd asked those questions and others that non-believers usually asked. No one had ever given a satisfactory answer, at least as far as he was concerned.

In almost no time it seemed, there was another church on the left, the sign out front reading:

Welcome to Laodecia
Today's Sermon
Is the Blip of Light a Sign in the Sky?

Jeff's heart beat rapidly as the dark road seemed to zoom by below, surely faster than the Cadillac could go; and then the car began to slow, 90 . . . 70 . . . 45 . . . It seemed as though he was barely moving. The shadow faded away as Jeff crested the slight hill, his stomach making the low moans of hunger. It had been miles and miles since the last restaurant.

There on the left was a building, maybe a restaurant, well lit by the bright, white metal halide lighting on the poles around the facility. When he saw the small restaurant, right out in the middle of nowhere, just like the weird churches he passed, he pulled the Cadillac Cabriolet into the parking lot, surprised to see 20-30 cars. There was no sign by the edge of Highway 85 indicating that it was a restaurant, or weird church; but Jeff smelled food.

Parking away from the other cars, avoiding the inevitable door-ding monster, Jeff locked the Caddy and walked across the parking lot to the beat of the reggae music flowing through the open windows. He glanced back at the Cadillac, almost in adoration, and was awed by the redness of the lunar surface, still clouded by the dust from the impact. *Reggae music,* his favorite. *Strange they would be playing reggae music in the middle of the desert.*

The restaurant, at second glance, was much larger than he originally thought. He entered the wooden, louvered swinging doors, just like the saloon doors he had seen in the old western films of yesteryear, and made a visual search of the crowd. There was no crowd; odd, considering all the cars in the parking lot. There were no employees to be seen, other than the young waiter to the left, wiping away remnants of the last customer's visit, maybe an invisible customer.

Jeff walked through the second set of swinging doors and toward the bar. Glancing right, the neon sign was hard to miss; and he almost dropped his teeth.

Welcome to Melissa's
Jamaican Delights & Drinks
All Religions Welcome

The bartender, tall and thin with jet-black hair, was wearing a *The End* T-shirt. He smiled as Jeff approached the bar, noting the ashen pallor of Jeff's face.

"Welcome back Jeffrey Ross. We've missed you."

CHAPTER THIRTY-TWO

"*T*oday is another sad day in Atlanta, the United States and the world. Sheryl Lasseter, the much-loved United States Public Relations Liaison, has been killed or kidnapped according to the AP. Authorities are trying to assess the available information at this time. This is what we know so far:

"*Ms. Lasseter, Admiral Justin McLemore and two body guards were in a two-vehicle caravan travelling to Briscoe Field in Lawrenceville, Georgia, where they were planning a flight to Warner Robins Air Force Base, the new temporary White House. Most of the Washington area is under a voluntary quarantine, trying to stop the rapid spread of the Spanish Flu. An unknown Christian militant group claimed responsibility, and Samarra Russell from Atlanta has been charged for releasing the deadly virus. Several 'off the record' reports from those in the 'know' claim the Christian militant group is a ruse and that the attack was the work of home-grown Islamic jihadists.*"

Chad Myers was on the phone with the new U.S. Ambassador to Israel when he saw the bulletin scroll across the bottom of his plasma display. Calling from Goddard Space Flight Center, Chad was informing the Ambassador about a possibility, a *good* possibility, that the entire Middle East, including Israel, was under threat of a meteor bombardment within the next few months, maybe less.

"Are there any designated areas of impact, or is it just *guess-work* at this time?" Ambassador Gwinner asked.

Chad wasn't sure if the new U.S. Ambassador was making an insinuation, he had not had the pleasure of meeting her before, and assumed not.

"Ambassador, it really is pretty much hit-or-miss, there's so much stuff flying around out there."

"Stuff?" she asked.

"Yes ma'am, lots of stuff, lunar debris and cometic debris. Most will burn up in the atmosphere, but that is now a problem in itself.

"The small motorcade was travelling east on Old Peachtree Road in Suwanee when an explosion of some kind occurred."

Condi was interrupted by the news correspondent in High Point, something that annoyed her mightily.

"Condi, is there any word yet on the type of explosive or where it was hidden?"

High Point was now a target of the jihadists because of the significant Jewish population. High Point was the *furniture capital* of the world after all, and many furniture manufacturers were owned by Jewish families. Ronn felt fortunate to be a part of this unfolding scene, as he had never really been in the limelight. Plus he had a not-so-secret desire to meet Condi Zimmerman. She was hot! They were *all* hot at FOX, but Condi was in her own league. The news continued in the background, continuous news alerts scrolling across the bottom of Chad's screen.

"What do you mean by 'a problem in itself' Chad? We don't really need any more problems."

Ambassador Pamela Gwinner was about fed up with all the problems. There were so many *problems* that no one seemed to be keeping their eye on Israel and what was going on. Her mind raged.

Israel was getting ready to blast the doo-doo out of the *new* Iran. The Israeli cyber-attacks had taken a huge toll on Iran's nuclear program, but Iran had gotten back on track much sooner than Israel had expected. With the collapse of the Syrian regime after the Arab Spring uprisings and the removal of all U.S. forces from Iraq the previous year, Iran had moved in smoothly and quickly. Greater Iran, as the area was now called, incorporated all three countries; and Lebanon was in her sights. The European Union said nothing, other than a couple more sanction threats; and the United States was too broke to do anything. Almost a third of the U.S. military was sick or dead from the flu, and the submarine fleet crew was in short supply.

"Ambassador," Chad paused to watch the scrolling news bulletin.

"Mr. Myers, are you there???" Ambassador Gwinner was getting impatient.

"Sorry ma'am, yes, I'm afraid there is another problem; and there will surely be more to come. All the meteoric debris burning up in Earth's atmosphere, while visually beautiful, is warming the entire stratosphere, which is gradually negating the ozone that protects all life from the Sun's ultraviolet radiation. You've heard of the ozone hole?"

"I have."

"Well, the ozone hole is growing at an unprecedented rate since the lunar-comet collision; and that is not good. Skin cancer and other cancers will become more prevalent if the hole continues to enlarge." And if mankind continued to exist, he thought. Skin cancer might be irrelevant.

Chad's mind wandered into the land of despair as his thoughts pondered the two possibilities; *what would happen if the ozone layer disappeared and was Sheryl Lasseter alive or dead?* He continued, news still scrolling across the bottom of his screen.

"Additionally, with the atmosphere warming almost six degrees in the past two months, we can look for significant temperature increases for the next couple of years, maybe more. Temperatures could routinely top 120 degrees in certain areas that have never seen these extremes, higher in others."

"Ronn, the type of explosives has not been confirmed. However, an anonymous source who has visited the scene believes that explosives were planted inside a historical marker along Old Peachtree Road."

"What kind of marker, Condi? How many Peachtree Roads does that place have?" Ronn persisted.

"That I don't know; but plenty. Initial reports say it was a marker denoting a December 6, 1953, crash of four Air National Guard jets on Old Peachtree Road. Foggy night, just after midnight, and all four planes were returning to Dobbins Air Field. It seems there was an altimeter problem of some kind."

"You're kidding?" Ronn's great-grandmother lived on Old Peachtree Road, but he had never heard *that* story. He would have to ask Granny Violet the next time he saw her.

"The jets were flying in close formation. As they flew over Lawrenceville and made the turn southwest back toward Dobbins, the jet's altimeters were off by ten thousand feet. The lead pilot descended, the plane crashed into a farm house, and the other three followed."

The Ambassador appeared distracted.

"That's not *good*, Chad." Ambassador Gwinner's voice took on a special urgency. "Temperatures are already increasing at a record pace. It's not even summer; and Tel Aviv registered a record high temperature, another I should say, of 119 degrees. The Dead Sea has nearly disappeared because of continuous evaporation, and the drinking water is becoming more polluted by the minute. Fresh water is being imported to Tel Aviv because Israel's desalination plant can't keep up with demand. We're getting ready to have a water war in the region, and Israel is preparing to blow the doo-doo out of Iran's military!"

Doo-doo? The Ambassador to Israel was saying *doo-doo?* Chad now knew the rumors were true. Ambassador Pamela Gwinner never cussed.

"Ambassador, can I call you back in a little while? I see some news I need to get to the bottom of, and I'll call you within the hour."

The line went silent, and the ambassador's thoughts drifted back to Israel, a land and people she truly loved; and their increasing dilemma. Now surrounded by sworn Arab enemies of thousands of years, and with the Persians to the west, the on-again-off-again "peace treaty" was off again. The natural gas supplies were cut off from Egypt and Russia after the *Arab Spring* uprising a couple of years earlier; and now Israel was threatened by the cut off of water sources from Jordan and Turkey. Her mood went from not good to much worse. The new Ambassador to Israel was clearly stressed.

Chad's heart was racing; and his breathing became shallow as he continued to watch the news, moisture now forming in his eyes. The thoughts of golf games, cookouts and laughs invaded his memories. It had been a long time since Chad Myers had cried.

"McLemore is at the Gwinnett Medical Center in serious but stable condition. The bodies of the two guards and the chauffeur have been identified in the carnage. Sheryl Lasseter's body has not been found, I repeat for our listeners, Sheryl Lasseter's remains have not been found. This is fueling speculation that she may have been kidnapped. The question is: who?"

"I just cannot believe it." Pam MacLott, the owner of *The Divide*, listened intently to the news. Every TV in *The Divide* was tuned to the same news, and the place was totally packed. The lunch crowd had lingered since the breaking news, and several said they heard the explosion in downtown Duluth.

"Me either." Abe was a sentimental sort, and the bartender-turned-manager turned away to wipe a tear away from the corner of his eye. "I'm headed to Gwinnett Medical."

"Not without me you're not." Pam and Abe grabbed some personal items, made sure Scott could handle everything with the small staff and left *The Divide* through the back entrance. Pulling out of the parking lot, sniper fire could be heard in the distance.

Chapter Thirty-Three

"In a dream, in a vision of the night, when deep sleep falls on people as they slumber in their beds, he may speak in their ears and terrify them with warnings, to turn them from wrongdoing and keep them from pride . . ." Job 33:15-17

"How do you know me? I've never been here before?" Jeff found himself leery of the place, maybe a little frightened.

Jeff closely examined the bartender's name tag, Kipper T, and noted the light blueness of his eyes, almost sky blue. He had never seen such blue eyes, and the combination with his jet-black hair made for a unique look. This had been a most perplexing day, so far.

"Oh, we know you well Mr. Ross."

The hostess was a young woman, about five-five or so, also with jet-black hair. Her nails were painted dark-red, and the young lady had a ponytail, tied with a red, white and blue ribbon.

Jeff was beginning to wonder if everyone in the place had jet-black hair and pale skin, when the woman spoke. "Yes, that's true."

"What's true?" Jeff responded.

"We all have black hair, blue eyes and pale skin, those of us who work here."

She was wearing a white cocktail dress, her name tag reading Missy T, and she had appeared out of nowhere. Missy T had a certain *glow* about her, and some *very* nice wheels, he noted, her legs already summer-tanned. How could her legs be so tanned when her face was so pale? *This has got to be Wonderland; and she must be Alice, except Alice had blond hair.*

"Who are you people?" Jeff asked as Kipper sat a bottle of Duckhorn Merlot on the counter, Jeff's drink of choice. *How did he know that?*

"I'm Missy and this is my husband Kipper. My brother, he's sitting over there, owns the place; and she pointed across the bar to another room of what seemed to be an enormous, ever-expanding building. The room was basked in a bluish glow; and Jeff saw the man, the brother, sitting alone in a recliner, listening to whatever was coming out of his headphones.

"Let me introduce you," and the next thing Jeff knew, he was being led to the blue room, following Missy T like a puppy dog on a leash. *Is this real or is this a dream?* They entered the room.

"No JJJJeffrey, it's not a ddddream at aaall. I'm ssssorry Mr. Ross, I sssstutter ttteriiibly."

"This is my brother. His name is Enoch, and he does have a severe speech impediment most of the time; but not always."

"I ttttruly ddddo have a speeeech impppediment." Enoch continued.

Jeff shook the middle-aged man's hand, and the hand felt clammy. Enoch's forehead perspired slightly; and his bald dome seemed to glisten, a blue glow reflecting the blue lighting in the room. The fact that Enoch answered his question before he even asked did not go unnoted.

"Nnnice to ssseee you aggggain, MMMr. Ross," and with that, the introduction was over.

"Let's talk Jeffrey," and Hostess Missy T escorted him to another room where several people engaged in animated conversation. Jeff heard bits and pieces:

"The Christians fell from God's grace, don't you see that? They stopped following the Law." The woman was dressed in black garb, almost head to toe, with a dark hat.

"But Jesus *fulfilled* the Law, don't you understand? The Jews were no longer required to keep the Law. He was the Messiah. He *is* the Messiah." The younger woman was just as adamant.

"Not according to Jesus? He never told anyone not to follow the Law. That was Paul, the same Paul who had persecuted the Jews who believed in the Christ," the woman in black responded.

The young woman in the tropically colored pants suit seemed to be frustrated with her friend dressed in black.

"She is an orthodox Jew," Missy T interrupted. "She wears the cover on her head to show she is married."

As he followed Missy T to the next room, Jeff recalled his junior high school days and his good buddy, Stewart. The other kids called him Stutterstew, pointed and laughed at him; and Stew's ego continued its early plunge toward insecurity. Jeff had been in many a junior high school fight, taking up for Stutterstew and remembered how bad all the other kids felt when young Stewart hung himself in the school cafeteria, dead at the age of 14.

Where the first room, *Enoch's* room, was bathed in a soft, iridescent, bluish light; this room, smaller than the first, was bathed in red, maybe more violet than red; and plush, black curtains covered the perimeter walls, floor to ceiling. They took a seat.

"What is this place?" Jeff asked the first question.

"This is the *Good Place*. It's a place you have been chosen to see, a place of enlightenment beyond your Mensa imagination."

"I don't recall ever being here before, but you all seem to know me. It's even named after my wife, Melis . . ." His mind did not want to go there and didn't. He wasn't ready.

"You will one day see Melissa again Jeff. Lukeville is 32 miles away, and we have plenty of room in our bed-and-breakfast. Please stay with us, get a good night's sleep and tomorrow will be a good day. I promise."

Before he could answer, Missy T was leading him down another hall, this one with small disco balls hanging from the ceiling, tiny MR16 spotlights shining on each. As the balls rotated, tiny jewels of light cascaded along the walls, floor and ceiling. His thoughts wandered through time and space, back to *The Divide* and Duluth's world-famous Disco Ball. He suddenly felt the need to call someone to let them know he was fine. He would do that tomorrow.

Abe the Bartender and Pam left Gwinnett Medical after arranging for The Admiral to be transferred to the hospital in Duluth. The Admiral would be closer, and the Duluth hospital was cozier than most, warmer and less sterile-looking. His injuries were minor, considering what they could have been; but he remained sedated. Abe and Pam sat in silence on the way back to *The Divide*. Their thoughts were the same as they wondered how Admiral McLemore would take the loss of Sheryl. They had just become an "item" of sorts.

Taking a right by the new Duluth Animal Hospital and Research Center, Pam asked Abe to stop so she could run in to pick up some diet food for Jeff's Great Dane, one of the fatter Danes she had ever seen. She and Abe would take over the responsibility of feeding and caring for the *gentle giant*. They would need to call Jeff soon, regardless of his desire to mourn. It was time to grow up and get his act back together. He had children to take care of.

Abe's iPhone toned, and he had it to his ear in a split second.

"Abe, this is Chad. What's going on man? I heard there was a disaster. Speak to me."

"Hey Chadbo. Speak to you about *which* disaster? There've been plenty." Abe sounded *different*, Chad thought. Abe continued.

"You probably know as much as we do about Sheryl. Her body was definitely not among the carnage, and DNA samples of all the blood stains have been sent to the Pentagon. The police aren't saying, but we've heard rumors that Sheryl has been kidnapped by a previously unknown organization, *Soldiers of God*, or something like that. No one has indicated whether this is an Islamic, Christian, Jewish, Buddhist, or whatever group. I guess in the whole scheme of things, kidnapped is better than dead."

"Yeah, maybe, maybe not. Let's take a guess." Chad's reply was smug. "Probably not an attack by the Presbyterians or Lutherans."

The sound of gunfire insulted the quiet summer day, and Duluth was no longer the quaint little Southern town they had once known. Windows of the bank across the street from Duluth Animal Hospital shattered as four masked men made their way through the newly-created entrances, automatic weapons in tow.

They must not've heard about the Duluth Police Department Abe thought before exiting and ducking behind the car, hoping for cover from the wild assault.

The daytime attacks had gotten much more brazen and brutal. One hundred thirteen dead in Atlanta the last week. Crime was running amok. The news continued through the Jaguar's speakers:

"Noah's Ark is again in the news, the most amazing archeological find in the twentieth century, maybe forever. DNA from feces samples from the floor of the newly discovered ship has indicated a wide variety of different animal sources, including, get this: possibly a small dinosaur. This is Condi Zimmerman wishing you a good day."

The sirens approached, and Duluth's finest were at the bank in less than three minutes; but they were too late. The armed men had entered and shot everyone standing. The well-planned attack took less than two minutes, resulted in a $ 100,000 take and seven people were dead.

CHAPTER THIRTY-FOUR

"The sea is clear today for a change."

Moshe was named after his great uncle, Moshe Dayan, the fourth Chief of Staff of the Israel Defense Forces. The young sailor loved his job, piloting one of the world's leading luxury submarine-yachts.

The *Phoenix 1000* had been purchased from U.S. Submarine by a wealthy Jewish benefactor who lived in High Point, N.C. The anonymous benefactor was referred to as *Mr. Anon*. The luxury submarine-yacht combo was purchased for the sole purpose of underwater archeology and retrieval of ancient Israeli artifacts that had been lost at sea.

After spending six years with the Israeli Marine Archeology Unit, Moshe had become ready for more adventure in his life. With no wife and kids, Moshe was a chance-taker; and when he heard about the opportunity to explore the waters in the Mediterranean off the coast of Morocco, he used his great uncle's influence.

Moshe had never seen anything remotely approaching the beauty and technology offered by the *Phoenix 1000*. More than 200 feet in length, the ship had 5,000 square feet of luxury living space; and the crew and guests could live comfortably indeed.

"I love this thing dude." Moshe said to his college roommate, the co-pilot of the sub, while carefully maneuvering the underwater yacht with the joystick console. "It's like an Xbox 700!"

The co-pilot didn't respond and carefully watched the steeply sloped surface of the Moroccan seabed unfold through the large, reinforced acrylic viewports. They seemed too close for comfort, but the roommate knew Moshe was one of the best when it came to undersea vehicles.

"There. I think we're ready," Moshe said as the sub settled softly on the seabed, 860 feet below the surface. They could actually see the base of the Rock of Gibraltar, at least they thought so.

The sub's 5000 square feet of luxury accommodations had been modified into an elaborate laboratory and engineering facility, and the "crew" consisted mostly of four archeology students and an underwater microbiologist. The plan was to use one of the manned submersibles for deeper exploration. The *Phoenix 1000* could maneuver to a depth of nearly a thousand feet, but the manned submersibles allowed far deeper investigation.

As the submarine turned off the interior lighting, the sea was near-black at the sub's depth; and everyone waited silently for their eyes to adjust. The "turning of the lights" was a ritual that allowed the crew to take in the beauty of the underwater, bioluminescent animal life. The tiny lights appeared as sparkling jewels floating slowly through what appeared to be dark nothingness. Ten minutes later, the crew still mesmerized by the bioluminescence, a large, dark object appeared off the port side of the submarine.

"What was that?" Moshe whispered the question to everyone.

"What?" Another whisper.

"That?" he said, pointing through the largest viewport. The long, dark shadow maneuvered by the luxury submarine, just a few feet away. The large, dark-skinned creature did not stop and take note of the 213 foot-long sub and continued for what seemed forever.

"I don't have a clue. It's too big to be a whale or a whale shark. I hope it doesn't see us," the roommate whispered, concerned that the large, sea beast might hear his very words. The creature continued eastward, ever so slowly, its speed not wavering much above one knot.

"What we gonna do with this woman, Aaron?"

"Handcuff her to the radiator." Aaron pointed to the rusted radiator once used to heat the small warehouse office.

"If she makes any noise, duct tape her mouth." Aaron threw a roll of gray duct-tape to Jonathon, another young *Soldier of God*.

"How long do we hold her Aaron? Are we gonna kill her?" Jonathon was troubled by the thought.

"Maybe, Jonathon. It's in God's hands. If they meet our demands, she lives. It's as simple as that."

"Can you git up ma'am?" Jonathon leaned over Sheryl, lying on the cement floor, still dazed from the explosion.

Jonathon helped her to her feet, grabbed the duct tape and took her to the men's restroom in the rear of the 20,000 square foot warehouse. He wasn't going to handcuff this poor old lady to the radiator, that was for sure. There were no windows in the room, so Jonathon pulled her over to the far wall of the four-staller and duct-taped her hands.

"Don't make no noise ma'am, or I'll havta tape your mouth. Do you understan' me?"

Sheryl shook her head in acknowledgment, continuing to fake the severity of her consciousness. Jonathon left, kicking some ceiling tiles that had fallen long ago, out of the way.

Aaron and Jonathon weren't *real* names but names they had adopted in their well-funded Christian cult; only it wasn't a *cult* to them. Most of the funds were from a few rich white men who still thought there should be "colored" and "white" restrooms, but money was money. Jonathon didn't feel good about it though. He wasn't a racist. That money just had sort of a dirty feel to it, and he thought maybe that's what Judas must've felt like when he took the thirty pieces of silver to betray Jesus. Walking to the far end of the warehouse, Aaron waited for the all-clear call.

"The feds won't meet none of our demands Aaron, no matter how importan' that lady is. This 'ministration will never move our embassy to J'rusalem. That'd *really* piss off them Muslims."

"They've been pissed for years, my friend." Aaron knew his young friend was right; but the Muslims had been *pissed off* at America and everyone else for hundreds of years, especially since the Barbary Pirates episode, and he responded.

"Jon, this country used to be Israel's best friend. Now we're almost an enemy. Everything is more-and-more pro-Palestinian and *anti*-Israel over the past few years. I'm sick of it. A lot of us are sick of it.

"Now we've reduced her foreign aid by seventy-five percent, our *greatest* ally; and they're one of the few countries that pays us back. God gave us this great country, just like he gave Canaan to the children of Jacob; and we are here to help *them*, his *chosen*. But now we've betrayed God. Now we're supporting every Muslim country under the sun! And you've seen all the Hindu temples that're goin' up everywhere."

Aaron's voice rose but was still quiet enough that *Ambassador* Lasseter, or whatever she was, wouldn't hear.

The *Soldier of God Army* was just another militia of late. They were coming out of the woodwork, at least it seemed so to Jonathon. Aaron was the leader, *Dear Aaron* to the others; and the small group formed after Israel, under extreme pressure from the United States and Europe, gave her land away and returned to the pre-1967 borders. Jonathon thought about that long-and-hard. He knew that Israel should be gaining land, not giving it up. Giving up land was not part of the prophecy. This troubled him.

"Can you believe those idiots brought their fight to the *Bible* belt? We will win Jonathon, you'll see. This lady is a very important person. We must focus on that."

"Why did we start killing, Aaron? Murder is against God."

Aaron loved Jonathon like a brother, even though they were just cousins; but he was *slow*. Jonathon didn't understand how Aaron could condemn Muslims, yet he was working *with* them. Jonathon didn't understand "*The enemy of my enemy is my friend*" philosophy.

"It's *not* murder Jonathon!" Aaron was emphatic and abrupt. "It's not murder if you have to kill for the better good. Don't ever forget that. Negotiation never works. Violence works. We've seen it with the jihadists. Every time they attack, America sends them more money. This is the work of the devil."

As time went on, Aaron became more hostile and less Christian, at least as far as Jonathon was concerned; and he worried about his favorite cousin.

"Aaron, that's the same thing the jihadists say every day. Know what I mean?"

"Let me tell ya somethin' Jonathon," Aaron drawled in his best John Wayne imitation, "When Jesus returns, son, he ain't a gonna be turnin' no cheeks. He's a-gonna be kickin' butt and takin' names.

"He knew it wouldn't work when he taught the apostles that turn-the-cheek bit. The only way *that'd* work is for every, single person in the whole-slapdab world to adhere to that teachin', know what I'm a sayin', boy?"

Jonathon knew Aaron was correct. Jesus would not be turning cheeks or loving enemies when he returned, at least according to the *Good Book*.

"I'm sorry about the bomb Jon. I had no idea it was going to kill those people. It was supposed to just stun them long enough for us to make the grab. But I can't change it now. Find out who their families are, and we'll send them money."

"Now you sound *exactly* like the Muslims. That's what *they* do when they *accidently* kill an innocent person."

Sheryl listened to the men's conversation, just a distant mumble. The door to her "room" was closed. The air was dank and moldy smelling; and her pretty, navy-blue dress wasn't pretty anymore. Sheryl visually inspected the room, the ceiling, looking for an escape route. There was none. There *was* a ceiling hatch and a cracked skylight; but they were well beyond her reach, even with the highest stool. Straight above, the bathroom ceiling tiles were missing, and she noticed the pull-down ladder, maybe ten feet above. Searching the ladder, investigating every inch, she looked for a locking mechanism. There appeared to be none.

The men hadn't sounded particularly violent, she thought, until the bomb comment. *Where was Justin, and the others? Were they dead?* The Admiral would never leave her in a time of distress. *Could* he be dead? She couldn't remember, couldn't remember anything at all, except . . . what? She and Justin had entered the black SUV. They sat in the middle seats, the chauffer and guard sitting shotgun in the front, the two secret service agents in the back. She concentrated.

They had departed Sugarloaf and headed to the newly renovated Briscoe Field to fly to Warner Robins. Then, as they took the left curve, cresting a small hill on Old Peachtree Road, the one where the four jets crashed, and . . . and . . . *That's the last she could remember.* Sheryl wasn't a weepy sort of woman, and she didn't weep. She would not show weakness to these goons. But her heart was heavy. Sheryl had waited her whole life to meet a Justin Philip McLemore and felt it was a God-thing. Surely it hadn't ended. She refused to accept the possibility.

She heard the TV and was glad. Maybe she would learn what happened; and now they wouldn't hear her, if she could devise an escape plan. Dizziness came and went.

". . . are a prophet. Mr. Hutz, do you consider yourself a prophet?"

"Of course not. I have stated that I don't know if what I say is true, it's just what comes out."

"In Hebrew?"

"That's correct."

"Change that channel! That guy's a nutjob."

"No, wait. I've heard him." Jonathon replied.

Jonathon thought Hutz the Putz *had* to be a prophet. He said the Dark Comet wouldn't hit Earth, and it didn't. He mentioned the Oort cloud, and that's where comets come from. He predicted huge solar flares, and it surely happened; shut down half of China.

"*Mr. Hutz, you've angered a lot of people, especially your views on adultery.*"

"*And homosexuality.*" Chuck Hutz interrupted, knowing where the conversation was headed.

"*Yes, especially that. Why do you have so many views on sexual behavior. You seem to have an obsession.*"

"*Condi, they aren't my views. That's just what comes out in these trances. I don't know why. We've had this discussion.*"

Condi didn't like the new direction the news station was taking, especially the direction of the questions she was required to ask. She knew Chuck and knew the shy man was nervous. Someone had just tried to kill him the day before.

"*Your accuracy though, with astronomical events, has been uncanny. How did you know the comet would not hit Earth, when are these flares supposed to hit and this Noah's Ark thing you talked about last week at . . .*"

"Change the channel!" This time it was a command from *Dear Aaron*; and Jonathon changed to another news network, *OLNN*.

"*. . . attempt on his life yesterday in Raleigh, North Carolina; but miraculously, he survived. Police say more than 100 rounds were fired from the two men arrested at the scene after participants at the rally wrestled the men to the ground.*" Kari, the OLNN anchor-gal, paused and sipped her bottle of TETB spring water, brought in by truck to the new OLNN studio in Roswell. Kari and her family loved their new home, but access to drinking water had been difficult, after Atlanta lost her main water source.

"*Yes, miraculous is right, Kari. These men shot until they ran out of ammo and were less than thirty feet from Chuck Hutz. Not a single bullet hit him or the young girl with him, Audry Ross; but fourteen bystanders were killed by stray bullets. Neither ran for cover. They just sat perfectly still, staring at the gunmen while the crowd completely panicked. Finally, several people chased the gunmen down.*" Rich waited for Kari's response.

Aaron fumed. Seemed like every channel was talking about this weirdo. Aaron found him *scary*.

Rich Badey had a reputation as a wandering journalist and had been with many news sources through the years. He was well respected, both locally and internationally. He was the reporter who broke the story about the dark comet hurtling toward Earth after overhearing it in a Dunwoody tavern.

"*Rich, why don't you fill in our viewers with a brief history of Chuck Hutz.*"

"*Will be glad to, Kari. As you will remember, last year the traffic signal networks were hacked; and all traffic signals were turned green at the same time. This happened in several cities. Chuck Hutz was almost killed in an auto accident as a result. He remained in a coma for . . .*"

The men changed to the only *other* news channel, the last option with the rigged antenna.

"Hutz the Putz. I'm getting really sick of hearing about this pervert. He *had* to know Hebrew before that accident. I don't care what he says, he's a false prophet."

Aaron laid the remote on the small table, beside the stale Whopper with cheese and some old, dried fries. A ketchup foil packet was glued to the counter with leaky ketchup several days old.

"*. . . flights remain grounded in Europe, Africa and the Middle East after 17 passenger aircraft were shot out of the sky in one day. Analysts are meeting but believe these surface-to-air missiles were looted from North Africa during the civil wars that are still going on. There have been a total of thirty-three planes shot down so far this year, the largest one the new A550 AirLux. Looks like all airlines will have to install laser defense systems if flying is ever going to get back to normal.*

"*The hailstorms continue to wipe out crops in India, Africa and China, adding to the agony of the starving. Somalia's mass graves now hold well over a million victims according to sources inside the French charity, Doctors Without Borders.*

"*Last night, another large meteor came crashing to Earth in the Three Gorges Dam area. If you remember, just a few weeks ago, the dam was completely destroyed by another meteor impact. They are still counting bodies from that tragedy, but estimates are more than three million dead.*

"*The Naval buildup continues in the Western Pacific as Chinese troops appear to be training for an invasion of Taiwan. The U.S. Fifth and Sixth Fleets are now virtually surrounding Taiwan with more than forty U.S. Navy ships in the waters of the Western Pacific and Indian Ocean. Russia has now entered the fray. There has not been a naval buildup like this since World War II.*

"*North Korea tested its tenth nuclear weapon yesterday, though they remain in a sort of 'treaty' with the United States. The United Nations remains silent about the possible sale of nuclear devices to Iran and the Muslim Brotherhood in Egypt. Since the overthrow of Hosni Mubarak, something the*

United States supported enthusiastically, Egypt has turned outwardly hostile to Israel. Unfortunately, the new 'democracy' in Egypt voted in the Muslim Brotherhood, an extremist group in the minds of most western nations. Though the peace treaty with Israel remains intact, at least loosely, there have been numerous cross-border attacks on Israelis along the Gaza border.

"And finally, this bit of tragic news. Tragic seems to be the word of the day. Eye witnesses confirm the rumors; five men with hoods kidnapped the U.S Public Relations Liaison Officer, Sheryl Lasseter in the Old Peachtree Road explosion in Suwanee, Georgia. The witnesses said the men drove away in a black SUV, possibly a Yukon, with a U.S. Treasury decal on the back. This is Erica Robbins, and that's the news."

CHAPTER THIRTY-FIVE

"When he had said this, Jesus called in a loud voice, 'Lazarus, come out!' The dead man came out, his hands and feet wrapped with strips of linen, and a cloth around his face. Jesus said to them, 'Take off the grave clothes and let him go.'" John 11: 43-44 NIV

"Follow the path so you don't mess up the daffodils."

Jeff followed Missy T up the path to the front door of the little white church named *Ephesus*. He couldn't remember how he got here, or even his night's sleep; but here he was.

"Shhhh," and Missy T held her finger to her lips.

The front door opened quietly; and the little white church in the daffodil field was nearly full. *What an eclectic group of people* he noted, he was always noting; and Jeff sat down in the back pew. There seemed to be a few Sunday-go-to-meeting Christians, a Muslim or two, a few rough-looking motorcycle types. A man who looked to be a monk sat on the floor, but the preacher with the deep voice commanded their attention. Except for the deep voice, not a booming voice, just deep; the church was as silent as a mouse.

Enoch looked directly at the young man in the front pew. The kid was pale with fluffy hair and five earrings adorned each ear, another looped through his nose. He wore a tan T-shirt emblazoned with *ATHEIST and PROUD* with the U.S. Marine Corps emblem centered below.

"Listen up kid, you'll learn somthin' *don'tcha know*." Enoch spoke without a stutter. "Today's sermon is about how the Jew's got to be God's chosen people."

"The Jews were not God's chosen people in the beginning, don'tcha know. Nope, in the beginning, God had a different plan. At that time he didn't have a chosen people, he had a chosen person, don'tcha know. That would be Adam. God made him out of dust. Imagine that? Dust. He made life out of rocks, organic life from inorganic stuff, don'tcha know. It's not possible, o' course, to make life out of dust; but he did it, yes he did.

"Now I don't know what you might know about dust, but making a man out of dust is impossible! In the world of chemistry, there is inorganic chemistry . . . dust, rocks, grains of sand; and then there is organic chemistry which grows things, plants and critters, don'tcha know. It would be impossible to take inorganic chemistry, *dead* stuff, and turn it into organic chemistry, *live* stuff. But God did it anyway, he made his chosen person out of dead stuff; and then it was live stuff. That's amazing, don'tcha think?"

Jeff couldn't believe what he was seeing, and hearing. Enoch spoke in a compelling way, to say the least; and his antics were those of a great actor. The monk stared ahead, unmoved. *Was that Enoch?* He looked . . . *different.* He leaned over and spoke softly into Missy T's ear, "Is that Enoch up there?"

"It is Enoch."

"But he talks; well . . . he speaks so eloquently, and deeply. He isn't stuttering at all." Jeff started to add *don'tcha know,* but didn't.

"Yeah, that's the strange part. When he's preaching, his voice is flawless . . . don'tcha know?" She smiled at him, and he thought for a moment she looked kind of angelic.

"But Adam was lonely, so this time God made him a mate, only he didn't make it out of inorganic stuff. He made Adam's mate out of live stuff, Adam's rib. Says so right there in your Bible and Torah." Enoch held up both; and the crowd took a copy of each from the book trough on the back of each pew, even the kid.

"So God's chosen people in the beginning were Adam and his new companion, Eve. Now I know the 'progressives' say their names weren't Adam and Eve, that the names were just 'symbolic' or some nonsense; but that's not the truth, let me tell ya. We'll have a sermon on Charles Darwin later.

"God offered the two a life in paradise, the *Garden of Eden,* and only gave them one rule to follow. Now think about that. If you woke up from nothingness and you found yourself in a land of paradise and were told you could just live there in comfort, forever, do you think you could follow a single rule? I think so!

"Well, they didn't; and God got really, really ticked. You see, God didn't need people; people needed God. God created people for *his* pleasure, not the people's pleasure, don'tcha know. Says so right there in your Bible and Torah." Enoch again held both books in the air.

"Now God was sorely mad at the two and promptly kicked their disrespectful butts out of paradise, don'tcha see; because they couldn't even keep one simple rule. He closed the gates and left angels to make sure they couldn't get back in to the other tree. Think about that. God punished mankind for their disobedience, and the punishment was death, don'tcha know. We were supposed to live forever, 'til they did *their* stuff. If they coulda somehow got to the other tree, the *tree of life*, then the world woulda been filled with bad people who lived forever. Not good.

"Adam and Eve suffered the first bout of human depression, and became wanderers in the wilderness. Because of that rule, that one stinkin' little rule that they couldn't keep, we inherited death, don'tcha see. Death was the punishment for breaking the rule. Thanks Adam. You shoulda manned up and just said 'no.'"

Jeff thought Enoch had quite a way with words and followed the man's presentation with interest. It wasn't really a *sermon*, more of a lecture from a great professor. The time seemed to be almost at a stand-still. It was entertaining if nothing else.

"So God pretty much turned his back on people, yes he did. Made some appearances now and then, finally helped Noah build his boat, don'tcha know; because God didn't like what he saw on his return trips. He decided enough is enough, he no longer liked his creation and decided to end it all, maybe start over, maybe not. Except wait! He loved Noah, because Noah loved God, one of the few in those days. Most were pagans and worshipped rocks and statues, or they were atheists and thought all of it was BS.

"Now today, we can all thank Noah for being God's buddy; 'cause otherwise we would not be here. We are all direct descendants of Noah, yessiree we are.

"Doc, we have a heartbeat." The voice again. It was really getting annoying, and Jeff wondered if he was going crazy.

"Finally, many years after the flood, God homed in on a man named Abraham, a *Godly* sort of man. Well, he was actually named Abram at the time; but God renamed him. He did that sometimes, don'tcha know.

"God told Abraham to gather his family and move away from all his friends and into the desert. I know that was a strange request; but Abraham believed his ears and did what God asked, unlike Adam. God said he would make Abraham's children numerous, *like the sands of the sea*; and it happened. Through Abraham we got Isaac, Abraham's legitimate son, and Ishmael, Abraham's illegitimate son. Ishmael was born 'cause Abraham's wife encouraged him to sleep with Hagar the slave-girl, don'tcha see. They needed kids, but Abraham's wife couldn't have none; so Ishmael solved that problem, or so it seemed. But that's another story.

"Abraham finally kicked Ishmael and Hagar out of town, so to speak, and into the desert. That's what they did back then. Ishmael became the father of the Arab race, and thus the eventual father of Islam, don'tcha see. Isaac received Abraham's inheritance, and Ishmael got nothing. That is just one of the reasons that Muslims hate Jews to this day, they were left out of the booty, don'tcha know.

"Wake up kid, and pay attention! Finally Isaac and his wife, Rebekah, had two sons, Jacob and Esau; but God really favored Jacob over his twin brother. God finally renamed Jacob, he does that sometimes, and Jacob became known as *Israel*. Jacob's twelve sons became the twelve tribes of Israel, and Israel was born.

"And that's how the children of Israel became God's chosen people. Now don't get me wrong. Being God's 'chosen' was sometimes a pain in the butt, don'tcha see. Adam and Eve had it easy when they were chosen, because they only had one rule. Not so with the Israelites, who found themselves burdened with 613 rules to follow. If the Israelites followed every single rule, they would live another life after death, a forever life don'tcha know. If not, they would eventually die, and that would be it. No eternal life, like was promised for obedience to the Law of Moses, that's what the 613 rules were called, just back to nothingness like Adam was before he was Adam. Now what are the chances of that happening?

"Israelis did not become known as Jews until there was a split between the tribes. The ten northern tribes became known as Israel, at least until those ten tribes were *lost*; and the two southern tribes became Judah, from which the word Jew is derived, don'tcha know."

"I think he might make it. His eyelids are fluttering." The voice.

"So now you know how the Jews got to be God's chosen, only it was really the Israelis, the children of Israel. Now a lot of churches today . . ."

Enoch's voice faded; and suddenly Jeff's vision became disoriented, like the pixilated TV image when the satellite loses signal. Enoch faded in and then out, his voice no longer clear, but muddled. Jeff reached to his right to see if Missy T was still there, but his hand felt nothing. He jerked uncontrollably. *What was happening?*

CHAPTER THIRTY-SIX

"The rest of mankind who were not killed by these plagues still did not repent of the work of their hands; they did not stop worshiping demons, and idols of gold, silver, bronze, stone and wood—idols that cannot see or hear or walk. Nor did they repent of their murders, their magic arts, their sexual immorality or their thefts." Revelation 9:20-21 NIV

Chadbo Myers had been associated with Goddard Space Flight Center's NEO project for several years and had been one of the first to discover the dark comet the year before. He flew from Goddard to Atlanta as soon as he heard about the attack on his friends, his *closest* friends. He was relieved The Admiral was out of the hospital. The Admiral was in great shape, but . . . well, he was getting old.

"How's he doing?" Chad asked when Pam opened the door. Chad's shoulder-length hair was drenched at the tips, a result of the continuing hot weather. He might need to get a haircut.

"He's fine. You know The Admiral. You'd think he was twenty. He's been waiting for you to get here. C'mon, he's sitting by the pool soaking his foot. There's a bathing suit in Jeff's room."

"What's wrong with his foot?"

"He broke it when he kicked that thug in the head a few months ago, trying to protect Sheryl. Still bothering him. Be gentle. He's very upset about . . . well, you know."

Chad did know. The rumors were flying about the budding romance between *Justin and Sheryl*, as unlikely as it seemed. Two hours later, as Chad and Justin dined on hors d'oeuvres, Chad's iPhone chirped. Wild Willy was on the other end, calling from Israel.

"What's up Will?"

"Everything's up, it seems to me. I'm at Natbag and will be on the next flight to Atlanta."

Will used the Hebrew acronym, Natbag; and all the locals knew it stood for Ben Gurion International Airport, located in the city of Lod a few miles south of Tel Aviv. Lod maintained its name from Biblical days and was considered by Muslims to be the place where the great battle that would kill the anti-Christ before the final judgment would take place. Of course lately, many were beginning to think the anti-Christ, if there was such a thing, would be the *Twelfth Imam* of the Shia sect, a Muslim.

"I should be at Briscoe Field about two. I'll rent a car and drive to Jeff's house. Have you heard anything from Sheryl or Jeff?" No ransom requests for Sheryl troubled him, and he hoped she remembered the small GPS device he had given her for her last birthday.

"We haven't talked to Jeff, and no word or demand from Sheryl. But Audry located Jeff yesterday. He's at a California hospital. Apparently he almost died, actually Audry said he did die briefly but 'came back to life.' At least that's her story. She's kind of a strange kid, you know? Way too precocious to be pre-teen."

Will *did* know. Audry seemed *special* in some kind of way, or ways. The plural was more appropriate. Since she began associating with Hutz the Putz, or whatever his name was, she seemed almost psychic.

"How did she find him? Last I heard no one had a clue where he was. And why hadn't the hospital contacted anyone?"

"She said she had a dream about the hospital, even the exact Respiratory ICU where he was located. The hospital said he had no ID of any kind, and they couldn't get finger prints because of the severe abrasions on his hands and finger tips."

"How'd that happen?" Will asked in the staccato style he used when anxious.

"Not sure exactly. Something to do with some of the debris coming from the moon, hit his van or something like that. We should know more by the time you get here."

"How long has he been in the hospital?"

"About two months, I think."

Chad suddenly heard sirens in the background at Natbag, or some kind of alarm; and Wild Willy's phone went dead.

Will noticed the faint light in the sky, high above Ben Gurion Airport, and recognized it immediately. *Incoming.* Probably one of North Korea's latest missiles, sold to Iran with China's blessings, he figured. China was the only nation who had any control over North Korea; and their control was minimal, as the rogue nation continued to be the world's largest proliferator of madness. Recent missile attacks on Israel had become highly sophisticated, and no part of Israel's now smaller country was immune. Israel's Iron Dome missile defense system had proven to be adequate, so far, with a success rate of seventy-eight percent.

Fearing the missile may be homing in on a cell phone signal, the Israel Defense Forces cut all cell phone and Wi-Fi communications. Accustomed to the ever-increasing attacks from her neighbors, tourists and locals rushed to the designated bomb shelters as warning sirens blared all around the town of Lod.

Wild Willy did not run to a shelter. Instead, he was planning his way out of Israel if the missile struck Natbag and he survived. Watching the white glow of the incoming missile as it descended toward the airport, suddenly there appeared to be a dozen missiles rather than one. Decoys.

"Get to the shelters!"

The Israeli security guard's voice carried above the din and was emphatic. Will showed his badge and security clearance to the guard; and the guard, though somewhat reluctantly, allowed him to pass through the airport and to the underground passages that would take him to the Iron Dome III missile defense system. Will had a hand in the development of the Iron Dome, with a little help from the Naval Weapons Lab in Dahlgren, Virginia. Many of the Israelis had already donned their gas masks, something that was never far from reach, with a constant threat of toxic weapons.

The Iron Dome III was far superior to the first version, developed to shoot down the thousands of rockets fired into Israel each year by the Palestinian militias. Since Israel had returned to the pre-1967 war borders, the Palestinian militias immediately lined the new borders with not-so-well hidden arsenals of short-range rockets. Where Israeli greenhouses had once grown crops in the West Bank, they now stored weapons for Israel's destruction.

"Hey Wild Willy!" The Israeli soldier used Will's moniker, like all his *good* friends, and didn't seem particularly disturbed about the incoming missile, sure to strike in a few more seconds. Iron Dome had proven over-

and-over again to be effective in disposing of incoming rocket and mortar fire, even weeding out the decoys from the real thing.

"Fire Dome one!" came the shout from across the control center, and Will could feel the ground movement as twenty-some anti-missile missiles scurried into the air, destined for a rendezvous with the incoming warfare, though war had not been declared. They were at *peace*.

The North Korean missile continued downward, but its course became erratic, going to the left and then to the right, taking evasive measures. The Iron Dome missile system destroyed thirteen incoming rockets; but four continued their advance of death, including the evasive weapon. At fifteen hundred feet above the Ben Gurion Airport, the North Korean rocket exploded, more with a *poof* than a *bang*; and a cloud of gas formed over the airport and the city of Lod. The air was still, as it had been the last three days, hardly a breeze.

The Israeli crew donned their gas masks as the cloud slowly dispersed, most of it descending toward the ground; but the masks would prove unnecessary as a sudden breeze, an updraft, came from the east, another miracle Will knew. The pathogen-ridden cloud blew westward toward the Mediterranean and away from the Jewish homeland. *God blew it away.*

A weapon of mass destruction had finally been used against Israel, and the Middle East would never be the same after this day.

Chapter Thirty-Seven

"For thus says the Lord of hosts, 'Once more in a little while, I am going to shake the heavens and the earth, the sea also and the dry land. I will shake all the nations . . . . I am going to shake the heavens and the earth. I will overthrow the thrones of kingdoms and destroy the power of the kingdoms of the nations." Haggai 2:6, 7, 21, 22 NASB

Terry and Toni, Jeff's neighbors from Sugarloaf, pulled into the vehicle area, made the U-turn, flipped up the stern camera switch and proceeded to back the sleek behemoth into the *stop spot* at the end of the asphalt ramp. In less than five minutes, they were ready to relax.

"Power's hooked up, water's hooked up, fire up the grill!"

The Faheys met the couple in the adjacent space and admired *their* behemoth, a late model Wanderlodge. They became quick friends, something that just happens sometimes and immediately planned to have dinner together.

The young couple from Raleigh, a Wolfpack bumper sticker adorning their red-and-white ice chest, carried the cooler over and opened the lid. There were four of the largest, thickest filets that Toni had ever seen, and she had seen many.

"Don't slobber bigboy." Toni knew that hubby Terry was probably salivating before the lid was open.

In the distance Toni thought she heard a low rumble, but it didn't really sound like one of the spring thunderstorms she had experienced so often as a kid along the plains of Missouri. She seemed to be the only one that noticed. There were no clouds to be seen through the encompassing trees, only filtered sunlight.

"I brought the wine too, if that's ok. My cousin's husband turned us on to it. Duckhorn." Sheri handed Bennett the opener.

Terry and Toni watched as Sheri pulled out a bottle of *Duckhorn Merlot*, and they looked at each other, in a sort of mild shock. They only knew one person in the world, and they had been all over, who drank Duckhorn Merlot. They had actually met Mr. Duckhorn at one time, a good friend of Jeff's. They hadn't seen Jeff in months, at least it seemed so; and Toni's forehead wrinkled slightly, worry-wrinkles.

They all heard the thunder this time. The ground shook, slightly; and the four new friends looked at each other with wide eyes.

A world away in the hills of Chechnya, Aludra and Naomi, the old Jewish woman with the cross, shared a room in one of the villagers' homes. Aludra thought about her brother in Afghanistan and worried that she should not have abandoned him. *Would he have killed her?* The thought crossed her mind, as it so often had in the past weeks, months. The Jewish woman with the cross seemed to fit right in with the villagers, most wrinkled with worn skin; and almost all were Muslims, like Aludra. This was something that would never have happened in her Afghan village. She couldn't imagine a Jewish woman with a cross gaining anything but misery, if not death, in *her* village. A happy-tear formed in the corners of her dark eyes. *Maybe there was hope.*

"I never thought we would get here." Naomi said.

"Where *is* 'here?'" Aludra asked.

"This used to be part of Russia a few years ago. The area became an opium smuggling trail for a while . . . until the villagers took over. It was quite a struggle." The old woman sighed, and Aludra decided to let her sleep. She just hoped she wouldn't dream about what she had seen today. In the weeks she and the old lady had traveled together, she had never seen so much pain and agony as she had seen the last two days.

"Why don't the villagers have the disease?" The spring air was warmer, but smokier too.

Aludra's only answer from the old woman was a slight snore, escaping from the quilt covering the woman's head. From across the small, dank room, moonlight shined through the window; and Aludra decided she liked the rings and the reddish glow of the full moon. It was pretty.

Allah, please don't let me dream about the disease, oh please, oh please. She drifted into dreamland, only the disease wasn't a dream. *Ebola* had raised its wicked head, and Aludra prayed to the God of Islam.

Naomi wasn't really snoring as she ignored Aludra's question, just faking it so she could think, and pray. She would pray hard tonight.

What's going on with the moon, Lord? Why is it so red and now with rings, like a small Saturn? Why are there so many shooting-stars? The diseases, please Yahweh. This disease can't be smallpox? Can it? Is the world ending, Lord? How will we know the day?

Naomi fell asleep praying to the God of Abraham, wondering when the Messiah would come, and if he may have already.

"You're early today Abe? Couldn't sleep again?"

"Hey Pam. You're early too."

The Divide wasn't open for breakfast, but Abe had begun a new routine. The Duluth Police were as good as good could be, but they couldn't be everywhere at all times. Neither could he; but he could be at *The Divide* more, to protect the place and maybe some of the shops on the Towne Green. Since the wild dogs, some thought they were coyotes, had attacked and killed Old Man Jackson up on the highway, the break-ins had slowed. No one wanted to take their chance with the dogs, the killing had been brutal. Too brutal for a *normal* dog, at least.

Abe's right hand probed beneath his loose, purple Hilfiger shirt, rechecking the pistol in his back holster, something that had now become a reflex action. An extra ammo clip was in his man-pouch. My how things had changed in just a year, and getting worse, fast. He waited for the large TV over the bar to adjust, and he was surprised not to see an Alert scrolling across the screen. He knew one wouldn't be far behind. Things just weren't the same since the only conservative cable news was forced off the air by the FCC, too *biased*. Now it was definitely biased he thought, in the *other* direction. He hoped it would be temporary, with the new election coming up.

"The smoke's strong today." Pam's point evident by the haze.

"Yeah, and it's early. Did they find out how the fires started?"

"Not for certain," Pam said. "Some fisherman in Suwanee said he saw men with *flaming arrows*, shooting them in the woods but said the man was *not all there*. Why would someone do that Abe?"

"They're trying to run us out of money." Abe replied, and was beginning to think that America's enemies would succeed. If the jihadists and militias didn't do it, it looked like nature would.

"Do you believe evil exists, Pam? I mean an evil force of some kind that makes a percentage of people extremely mean and evil?"

"You mean kinda like the *unholy* spirit?"

"Yeah, I guess that's a good analogy. Opposite of Holy Spirit. Something like that."

Condi Z's face appeared on the flat screen, as lovely as ever; and Pam thought she just *had* to get Condi's plastic surgeon's number. She wondered if Condi would be the anchor at the new network. Like Abe the Bartender, Pam was surprised there wasn't a *News Alert*. They seemed to be coming more-and-more often.

"*Dr. Dennis Duncan is a professor, geophysicist and an earthquake and natural disaster specialist from Mississippi State University. Welcome Dr. Duncan.*"

"*Thanks Condi for having me here. I wish I could say I'm glad to be here.*" The doctor didn't look healthy.

"*Dr. Duncan, the first six months of the year have been virtually free of terrorism.*"

Could she say that? she thought in a mild-panic. Can't say *Islamic* or *ethnicity-of-any-kind* terrorism she thankfully recalled. It was going to be difficult to follow the new network's rules. She continued.

"*At least man-made terrorism Dr. Duncan, but there's still plenty of terror going around of a different nature, correct?*"

"*Yes there is Condi, in a very significant way.*"

"*What would you say is the most pressing issue facing the country?*"

"*It's the world, the rest of the world that is. The United States is having significant natural disaster issues, and the flu virus has stymied the national economy. We're having a few riots, but nothing like Europe and China and Russia. So as you say, the terrorism seems to have slowed. That's good.*"

Condi Z coughed and listened.

"*However, the other continents have even bigger issues. The recent discovery of mosquitos becoming vectors for the HIV AIDS virus in Ghana has the entire African country in quarantine. Unfortunately they waited too late to shut the borders it appears, and mosquitos don't recognize borders.*"

"*What do you mean by that?*"

Dr. Duncan sipped a glass of white-grape juice, *or could that be wine?* Condi wondered. He seemed a little giddier than the last interview.

"*There has been an apparent outbreak in Asia, somewhere in the Chechnya area; and the virus appears to have mutated into an especially virulent and violent strain. It may have merged with a different virus, possibly a derivative of Ebola-Zaire, according to CDC in Atlana.*"

"*Is this evolutionary process common, Dr. Duncan?*"

"*This isn't an evolutionary process. It is either a mutation of the single virus or a combination of two or more, at least that would be my supposition. It is still a virus. It has not evolved into another species.*"

"*Europe and Africa, because of unusually high winds in the jet stream and the months-long droughts, are on fire. Millions of acres have burned, Greece's famous olive groves are no more. Talk about a carbon foot print.*"

"*Guess this is not good news for the 'greenhouse effect.'*"

"*The 'greenhouse effect' is total hogwash, but that's another story. The pressing issue is the transportation of the disease borne mosquitos via the dense smoke. Smoke is thicker than air and will transport more mosquitos because of the heat and increased air pressure around the fires. They could end up anywhere, even Iceland or the Arctic. In those cases, the mosquitos would die from cold, unless another mutation occurred.*"

"*Oh no, this 'greenhouse effect' is more than man could do in a million years. Every earthquake creates GE gases; the seven volcanic islands in the Ring of Fire that recently appeared in the ocean create GE gases; and the burning forests around the globe are the largest contributors. It needs to stop, somehow.*"

Dr. Duncan's skin was pallid, and Condi was a little concerned. He was sweating profusely.

"*Is there a way to stop it Dr. Duncan . . .*"

The screen digitized briefly, puzzling into a billion tiny, colored squares; and then Condi was back. Before she could continue, a News Alert appeared, this one a *real* alert with the new jingle from *Phantom of the Opera*. Abe and Pam held their breath in anticipation and didn't notice the man in black as he entered the front door.

"Where is the Men's room?" The man asked in a low voice.

Their eyes remained fixed to the screen, every alert now seeming to be more urgent. Without looking at the stranger, Abe pointed to the bathrooms.

"*There has been a major earthquake in . . . ri . . . is . . .*" The screen again digitized. What was wrong with the signal? Abe clicked to another channel and back.

"*. . . ports of deaths . . . in the . . . ds.*"

"He's not dead *for Pete's sake*." That was the man in black's only comment; and he walked out the front door as quietly as he had entered.

Abe glimpsed his back and was sure he had seen the man before, then remembered. Just before Jeff left for California, they were sitting at the bar and the same man came in. *What had he said? Something about Satan? Had he said his name was Mike, or maybe Michael?*

Pam and Abe looked at each other, jaws dropped.

"I've never known anybody but Jeff who said 'for Pete's sake,' have you?" Pam was sure of that.

The Kichlers and the Faheys continued the neighborly cookout, deciding that the *boom* must have been thunder echoing across the drought-ridden plains of Missouri. It hadn't happened again, but Toni remained uneasy. It was dark and the katydids were singing their favorite song, the sky clear and starry. There was no pink moon tonight.

"Are they looking for a honey?" Sheri asked, and started laughing hysterically. And then she cried.

"What's the matter?" Toni was concerned about the sudden mood swing.

"Oh, I'm OK. I was just thinking about a comment my niece made last summer when visiting us in Raleigh. She's so smart. She heard the katydid's mating calls, came running onto the patio and hollered as loud as possible, 'Are those katydids lookin' for a honey?'" Sheri broke down laughing again, along with Bennett and Terry. Not Toni.

"Our next-door neighbor's daughter says the same thing. This is *too* weird. Her dad, one of our best friends, is missing; recently widowed, at least sort of widowed." Toni's voice trailed as she noticed the bright but almost-hidden light that briefly flashed on the western horizon. "He drinks Duckhorn Merlot."

Sheri and Bennett looked at each other, and now they had the dropped jaws. Sheri asked the next question.

"Is her name Audry?" A rumble in the distance, low and close to the ground.

Fifteen minutes later, cucumber martinis in hand, the new friends sat under the million-dollar *Prevost* RV's retractable awning, overlooking the rolling hills across arid plains of southern Missouri.

"I am totally awed, still." Sheri repeated again. She and Toni sat alone on the chaise lounges under the stars while the hubbies talked football or some other nonsensical subject like men seemed obsessed to do. The men relocated to the banks of the RV resort's natural spring a few hundred feet away, a spring that would be dry by the time this night was over.

"Sheri, do you read much?"

"I do actually, but maybe not what you read. I love history, natural science, weather phenomenon . . . weird I know. And of course a good love story, the defining word being 'good,'" she said; and Toni understood her implication. Love stories weren't really as good as they had been a few years before. "Sometimes there can be just *too much* sex, know what I mean?"

"I do," and they laughed.

"Have you ever heard of the New Madrid fault?" Toni asked.

"Sure, it's right past the hills over there, on the western horizon. There's a major fault-line between St. Louis and Memphis, I think."

Sheri was sure she was correct but didn't mention the flash of light she saw earlier. No one seemed to have noticed. She recently read several articles about new activity along the New Madrid fault and the possible implication with oil drilling in the Gulf.

"You are a real pleasure to know, I have to say. Hardly anyone I meet knows anything about the dangerous nature of this area, should the fault slip." Toni liked her new friend.

"Yeah, like in the 1800s?"

"Exactly," Toni answered. "I think it's getting ready to go-and-blow Sheri. I know that sounds crazy, but . . ."

"You saw the lights on the horizon?"

"Yep, I noticed," Toni said, "and the sub-surface rumbling. I was in a large earthquake in China when I was little, at least it seemed large to me. I was only eight. Two days before the quake hit, there were deep rumbles in the ground. I could feel it in my sandals, and all the birds flew away. Suddenly the animals followed. Way away in the distance there were these really bright flashes. It was so scary. I remember it like it was yesterday." And she did.

"I think it's amazing that we met, Toni. I mean, what are the chances? There has to be a reason, maybe a God-thing. You know?"

They hugged, and Toni felt like Sheri was a sister. Toni missed her only sister, killed by a serial rapist on early release two years earlier but dismissed the thought.

"What do you think we should do?" Sheri finally asked after a few moments of silence. The sounds of the katydids were suddenly silent. That was odd.

"I think we need to get the hell out of here. Right now."

The lights in the distance were brighter this time, and the flashes lit up the two husbands walking toward them on the trail. Terry was the first to speak.

"You ladies hurry. We're all getting in the *Prevost*. We have to leave immediately, because something strange is going on to the west. Bennett thinks it's an Earthquake warning! Hurry!"

The earth was suddenly unstable, wiggling like a big bowl of Jello. A rider on a large, pale horse came galloping up, shouting.

"You guys must evacuate, now!" The horse came to a halt as the four ran for the *Prevost*. Bennett stopped.

"Who are you?" he asked, thinking she looked sort of like the paintings he'd seen of Jeanne D'Arc.

"Name's Lynn Tomay. I'm working with the U.S. Geological Survey. You must evacuate."

"Is it the Madrid fault?" Sheri already knew the answer.

"It is! Go!"

Lynn galloped away under the four hundred watt outdoor lamps, warning others like Paul Revere warned of the coming British. The ground shifted suddenly, breaking all four legs of the pale horse and pinning Lynn underneath. Looking up from her precarious situation, Lynn saw a million birds flying away. Some campers rushed to help Lynn, but most ran for safety. The horse bellowed in agony as the bones stuck through the skin of the horse's legs. Once free, Lynn removed the pistol from her holster and shot the horse in the head, three times.

"That was just a preliminary shock! We must leave a-sap!"

The camper-rescuers were in awe. Lynn nursed her leg, following the four new friends to their RV. Leaving the resort, the traffic was backed up and the ground continued to rock. The Prevost swayed but maintained stability as the group took a shortcut across the campgrounds, by the spring that was now a dry creek bed and onto the nearby dirt and gravel trail. There was another strong jolt, and the RV slid sideways as Bennett wrestled the steering wheel for control.

Then it was over, as suddenly as it had begun.

"Al-Jazeera TV-News has just confirmed a possible nuclear explosion at the Bushehr Nuclear facilities inside Iran. The facilities are located along the Persian Gulf coast. The massive explosion, which registered a 3.8 on the Richter scale, has been blamed on Israel. There has been no unusual air force activity this evening, according to Israeli sources; and the IDF is not commenting.

"Please tune in tomorrow morning, if we have a signal, at 10:00 for a special interview with Chuck Hutz. He will be interviewed by a rabbi, a Catholic priest and a Muslim cleric. Should be interesting."

Abe turned the TV off, locked the door of *The Divide* and wondered if Wild Willy was still in Israel. Another day of bad news had been stressful. Exiting, he looked up at the sky and considered how long before a really big chunk of something was going to wipe out a city, or continent. Some of the orbiting Moon rocks were large enough to detect; and Abe remembered what Jeff had told him before leaving for California, that some of the larger rocks would certainly leave the Moon's orbit. Still, the multi-colored streaks across the dark sky, the rising pink moon with rings, were awe inspiring, a beauty beyond poetic description.

"I will show wonders in the heaven above and signs on the earth below, blood and fire and billows of smoke."

Abe considered the quote. Jesus of Nazareth had said it 2,000 years earlier, though more-and-more were denying that Jesus even existed. Abe thought about Jeffrey Ross and his fervent atheism and wondered if Jeff would ever be back for his Cliffsnotes <u>Bible</u> study.

How could anyone not believe in God after seeing this?

CHAPTER THIRTY-EIGHT

*"Then David said to Nathan, 'I have sinned against the
Lord.' Nathan replied, 'The LORD has taken away your
sin. You are not going to die.'"* 2 Samuel 12:13

The light was so bright, for a moment Jeff thought it was *Blip* again;
but this light was much larger and closer. He could feel the heat,
tiny photons of light bombarding his face. As the light faded away,
he began to hear voices, unfamiliar voices, but was too tired to assess. Then
the light disappeared completely; and Jeff was back at *Melissa's*, reggae
music playing in the background as a Bob Marley wannabe sang *Exodus*.

"Bet you didn't know that Robert Marley converted to Christianity
about a year before he died."

Jeff was relieved to see Missy T.

"Nope, I didn't. Last I heard he smoked a lot of weed and was a
Rastafarian. But I love his jammin'. Did you know reggae was my favorite
music?"

"What's it now?" she asked.

"What?"

"What music do you like now?"

"I just told you silly woman! Reggae."

"No, you said that reggae *was* your favorite music, past tense. Are you
living in the past Jeff?" Missy T was in rare form.

Kipper T looked at Jeff and gave him that *'what can I say?'* look and
a wink. That's when Jeff noticed that Kipper had a glass eye. He had seen
many; and this was a good one, just the perfect shade of blue to match the
other. He couldn't believe he hadn't noticed that earlier at the bar.

"Yep. Robert Nesta Marley, dead at 36 from cancer. He spent most of his adult life as a Rastafarian, but his roots were Christian. He just rebelled against his Christian parents, like so many do. He was a little bit of a wild child, if you know what I mean.

"He had a mentor of sorts, an Archbishop appointed by Haile Salassie, the ruler of Ethiopia. Actually he was the Emperor. Did you know any of that?"

"Nope. But go ahead. It's interesting." Jeff *was* interested and had always been a Bob Marley fan.

"Selassie wanted a church established in Jamaica so the Jamaicans would worship Jesus the Christ and have a Christ-like attitude. Anyway, the new Rastis smoked a lot of ganja and worshipped Haile Selassie instead. It was easier.

"Bob Marley tried to convert to Christianity several times but was almost killed by the Rastis. Then the last year of his life, he was baptized. Dead at 36, buried with his Bible and his Gibson Guitar.

"Did you know any of that?"

"I know that the famous Gibson guitar is almost a thing of the past, thanks to the feds; something about the imported wood Gibson used. But no, I didn't know his bio."

"Well see there Mr. Mensa, you're not so smart are you? He was baptized into the Ethiopian Orthodox Church. Want some fresh lemonade?" Missy T poured a glass without waiting for an answer.

"I keep hearing voices Kipper. Unfamiliar voices. They just kind of appear out of nowhere. It's really getting on my nerves."

"Maybe they aren't as unfamiliar as you think, Jeff." *Did Missy T ever let Kipper answer a question?*

"Who do they sound like?" Kipper T asked the question as though he knew the answer already.

"They sound hollow and muffled, and there is all this 'clinking' in the background. I don't know; it seems like I may have been there before, wherever it is." Jeff looked tired. "Then ever so often, I see this bright light shining through my eyelids, kind of like *Blip.*"

"Who?" Missy T asked.

"Never mind. That's a story for another day."

Enoch walked up. "Hhhhhey Mmister Rosss," and stuck out his hand but then gave Jeff a big hug instead.

"Ddid you lllikkke mmy sspeechh? I sstuttter, ddon'tcchha know?"

Jeff was in total awe of Enoch's speech disorder, more in awe at how it disappeared in the little white church and then reappeared as soon as Enoch stepped out of the daffodil covered field.

"I know Enoch. Maybe we should all move to the church!"

They laughed, Enoch especially. He noticed that Enoch didn't stutter in his laughter and found himself wondering about his crying, and whether he stuttered then. What had Abe said that time, something about the *universal* language?

"A Chinese person sounds exactly like a Russian, Mexican or Frenchman when he cries or laughs. Think about it. Do you think you could identify someone's language by a cry of mourning or a laugh of joy? An American mother crying for her son killed in war is very similar to a mother in Afghanistan crying over the death of her child. Right? Emotions aren't nearly as identifiable as words. Do you think a French cardinal chirps in French? Not!"

I have to call Abe he thought.

"Are you staying another night or going to Lukeville?" Missy's question was abrupt, as was her mood today. She didn't seem quite as *friendly* as before.

"I guess . . ." Jeff started . . . "I'm not sure why I was going to Lukeville to begin with. Did I mention a reason?"

"Then that settles it, you can stay in the same room tonight. We will have a cocktail and talk. Whatever you do, don't go through *that* door," and Missy T pointed to the same door she defined earlier, the black one.

Why not? He supposed he would dream about the forbidden doorway tonight, as he again slept in the room of dreams. *Did I just dream about the church and Enoch, or was it real?* He was beginning to think nothing was real. *I don't feel normal.*

"What is this place Missy? Is this a dream?"

"No, it's not a dream Jeffrey. This is the *place of lost opportunities and second chances.* Trust me. God wants you to make the cut."

Chapter Thirty-Nine

"**A**udry found him!"

Pam walked out to Jeff's pool, interrupting Chad and The Admiral, both in deep conversation about Sheryl no doubt. The waterfalls adorning the pool were relaxing, but the news she bore wasn't.

"Found who?" Chad asked.

"Audry located Jeff. He's in a hospital in California. Somewhere near San Diego. She and the twins were hoping to fly out, but all airlines are still grounded. They're taking the train. I think we should volunteer to keep Audry."

"Why's he in the hospital?"

"I don't know Chad; just got the info."

That's kind of snippy, he thought.

"I'm sorry Chad. I know that was snippy. I'm just tired."

Pam glanced at the sky, still amazed at the beauty of the last few months, perpetual fireworks displays in the sky, even during the day; but *angry* at the reasons, and what was happening to the world, *her* world. She turned up the volume.

"*. . . the circuit court has overturned the ChristianRight vs. The Boylove Project verdict today. This contested decision lowers the acceptable age for a man or woman to have sexual relationships with a child, from age 15 to 11.*"

Condi looked like she might throw up but quickly got her composure.

"*In a ruling against the ChristianRight group, who brought the suit, the court said that the relationship between Benjamin Haffala, 56 and an eleven year old girl was consensual and not forced. With the recent modification of pedophilia rulings, Haffala will not be charged for having sex with the eleven year old girl. Many are concerned of the possible influence of Islam's Sharia Law which approves of young relationships but is very much against homosexuality, adultery and many other acts of sex. Muhammad's favorite wife was onl . . ."*

The feed went dead but continued for anyone listening on a short-wave radio.

". . . only 6 or 7 when Muhammad married her, though according to Islamic biographers, he and the 7 year old girl, A'isha, did not have sex until she became 9. Muhammad was in his late fifties.

"On a similar note, the city of Atlanta has become the 30ᵗʰ city to allow private, nude bath houses on public thoroughfares with road-facing windows. There have been no fatalities yet, but three cars and a tour bus of retirees have crashed into the building so far. Neighbors are concerned that the building is a 'distraction.' Now to the Decadence Parade in New Orleans, just a few months away . . ."

Condi didn't like the changes in broadcasting *rules*, a million thoughts going through her head as to why this report was so *wrong*. Shouldn't people be recognizing that something, many things actually, were terribly awry with the world? Shouldn't people be getting closer to God rather than farther away? It seemed to her, the more tragedy, the faster the drift away. Seemed odd, against logic. She continued.

"Now some good news," a slight smile forming at the right corner of her mouth, *"The high-jacked Nerpa 155 submarine has apparently been spotted in the Mediterranean by an Israeli Oceanographic research vessel off the coast of Morocco. The U.S. Navy has been searching the east coast of the United States for the submarine, but anonymous Pentagon sources tell us that the Navy has a world-wide dragnet out for the Russian-built sub. Though it hasn't been confirmed, the Israeli Navy is said to be on high alert, as is the Suez Canal."*

Pam made note of Condi Zimmerman's demeanor and noticed a sincerity she had never noticed before. She had met Condi before, at the Rexall Grill a few years earlier . . . the Runaway Bride fiasco. She didn't seem like one to hold her tongue, but it sure seemed so now.

"How did Audry know?" Chad asked but thought he knew the answer.

"Can you share that info with Pam?" Admiral McLemore asked, changing the subject.

"Sure. It's not a security issue, at least so far."

"Chadbo says the Sun is experiencing some *unusual activity*."

"Not solar flares or CMEs," Chad interrupted, thinking that he was the one who was supposed to share the story. The Admiral always did that.

"He says the Sun is heating up a bit, that we haven't really seen global warming yet."

"Yeah, and the chimneys." Chad inserted.

"Chimneys?" Pam asked.

"Black smokers."

Pam knew Chadbo didn't have a racist bone in his body, being bi-racial himself; but the black people smoking comment caught her off guard.

"What the hell do black smokers have to do with global warming Chad. That surprises me!"

"Black smokers; at the bottom of the ocean. There are these vents on the bottom of the ocean in certain areas, especially really deep areas. These underwater vents spew out really hot water, about 700 degrees."

"I thought water boiled at two hundred?" Pam questioned.

"At one atmospheric pressure, like on the stove, water boils at 212 degrees, Fahrenheit. The greater the pressure, the hotter the water can get before it boils and turns to gas. There is so much ocean on top of the vents, the water pressure prevents the boiling until the temperatures get extreme."

"That's not the strange part," The Admiral interjected. "The water has now been detected at much higher temperatures, in the Pacific off San Francisco. These vents usually form chimneys from the elements that accumulate around the vent. The one off San Fran has a chimney that's thirteen feet tall. This chimney is known as Godzilla, and the water now coming out the top is approaching 875 degrees."

"So what's so strange, other than the pressure has gotten greater?"

"Good question, Pam." Chad showed a picture of a Black Smoker on his iPad. It looked like a small, underwater volcano. "There has been no increase in pressure. It's impossible."

The conversation turned silent, the small waterfall at the back of Jeff's pool the only noise, as water fell into the pool below. A flock of starlings flew from the trees in unison, forming a small, dark cloud, flowing eastward.

"Nothing's impossible with God," Pam said. "Didn't you ever read the book of *Job*?"

Jeff's back muscles spasmed. They had spasmed before, especially after the Park Place explosion and the wreck when he was an active SEAL; but never like this. He nearly jerked himself out of the bed. *How did I get here?* He didn't even remember going to the room of dreams. He had been talking with Missy, and . . . did he go to the *bad* room? *Did I go through the door?* The light was bright and annoying, the blood vessels visible thru his eyelids.

"Turn off that light!" He tried to mouth the words, though it would have been a shout were it not for the tracheostomy in his throat; and no understandable words were emitted through the tube, just a slight hiss as the air briefly escaped through the opening in his neck. His throat ached from the ventilator.

The unfamiliar voices were everywhere now; and hands were touching him, grabbing him, exploring the wires all around. *Did I go through the door?* Clashing and ringing of metal on metal. Suddenly it was dark.

As the starlings flew from Jeff's trees, the morning suddenly seemed stifling, the air still. The sky was perfectly blue, but something didn't seem right. The air felt heavy, and Pam thought it must be her imagination.

"The San Diego Hospital had him listed as *John Doe*. I don't know the details, but apparently he's been hospitalized since he got to San Diego. The report said a meteorite hit the van he was riding in. Two days ago, Audry *dreamed* he died from the Spanish flu; and she saw a sign for the Emergency Room at the very hospital he's in. Apparently he *did* die, but now he's alive. That's a *really* unusual child." Pam considered whether her love for Audry might have developed a small, respectful fear of some kind. "They said he was dead for approximately two hours."

"He came back to life after *two hours*? Not possible." The Admiral was incredulous.

"Hutz the Putz was dead longer than *that* and came back to life. It was all over the news last year. Remember?

The Admiral and Chad *both* remembered that very, strange guy. Almost killed in an auto accident in Raleigh the day the Christian cult hacked into the motor vehicle department computers and turned all the traffic lights green, T-boned by a Cadillac.

"I remember him, the guy that died and came back to life waiting for the morgue attendant. Didn't he sit up on the gurney and scare someone?" Chad laughed out loud.

"Yes! The drunk. Saw it on the news. Scared him so bad he took off out the door of the emergency room yelling 'I'll never drink again, Lord save me!' Ran right into a sliding-glass door and knocked himself out, cold as a cucumber." All three laughed again.

Pam continued her foreboding news, and the laughter quickly subsided.

"I think that's what she said. Jami and Jenni are making train reservations. Can't fly because of the meteors. I'm going to see if Abe wants to go with them. Jeff really likes him, might be good to see familiar faces; and Abe could watch over the girls. It's not safe anywhere anymore, especially for young women."

The air suddenly became warmer and the *whoosh* was heard by all, and then the impact. They ran out the pool gate, not realizing the danger as three large chunks of ice landed harmlessly in the neighbor's yard.

Pam, Admiral McLemore and Chad ran through the gardens to get a closer look. There had been no thunder, no clouds, just sunshine and blue sky. As they peered over the wrought-iron fence at the back of Jeff's yard, the fourth ice bomb fell from the sky, a louder whoosh than before, and it destroyed the back half of the Fahey's home, the brick and stone exterior walls exploding outwards. Thankfully, they were on a camping trip.

Pam MacLott fell to the ground in a sudden heap, hit in the head by an ice fragment, and her head bled profusely.

CHAPTER FORTY

"The dragon stood on the shore of the sea. And I saw a beast coming out of the sea. It had ten horns and seven heads, with ten crowns on its horns, and on each head a blasphemous name." Revelation 13:1 NIV

Submerged but silent, Moshe knew immediately that the large, gray behemoth was no beast but a submarine, a very *large* submarine. There were no markings, but he knew it was not of U.S., European or Israeli design. He held his finger to his lips, indicating silence. There appeared to be ten large missile silos and seven that were smaller.

"Let's wait fifteen minutes," he whispered to his copilot. "Then we will begin a slow ascent, as quietly as possible. That may be the missing sub."

"Moshe, what is it? We blow these ballasts and they know we're here."

"Then don't blow the ballasts. We can rise slowly. The submarine was only going a couple of knots. We have to warn *someone* Myles. That sub's headed for Israel. They closed the Panama Canal, and now shipping is backed up all over the world. People are starving because the grain barges have to go around the tip of South America, and good luck with that. I read an article just last week about another grain barge sinking in the Drake Passage to the south of Cape Horn. No telling how many dead sailors lay at the bottom of *that* extreme sea."

"What if they fire at us?"

"I am sure they will Myles, if they hear us. They may have already detected us. I know the sonar the Russkies developed is one of the best, if not *the* best. I don't imagine the Phoenix looks like the terrain that is programmed into that ships navigation system. We go for it, understood?" Moshe's glare was stern.

The co-pilot, Myles Cabbot, was a bioengineering genius and had known Moshe long enough to know what *that* look meant, so there would be no discussion. The plan was shared with the crew as quietly as possible, everyone donned their life vests with built in air supply; and within fifteen minutes, the ballasts were slowly opened and the *Phoenix* luxury submarine began an agonizingly slow ascent from 700 feet below the surface of the Mediterranean. They held their breath, but the silence was deafening.

"Commander Kadyrov! We may have a guest." The Nerpa sonar-tech was breathing rapidly. If they were caught now, their plans would be over. No Tel Aviv. No Suez Canal.

"Do we have a description? Could it be our supply sub?"

"It's too small to be a supply submarine, Commander, but too large to be a private-use sub, unless maybe it's one of those tourist submarines. It's noisy. Looks like they're making a slow ascent."

"Do you think they could have detected us?"

"I don't know, Commander. I do know we have picked up *something* that is ascending. It wasn't ascending before we passed."

"Ignore it. Continue on. If it's a tourist sub, they won't know who we are. We cannot draw attention to ourselves."

"Myles, get everyone to the submersible platform *now*! Everyone can fit in the two mini-subs. Get them in, *now*!!"

"There won't be room for you Moshe!"

"Myles, do what I say." Moshe was calm. "We may not need them; but if we pick up torpedoes headed our way, we must be ready to abandon ship. I'll set the *Phoenix* on autopilot and she will continue to rise . . ."

"If she's not blown out of the water." Myles interrupted.

"Yes, if she isn't torpedoed. If so, I will use the 1-man submersible to escape. This is our *only* chance. Head straight to the surface and away from the submarine. Try to keep the *Phoenix* between you and that sub. I will give the signal if it looks like we need to abandon ship."

Abandon ship. Myles looked exasperated, but turned to follow Moshe's instructions. In less than two minutes they were secure in the two mini-subs, and Myles notified Moshe with the code they had devised. Moshe turned the valve to the now water-tight compartment and the egress system worked flawlessly. *God, I love this sub!*

The sonar warning system suddenly alarmed; but Moshe had no idea it was a malfunction, a false alarm. Moshe was sure what was headed his way, hell in a tube. He sent the signal to Myles. The two small mini-subs, preprogrammed to surface automatically, did. They moved westward, too slow for comfort, gradually gaining on the surface.

Moshe engaged the Phoenix 1000's pre-programmed autopilot and headed to the second dive platform, the one that housed the 1-man submersible. He would need to hurry.

The submersible was jettisoned in a sea of bubbles; but as the bubbles flowed up, Moshe dove, knowing that he could descend faster than ascend, and prayed to the God of Abraham that he would be far enough away when the torpedo hit. One crack in the acrylic skeleton, and that would be it. *Adios amigo.* He prayed again. *What was taking so long?*

The false alarm from the Phoenix was quickly detected by Commander Kadyrov's sonar tech, and the information was relayed to the commander. The stern-mount torpedoes were pressurized and ready. The micro-torpedoes traveled at tremendous speed and required no explosives and carried none. The kinetic energy from the small torpedoes would puncture the skin of the enemy ship and sink it, quietly.

Sheryl memorized the dank warehouse layout and listened. At least an hour had passed; and there had been no sound, just silence, except for the wind blowing through the cracked skylight in the roof above. Glancing through the broken skylight, surely broken from the hailstorms, the opening was partially obscured by the metal support beams. It was still daylight, barely. The heat was stifling.

"Water!" She yelled as loud as she could. She needed to know how many were guarding her.

Nothing. Silence.

"Helloooooo," she dragged the word out, "Is anybody here?"

Silence, except for the wind at the skylight. She counted to 300, and five minutes had passed. She shouted.

"I need water!!!"

Nothing. *Had they abandoned her?* Sheryl had already worked her hands free from Jonathon's inadequate wrap-job. By now she was fully aware of her surroundings and the unlikelihood of escaping. Rather than open the bathroom door, she carefully stood on the bowl of the toilet, trying to maintain her balance, and looked over the wall partition. The ceiling tiles were missing and an air conditioning duct hung loosely. There was no one in the vacant space. *What happened? Where are the guards? Hadn't there been several voices?*

Walking toward the four roll-up garage doors, she was certain they would be locked; and they were. *Is there a guard outside? What a bunch of bumpkins.* She checked every possible point of egress, but all were secured. In a hurry, Sheryl walked back to the roofless bathroom. She had to figure a way to use the ladder, it was her only hope.

Without taking off her blouse, she quickly removed her bra; and her mind raced faster than her heart. She could hear the blood pumping through her body. For the first time in her life, she wished she had worn panty hose. In the corner, she saw something she had missed during her earlier inspections, a painter's tarp, old and torn, but not rotten. She removed her tennis shoes after examining the tarp, removed a sock and slowly began to unravel the polyester-cotton yarn. She worked fast.

The *Phoenix* submersible could descend at a remarkable rate; and by the time the mini-torpedo hit the *Phoenix 1000*, Moshe was three hundred feet below. *Holy Schmoly* was all he could say, though no one heard, but the anticipated blast-wave didn't happen. Moshe waited. Was that a *pop?*

Moshe examined the thick, acrylic windows and breathed a sigh of relief when he found no seepage and no cracks. He waited, his electric motors off, in case the enemy submarine was returning. Where was the explosion?

Suddenly Moshe saw a large object, descending on his left. It was the *Phoenix*.

Moshe began his ascent, no sign of the enemy. Breaking the surface of the Mediterranean, the rest of the crew shouted out in celebration. Now they just needed to get rescued somehow. With no radio, and not in a particularly pro-Jewish area of the world, Moshe instructed Myles to fire a rescue flare at the first ship they saw. They would take a chance.

As the night invaded their space, a spotlight appeared on the dark horizon; and Myles fired a single flare, lighting up the night sky. Within twenty minutes they knew a boat, ship or enemy sub was on the way. Moshe decided not to fire another flare at the moment; and they all sat in the dark, thankful that the seas were calm.

Sheryl, after unraveling a twenty foot long yarn fiber, tied one of her metal buttons that once adorned her blouse to one end of the yarn thread. She then tied the other end to her finger. Using the elastic strapping from her bra, she engineered a slingshot and launched the button toward the ladder, hoping the polyester would be strong enough and the line wouldn't break. Though an excellent shot with a pistol, she missed the first two attempts; but the third was a charmer. The button went over the second rung and swung underneath the ladder, a few inches above the cement floor, like a pendulum from an Edgar Allen Poe tale.

Hurrying to the button, Sheryl tied the rope, made with small strips of the painter's tarp, to the cotton/polyester yarn and proceeded to carefully pull the tarp-rope over the second rung of the escape ladder. *What was that?* She paused, fearing the worst. The sound hadn't been loud, but *where did it come from?* She waited a few minutes and then proceeded, probably just something blowing in the wind.

The sling-shot device worked like a charm, and Sheryl grabbed both ends of the rope and pulled. She met little resistance as the ladder easily lowered to the floor. Fifteen minutes later, Sheryl was standing on the flat, pebble-covered roof of the building after working her way through the broken skylight. She thanked God for her good luck, especially the ladder-lock cable lying on the catwalk above. She secured and locked the ladder in place. Standing on the rooftop she couldn't help but laugh. With the ladder locked in place, the bumpkins will think she disappeared, vanished. She hoped she wouldn't be around to see their faces.

Marching around the perimeter of the roof, in the near-darkness, she was cautious and getting more pessimistic with each step. Then she spotted it, again thanking *The Almighty* for her good luck. There was a ladder on the outside of the building, firmly attached to the wall and encircled in a protective cage. She began her descent, awkward in a dress *and* braless; and she was nearing ground level when a gray or green Humvee, too dark to tell, turned the corner. The only vehicle in the area that was moving, Sheryl knew who it was; the *Bumpkin Brothers*. She pressed back against the building, not moving or breathing, and hoped the Humvee's headlights wouldn't give her away. They didn't. Then she remembered her pin, the pin that Wild Willy forced her to take, Mr. Paranoia himself.

Sheryl dropped the last 5 feet and hit the ground running, making mental notes of the building numbers so she wouldn't go in circles. She knew they would be scouring the area in a few minutes, and she had to secure herself. Running as fast as she had ever run, Sheryl pressed the top button of her blouse; and the GPS locater was activated. She turned the corner of the 500 building, and ran squarely into a tree; only it was too soft to be a tree.

"I guess I'm gonna have to tie you up *real* good this time, missy." Jonathon smashed his fist into the left side of Sheryl's face, knocking her cold and breaking her left jaw. Blood dripped from her ear.

"Light the flare!" Moshe gave the order once he determined that the approaching vessel wasn't the submarine. They would now have to take their chances; and the crew silently hoped, some prayed, that it wouldn't be a group of Muslim fishermen. With a cadré of Israeli Jews as hostage, they would be held a long time, maybe killed. The fishing boat drew near, and Moshe understood the Moroccan dialect. Oh boy. Their luck had run out.

"Everyone be cool and let me talk, capiche?"

That was fine with the crew. Maybe they could pass as Arabs since they all spoke the language. A safety rope fell among the group, and Moshe grabbed it, securing it to the submersible. Then one of the fisherman shouted in Spanish, "Welcome, are there any injuries?"

"No, no injuries, just wet and cold, thank you." Moshe spoke fluent Spanish and knew that Northern Moroccans often spoke Spanish, so this may not be the Spaniards. His hunch was correct.

"Come my brothers, let us help you. Oh? And sisters too. All are welcome." The fishermen moved swiftly to help the survivors aboard the fishing boat, and that's when they knew this was no fisherman's boat at all. It was a tourist boat.

Once on board, Moshe and the crew couldn't believe their luck, a 60 foot luxury motor yacht with four Frenchmen and their wives and a crew of four. The yacht's crew was Moroccan, and often the Moroccans weren't as *jihadist* as their Middle Eastern cousins. Moshe hoped this to be true. No one questioned their nationality.

After brief introductions, Moshe spotted a satellite phone by the hot tub. He made no move for the phone. After a round of drinks, he asked the large, portly Frenchman if there was a phone available so he could call his wife. She would be worried.

"Of course, of course, come with me." The Frenchman made a quick scan of Moshe's hands and spotted no wedding band, though that surely wasn't unusual in France. "You can use the phone in the Master Suite."

Moshe made the call but not before looking around the suite for recording devices. He didn't have time to thoroughly search, so again, he would have to take his chances.

Moshe's close friend, Will Briggs, answered the third ring. "Go."

"Will, it's Moshe. Listen carefully. Notify Mossad that the missing Nerpa submarine is in the southern Mediterranean, maybe a mile or two off shore, heading east."

"Are you sure?"

"Just blew our lab right out of the water about six hours ago. Notify Mossad right away and let them handle it. They will know what to do. Anything new in Israel?"

"New? You must be kidding. Tel Aviv airport was attacked with an anthrax bomb."

"Oh no, how many dead?"

"That's the strange part Moshe, the missile disbursed at about two thousand feet, and the wind, though slight, was blowing directly for Tel Aviv. Then in an instant, it shifted."

"What shifted?"

"The wind. The wind started blowing, *gusting* out to sea. Blew the entire cloud into the Mediterranean or beyond. It was a miracle, at least many are saying. Could be. It was really strange."

"Will, can you get the message to the proper people. Tel Aviv might have a much larger problem to deal with soon. I have a feeling."

"I will take care of it Moshe."

Wild Willy Briggs made the secure call to notify Mossad and headed once again to the airport. He had to get back to Atlanta and rescue Sheryl. He hoped she remembered the pin.

As Moshe ended the call he heard someone coming in the door behind him. Turning around in the ornately decorated suite, his heart skipped a beat as the portly Frenchman stood facing him, a collector's edition *French Modèle 1935A* semi-automatic pistol in hand. It was pointed directly at Moshe's worried face.

"I thought you were calling your wife, monsieur. Come with me, your crew is in our custody."

CHAPTER FORTY-ONE

Scripps La Jolla Hospitals and Clinics

La Jolla, California

"Ladies, please remember this, I know you're excited about seeing your father; but he's been through a real ordeal here." The doctor sounded like a Texan, Jami and Jenni thought, as they looked at each other and smiled the same smile, as twins do.

"He has been in-and-out of a coma for the better part of three months, and we thought he died twice. He's a fighter if I ever saw one, lots of fortitude." The doctor from Arizona said nothing but thought about the possibility of someone coming back from the dead after two hours. Not likely. He had heard stories that Jesus did *that*, but his Hindu family never discussed that subject.

"Now he's back, but he's not totally back. He's having some problems with memory and also, his physical stability."

"Is he going to know us?" Jenni asked.

"Oh yeah, he remembers that stuff. He doesn't remember what led him here. You mentioned something about coming to buy a car?" The doctor looked at both twins and couldn't believe how truly identical they were, and beautiful too. "He remembers little about the trip, nothing about the meteorite that slammed the van, doesn't remember the guy who pulled him and the driver *from* the van and saved their lives, though he knows him now. He has mentioned a blue Cadillac several times, but he says he doesn't know why, he 'might've dreamed it.'"

"Yes, that was the plan. He was coming here to buy some kind of a special Cadillac classic. Him and his boy toys. Who saved him?" Jami and Jenni asked the question at the same time.

"A gentleman named Bruce Lee Durham. He owns a Karate Studio in Beverly Hills. He spent several weeks in the hospital after the accident because of severe burns to his arms.

Apparently people were standing around doing nothing when Bruce came upon the scene. He grabbed his fire extinguisher and tried to put out the blaze but ran out of CO_2. Then he literally crawled into the flames and pulled your father and the young driver to safety. No one knows how he did it, how he could have withstood the pain; but he did. He's been to see your father almost every day since he came out of his coma."

"What about the driver? Is he all right?"

"Girl. Taci Edwards. Remarkably, she hardly had a scratch but nearly died from the Flu.

"Can we meet Mr. Durham? Did he get the Spanish Flu?"

"Sure Jami . . ."

"Jenni."

"Oh sorry, you two look alike; anyone ever tell you that? And no, he didn't."

They all laughed, and the girls asked spontaneously, "When can we see Dad?"

"Right now," and the doctor led them to Jeff's private room, just a week out of ICU. "I will leave you alone for only a few minutes. He needs rest. The doctor opened the door, turned back to the twin beauties and briefly wished he was about forty years younger, then asked, "Do you know a man named Thomas White?"

"Doesn't ring a bell," they said in unison. "Why?"

"Because he offered to pay all of your dad's medical bills and asked to be billed for any additional charges. Your father has no recollection of him either. He also had some bad news. The Cadillac classic your Dad was going to purchase was destroyed when a power pole collapsed onto it. From what Mr. White said, a power surge on the grid system caused the transformer to explode and the pole destroyed the Cadillac."

"What causes all the power surges here? It's not like that in Atlanta."

"Electric cars. We have a bunch in California; and when everyone plugs them in at the same time, we lose power."

The two girls entered the room and softly cried when they saw Jeff, each holding the other as their dad slept. He didn't stir.

Abe finished parking the *Prevost* in a parking lot several blocks from the Scripps hospital, one of California's finest, and made his way to the hospital. The trip from Raleigh to California had been a dream in Sheri and Bennett's RV, and he was glad they let them borrow it for the trip. Sure beat the heck out of a train. He couldn't wait to see his good friend and wondered what it must be like to die and come back to life. *Did Jeff see the bright light that so many NDE's report?* A near death experience. They would have a lot to talk about.

Walking through the Visitor's Lounge, Abe did a quick scan of the four TVs in the lounge and immediately recognized Hutz the Putz, live and being interviewed by none other than Condi Zimmerman. Condi normally would have gotten Abe's attention for more reasons than one, but it was the news on the other screen that stopped him in his tracks as a large crowd gathered around the latest news alert.

"*Our sources tell us there were 327 people on the South Pacific train, including three Girl Scout groups, when it plunged off the Pecos River High Bridge and into the Pecos River almost 300 feet below. First witnesses at the scene described unbelievable carnage, and it appears there are few survivors. The train burned for several hours in the shallow river, a few miles from Langtry, Texas.*

"*Two campers who saw the actual disaster said there was a small boat, approximately 25-30 feet long, tied to one of the main moorings. The witnesses said they saw no one in the boat when it exploded as the train approached and collapsed the entire mooring. The South Pa . . .*"

Abe turned to walk back outside and for the first time in years wished he had a cigarette. That was the train they were supposed to be on.

CHAPTER FORTY-TWO

*"O Jerusalem, Jerusalem, you who kill the prophets and
stone those sent to you, how often I have longed to gather
your children together, as a hen gathers her chicks under her
wings, but you were not willing."* Matthew 23:37 NIV

Muhammed worried about Aludra. His sister was now missing
for months, but he had wasted no time in getting on with the
war plan. Besides, Aludra had become . . . different; different
since her trip to France. Different since she read the *New Testament*, the
one she left for him. He burned the *Bible* right away, lest someone think
he was an infidel. In spite of that, there was one page that didn't burn; and
the highlighted passage stood out in his mind as he read in Arabic from
the very last page of the Christian Bible, a note in the margin from Aludra
stating that Jesus, a Jew, was talking:

*"I warn everyone who hears the words of the prophecy of this book: If
anyone adds anything to them, God will add to him the plagues described in
this book. And if anyone takes words away from this book of prophecy, God
will take away from him his share in the tree of life and in the holy city, which
are described in this book."*

There was another note scribbled in the margin: *Muhammed, the book
we weren't supposed to "add to" or "take away from" was the Bible. We added
the Quran. Don't you see that? Please read the New Testament, Muhammed.
It will save your life into eternity. Please. I love you Muhmi . . .* Muhammed
folded the page from the book of *Revelation* and placed it in his leather,
American pouch that was made in China. What a world . . .

"My brother, good morning?"

Muhammed hadn't seen Yousef in months, not since they had spoken of the submarine plot, which seemed to be working flawlessly. At least the Panama Canal was closed and half of Diego Garcia was uninhabitable. The Suez would be next if all went as planned, insha'Allah. There wasn't much time left, he knew, before the sub was detected.

"Allah is great, Yousef. You have done the work of Allah well, my friend! It will soon be Papaver season, and I love the smell of the poppies."

"Yes Muhammed, you love the smell of *dinars*." They laughed, but not too loudly. The hills have ears in Afghanistan.

"The opium season will be good. Since the Americans pulled out, our harvests have grown back to normal. More poppy, more dinar!" Yousef laughed. "They always pull out. They run away like the cowards they are. The Taliban kicked their ass. What is our schedule?"

Muhammed told Yousef about the correspondence with Mohammed Rehza, but didn't mention Mohammed's brother, Aboud. Aboud was *snug as a slug* along the U.S.-Mexican border, and Muhammed smiled at the American sayings. Vinny was *snug as a slug*, and he was the *man with the pan*.

"Ever notice how everything rhymes in English? I wonder how they do that?"

"What's the schedule Muhammed?" Yousef repeated the question.

"Has Dmitry been released yet?" The Russian would be greatly missed in the weapons department if he remained in jail. Muhammed was glad they received the supply submarine before Dmitry was busted.

"Of course. He was released almost before he got to the jail. The Russian President stepped in. Dmitry has many friends in high places, you understand. The men laughed again, and looked up at the sky.

"Look at the Moon, Muhammed. What do you think it means."

"I don't know Yousef. A sign from Allah most certainly. Allah protected us from the Dark Comet. Now the Moon is pink and has rings. It is certainly a sign." Muhammed was sure Aludra once mentioned this, that she read in the *Bible* that the Moon would turn red. It would turn red in *the end*, a *sign in the sky*.

"What do you think of the *Bible* Yousef, now that you have studied? You know the Rosary by heart, and most of your associates are Catholic. Are you fitting in? Do they suspect anything?"

"Actually Muhammed, I still have many Muslim contacts. I'm very careful. I don't just associate with Catholics. I have met many Protestants too. They all believe different things. It's something."

"What's the difference, Yousef?"

Yousef had known Muhammed since they played in the dirt alleys together as children, throwing hardened opium balls in a race from one end to the other. He knew him as well as he knew his own brother and loved him equally. Muhammed was not being sarcastic with the question. He only knew Islam.

"There are some differences Muhammed. The Catholics were the first Christians, at least the first truly organized Christians. Many were Jews. Until Emperor Constantine, the early Christians were sort of like nomads, wanderers. They followed Jewish law, they kept Saturday as the Sabbath, celebrated Passover and other Jewish holidays. Then after Constantine, everything changed. Several hundred years later, some Catholics started noticing things in the Scripture that they had missed the last time they read it, and the times before. They started *asking questions*. The church didn't accept that at all, Muhammed."

"I bet not Yousef. Can you imagine someone in the village, questioning the teachings of Muhammad? What do you think would happen? All religions are like that; you don't question anything."

Muhammed was laughing before he could get the American saying out, then blurted, like his favorite cowboy, John Wayne, "Wellll, ah guess they lost their heads, pahdnuh."

Yousef didn't get it. "What is the schedule?"

"The stars have stopped falling. Have you noticed Yousef? Three nights and not a single shooting-star. Is *that* a sign?"

"I don't think it's a sign Muhammed. China has been devastated by the *falling stars*. "Do we have a schedule Muhammed?"

"We do." Muhammed pulled out some stained documents, the *only* documents. There were no copies, only the plan for the coming fall of Europe, if the meteorites didn't take care of it first. "These are the plans that Allah gave me in a dream Yousef. For three nights I dreamed the same dream, with the same directions."

"What did you dream Muhammed?" Yousef didn't like the sound of this plan. Muhammed seemed to have a *lot* of dreams.

"I dreamed that it was a great gift from Allah that the Americans went into Iraq. How else would we have gotten all of Saddam's weapons? And gases? And plague spores? If the Bekaa Valley exploded, the whole world would die from plague. The intelligence agencies had to know what Saddam was doing, that's the strange thing, Yousef. One of his own, General Sada the Christian, told the world where the weapons were and how they carried them to Lebanon. I don't think the Americans and

Europeans are that stupid Yousef, I think Allah is keeping them confused. He is blinding our enemy. *Time is on our backside.*"

Muhammed felt comfort, the night was cool, the sky was dark, there were no shooting-stars for a change; and that seemed odd. Everything was going better than planned. He wouldn't share the message with Yousef. Aboud's coded email said all the *KFC drumsticks* had been delivered for the picnic. The surface-to-air missiles had finally made it from Libya to America, thank *you* Mexican drug cartels. *The enemy of my enemy is my friend,* and Muhammed knew that Vinny would put the missiles to good use. Vinny was heartless.

"Plague, Yousef. Think about it. Why aren't Muslims catching the Spanish Flu if it's not Allah's will? Fifty thousand dead in America, not counting Europe."

"And Africa." Yousef interceded. "Africa is plague-ridden. The gay plague is spreading everywhere, and I heard it was coming from mosquitos or fleas."

"Why do you call it the *gay plague* Yousef?"

"That's what the Protestants call it. They were talking about God's retribution on the men who love men, you know, like they should love the women. The Sodomites. They say the disease started in America and now is everywhere, that it started in the Sodomite community."

Plague.

Yousef thought about the word, and he had new respect for the meaning. What would plague do to *their* world? For the first time in his life, he found himself worrying about a *different* people, not a different tribe, but a *different* people. His new friends, the *Catholics* . . . and the Protestants. People were dying everywhere, not just Europe and Asia; and now there were these rumors of the *gay plague* spreading through mosquitos. *How could that be?* He wondered. That plague was spreading like wildfire through most Islamic countries, especially Indonesia and Africa; and Yousef was disgusted that there could be so much sexual perversion in the Muslim community. *Allah* was not pleased, no matter what Muhammed thought.

"Have you ever heard of the Hopi Indians, Muhammed?"

"No Yousef. Why?"

"I learned of them just recently from a Catholic teacher I met. The Hopi live in America somewhere and have predicted the end of the world, this year Muhammed. They predicted world-wide plague and terror from the sky.

"There are many Christians who believe the world is ending soon, did you know? Then there are these Hopi people, and others, who have predicted the end of the world December 21, this very year! Do you believe this is possible, Muhammed? Did you hear of Nostradamus or Mother Shipton? Or the Maya? They all believe this date will be the beginning of *the days of sorrow*."

"What is your point Yousef?" Muhammed's irritation was evident.

"I don't have a point Muhammed, just talking. A lot of bad things are happening all over the world is all I mean. The floods are greater than ever; the hailstorms in Europe and China have killed many people and animals; earthquakes are happening in places that don't get earthquakes; plague and disease is becoming rampant, more so than anything *we* could have caused; and then there are these meteors. *What if they are right?*"

Muhammed thought a moment, trying to digest Yousef's words. His training to *act Catholic* seemed to be having an adverse effect. His head was getting clogged with mysticism and nonsense.

"All things must end Yousef; you know that, the Prophet knew that. The infidels will be judged and sent to hell where they belong. The Shi'a believe the Twelfth Imam is already here, somewhere. Some young girl is traveling around Iran curing people of disease and performing miracles. She says the Twelfth Imam is here. We just don't know where *here* is."

"So she's like John the Baptist."

"Who?"

"The little girl, Muhammed. John the Baptist, according to the Christians, paved the way for Jesus' appearance as the Jewish messiah. She must be doing the same for the Twelfth Imam. Do you believe in the Twelfth Imam, Muhammed? It isn't a Sunni belief you know."

"I believe all things are possible with Allah. I believe we will have our messiah, just like the Jews had theirs; but we won't kill him when he comes. He will lead the Muslims to world dominance. That's what I believe. Then there will be a world of peace for Allah, a time when there will be no unbelievers."

"Israel is on war alert. I heard reports that Iran or Syria launched a chemical weapon, but the chemical blew away from Israel and into the Mediterranean Sea. Why would Allah protect the Jews, Muhammed? The Jews always killed his messengers. Every time Allah sent them a prophet, they killed him. So why would he protect them?"

If you don't like the massage, kill the massager. Muhammed smiled at the American saying, but he knew it was true. Even Muslims sometimes killed the *massager*.

Chapter Forty-Three

"In My zeal and in My blazing wrath I declare that on that day there will surely be a great earthquake in the land of Israel. The fish of the sea, the birds of the heavens, the beasts of the field, all the creeping things that creep on the earth, and all the men who are on the face of the earth will shake at My presence; the mountains also will be thrown down, the steep pathways will collapse and every wall will fall to the ground." Ezekiel 38: 19-20 NIV

D avid Cooke and Randy Chafin, two American tourists from Georgia, parked their *Co-Motion Americano* touring bikes by the Ripoll Inn, a small bed-and-breakfast in the gorgeous Spanish village of Ripoll, located on the foothills of the Pyrenees Mountains, the natural border between Spain and France. The two friends had toured much of the world by bicycle, but the Pyrenees had turned out to be the best. They were sure the new $3,500 bicycles had something to do with their enjoyment.

"When do you want to head to the volcano park?"

"Let's rest awhile, maybe visit that building over there. It looks interesting." David pointed at the ancient-looking, Romanesque structure on the hillside.

"It is the Monastery of Santa Maria de Ripoll, señor. It is a Benedictine monastery. You should go see." The old man carrying the water pail, sweat on his brow, had to be eighty at least, his English nearly flawless, unlike his clothing which hung loosely from the man's frail stature.

"Thank you, señor."

David and Randy entered the Inn, ordered a pomegranate juice and headed to the monastery.

The Parc Natural de la Zona Volcanica de la Garroxta, also known as the Olat Volcano Field, is a regular stop for tourists of all sorts; and the two friends from Georgia would certainly not miss that part of the tour. They shared a common interest in *seismic stuff*, as they called it.

The Park consisted of forty volcanos, inactive for thousands of years, though the area still experienced minor earthquake activity from time-to-time. On this late afternoon, the temperature unusually balmy, even for summer, the park was being visited by about six hundred tourists, including three elementary school groups.

A hundred miles east of David and Randy, the volcano park in between, the Pyrenees blended from the hills to the waters of the deep blue Mediterranean Sea.

Banyuls-sur-Mer was nestled along the sea, just north of the Spanish border. The small French port village was romanticized with Roman-built, cobbled streets and small, quaint restaurants. Fishermen were coming in from sea during the late afternoon, their royal-blue and white boats almost glowing in the late afternoon sunlight.

"What the hell's that?" The fisherman had to shout against the wind.

The French fishermen, still about a mile out to sea, pointed toward the shore and the smoke plumes on the horizon. There seemed to be ten or twelve separate plumes, gray with a reddish glow, climbing toward the darkening clouds. The ground began to rumble and moan; but the fishermen, so far out to sea, were oblivious to the shaking.

Approaching the shore, now less than a quarter mile away, the fishermen stared in awe as trees began crashing to the ground and people, enjoying sushi just a few minutes earlier, ran and screamed in panic, many toward the sea. A restaurant collapsed and sat cockeyed, half on its foundation and half in the harbor waters.

"Turn around!" The fishermen yelled in French unison, realizing their best bet of escape was to stay out to sea.

Leaving the monastery, David and Randy, empty juice bottles in hand, made their way back to the inn. They would turn in early and leave about sunrise the next morning. That's when they began to notice a slow movement of the ground and then a moan in the distance. Then nothing.

"What was that?" Randy asked, but David had no idea. Suddenly to the east came a loud, deep explosive sound, and they looked eastward. The frail, old man came out of the inn, running as fast as an old man could, screaming that an earthquake was on the way.

The ground began to sway again; and the growing moan was surreal, almost like the cry of a tortured animal under attack in the jungles of Kenya.

"Our sources have now confirmed the quarantine of a Turkish cruise liner, the Fantastika III, between Cyprus and Tel Aviv."

Amber Michelle, The al-Jazeera news reporter, olive skin and resonating, dark eyes and hair, would have been right at home on the Foxy-FOX News channel, at least that's what her guest thought, as he sat in al-Jazeera's new Atlanta studio.

"All we know at this point: 156 people dead, mostly Iranian and Syrian tourists. That toll will surely rise, as there were nearly fifteen hundred tourists and a crew of six hundred. The deaths came suddenly, according to anonymous reports, as the exotic ship cruised under a cloud, a cloud which most eye witnesses have reported as 'greenish and wispy.' The Iranian and Turkish Embassies are up in arms at reports that the cloud may have been a result of chemical weapons testing by the Israeli Defense Forces. The IDF is on high-alert, as they always seem to be.

"Now to our guest speaker, Dr. Dennis Duncan, an expert in Volcanic and Earthquake Geophysics. Dr. Duncan is a professor and lecturer from Mississippi State University. Thank you so much for being here.

"Volcanic and Earthquake Geophysics. That's quite a mouthful Dr. Duncan. I apologize for taking your time with the breaking news. It seems we have a lot of that lately."

"Thanks Amber. I'm not nearly as smart as the title presumes."

"Dr. Duncan, the earthquake in Missouri, the New Madrid 'Fartquake' is what it's being called by those who live in the area and could smell the hydrogen sulfide gas, was expected to be much worse. An earthquake specialist at the sight has stated that this was just a precursor to a much larger quake and probably has caused stress along other fault lines. Is this fact or theory?"

"It's theory at this point, but there are many geologists who believe one earthquake, even a small one, can affect pressure points all around the world, instantly. Take the Pyrenees quake that happened last month in Spain."

"*Yes Dr. Duncan, that was quite a surprise.*"

"*It <u>was</u> a surprise. There were no warnings, no pre-quakes, no noises or lights that often happen prior to quakes, no odors; and the Pyrenees have very few noticeable earthquakes, most of which are 4.0 or less.*

"*After the New Madrid event,*" the professor refused to use fartquake, "*though small in nature, the Pyrenees quake occurred less than a week later, a 9.0. There is no history of this region along the Spanish-French border ever having an earthquake of anything near this magnitude. Tens of thousands are dead so far, and we will never have an accurate count. The mountain range collapsed and sunk into the Earth. Thousands and thousands of people are buried beneath the collapsed mountains.*"

"*Are you saying the entire mountain range collapsed, Dr. Duncan?*"

"*That's exactly what happened. Well, not the entire range; but it looks like about fifty percent in the southern half toward the Mediterranean. The seven-minute quake, one of the longest continuous quakes ever recorded, liquefied the soil under the Pyrenees; and the mountains just collapsed, fell right to the ground. You could drive a go-cart over them. It's the most amazing thing I have seen in my lifetime. Most of the ground is covered by a fine dust.*"

This was news Amber hadn't heard before. She always thought the things her grandma told her about *all the mountains will collapse to the ground in the final Earthquake at the end,* was pure mythology. "It's right there in the *Bible* Amber, you can read it yourself. I'm not making it up."

"*Is there any history of this ever happening before, Dr. Duncan?*"

"*There is, actually several, though it is a rare event. In 1692, on the southern shores of Jamaica, the town of Port Royall sank several feet during an earthquake. As the sea rushed in to fill the new depression, Port Royall disappeared. Known as the 'fairest of all the English plantations,' in less than three minutes, the entire town disappeared and was covered with water.*"

"*That's awful. We didn't learn that in history class.*"

"*Eye witness statements told of the town and the surrounding mountains just 'disappearing' into the Earth, with large cracks in the Earth opening and shutting with such force that people falling into the cracks were suddenly crushed at the waist as the ground closed. Can you imagine the horror of that? Ships that arrived in the port later in the day described only a small remnant of Port Royall sticking above the water. Later maps of Jamaica designated the area as 'Port Royall Sunk,' and there have been other instances of entire mountain ranges collapsing. But not to the extent of the Pyrenees Collapse.*"

CHAPTER FORTY-FOUR

"Do you think the Great God Yahweh is pleased with your choices and dreams; and the things you feel are important? Your false idols? Yahweh said we are life while in the womb. Think about that and the plague of death. You are dancing with the stars when you should be dancing with God." Hutz the Putz

"When you get to Arizona, start looking for Buckeye. At Highway 85, take a right and head south toward Lukeville. I'm going to nap for a few minutes."

"OK Boss."

Abe didn't bother to ask why Jeff wanted to exit I-10, the most direct route to Atlanta. The original plan was to stop by Surprise, Arizona and meet with Abe's high school buddy, Rod Smith; but the message on Rod's answering service said he would be in Atlanta for the next month.

Jeff seemed different somehow; but then, who wouldn't be? Abe was anxious to ask him if he had experienced an NDE. Near-death experiences had been reported for years, with most descriptions similar and happening in hospital emergency rooms or surgeries: Floating, or possibly walking, through a tunnel, a bright light in the distance; mysterious creatures or people in the distance and at the sides, moving in slow motion; wispy and almost fog-like and sometimes, music. Most reports indicated a pleasant experience, almost happy, though they didn't remember seeing anyone they knew. Occasionally, the experience was pure hell.

Abe set the *Prevost* on cruise, sixty-five; and changed the satellite station to FOX. It was nine o'clock and the morning was hot. A meteor flew across the horizon to the east, visible in the bright daylight.

"Good morning. I am Condi Zimmerman."

"*The bicycles of the two missing bikers from Atlanta have been found beneath several feet of debris in what used to be the town of Ripoll, just a few kilometers inside the Spanish-French border along the Pyrenees Mountain range, or at least what's left. Though the two bodies have not been recovered, it is thought they are under the ruins with so many others.*

"*It seems there are earthquakes occurring everywhere, especially places that don't usually experience such seismic activity, like the Pyrennees. London has experienced more than a hundred earthquakes during the past week. Though all have been 4.2 or less. There has been enough shaking to stop the reconstruction of Big Ben. Since destroyed last year by a bombing, the reconstruction has been slow, mostly due to the near economic collapse of Europe and Japan. It looks like Europe's third country is on the brink of financial ruin, as what used to be the European Union reconfigures. A loaf of bread in France is $19.00, U.S.*

"*Airlines are still grounded in the Southern United States as well as most of the southern hemisphere due to expected meteor showers. Seven planes last month were damaged or destroyed in flight, not at the hands of terrorists but at the hands of God, as more fragments of the Moon continue to bombard certain areas of our planet. There is a report out of Australia that a whole town has died, and the Youtube videos show hundreds of people lying in the streets and lawns. It reminds me of one of those horrid zombie movies. There is no explanation for the deaths; but a doctor, who wants to remain anonymous, said it appears the people were poisoned.*"

Hands of God. Almost asleep, the words stirred him; and he awakened. Jeff had never believed in God, at least not in many years; but the biblical predictions were interesting, so the word was more impressionable than it had once been. He sat up, adjusted the extra-fluffy Eiderdown pillows, and he was absolutely sure the $2,800 pillows didn't sleep as comfortably as the Belk's brand he used at home. And besides, who can sleep with a square pillow?

Jeff's beliefs weren't changing, he was sure of that; but the *dreams.* They gave him pause. Was it possible that some mysterious, universal force of some kind played a role in man's evolution; except he didn't believe in evolution either. He did think it odd that so many so-called believers always seemed quick to blame God for bad stuff. *Not sure I'd want to be God*, he thought. *All blame and no glory.*

Pulling the drapes and glancing out the large bus window, Jeff noted the road sign, Highway 85S, one mile ahead. There was a large billboard promoting an end of the world party.

<u>Come Join Us for the Mother of All Parties</u>
Mayan Martinis, Hopi Hops, Nostradamus' Naked Mermaids
December 19-21, 2012 . . . until
THE END!!
End of the World Party at Romano's in Phoenix

The news continued as Jeff gathered his thoughts. He would join Abe at the front in a while and navigate. *Would he see the white churches and fields of daffodils?*

"*Dr. Chad Myers with the Goddard Space Flight Center said in a speech today at Warner Robbins Air Force Base that the large comet that collided with the Moon in January has dislodged the Moon from its orbit. If you have been pondering at night why the Moon looks larger, it's because it's more than seven hundred miles closer. Dr. Myers also said this realignment is likely responsible for the unusually rough seas, high tides and increased rogue wave activities. Coastal cities on every continent are flooding, including Manhattan.*

"*Dr. Myers also said this could just be the beginning. He stated that JPL and Goddard Space Flight Center had noted a remarkable upswing in NEO activity with 37 discoveries of these Near-Earth Objects this month so far; and the month ain't over, as we say in journalism school. The newly discovered NEOs are not the Moon-meteors but are from the Kuiper Belt.*

"*If you remember, last year the man who is now known as Hutz the Putz, mentioned the Kuiper Belt and the Oort Cloud in reference to the Dark Comet, which he also named. We will have a special report . . .*"

As late afternoon converged on dusk, Jeff sat on the queen sized bed, buttoning his shirt, and realized he had missed Condi during his state of unconsciousness. He was glad to see her, so ravishing; and he wondered why she never married. Maybe she just didn't wear a ring.

Glancing out the window, the Moon was as large, but not as red, as he remembered from his dreams . . . or whatever they were. *Were they dreams?* He yawned, his heavy eyelids closed, then reopened as he fought sleep. *The Dreams.* He didn't want to go there again. He fell back, and his head buried into the square pillow. Jeff faded into a troubled sleep of colored rooms and the *Dark Door;* the news, the bad news, continued.

"*The earthquake in Jerusalem has caused significant structural damage to the Dome of the Rock shrine and the al-Aqsa Mosque complex. The 7.8 earthquake has been called an act of Israeli terrorism by the 'New Arab*

Council,' yet another jihadist . . . scratch that please . . . another group emerging from the Arab uprisings. The group blames Israeli natural gas extraction from the Mediterranean as the cause.

"The Saudi government is blaming Iran for destroying the Sunni religious structures, built on the site of the ancient Israeli Temple Mount. Dome of the Rock was completed in 691 AD or CE, depending on preference, and was built directly over the Holy of Holies of the original Jewish Temple constructed by Soloman about three thousand years ago. It is normal Islamic tradition to build shrines or mosques on the site of their conquests, so choosing to build on top of the ancient Jewish Temple has been contentious, especially in the past sixty years.

"We just received breaking news: Three U.S. Congressmen and an Israeli delegation of fifteen have been killed in a plane crash. Initial, though undocumented, eyewitness reports claim that a contrail was seen leaving the ground and to the U.S. Air Force jet as the plane approached the airport in Tripoli."

"Back so soon?"

Jeff *was* glad to see Missy T, though his last visit had been a little different, almost belittling. How many times had he been here? He couldn't remember. He didn't really even know where he was.

"I guess I am," Jeff said with a slight smile curling the left corner of his mouth. "Where's Kipper and Enoch?"

Across the room, this one bathed in soft-green light, two women were talking, animated in their conversations. Jeff turned his head toward the women, and he could hear them as plainly as if he had been sitting between them.

"Naomi, do you ever think it's possible that Jesus *was* actually the Messiah?"

"No. Do you ever think Jesus might *not* be the Messiah?"

"No. Not really. That's the pillar of my faith."

"And Jews also have pillars, my dear friend."

Naomi *had* read the *New Testament*, a couple of times. She didn't believe Jesus was the Messiah, but she loved the stories of Jesus' merciful miracles, ending so much suffering, the blind people receiving sight; the deaf, hearing. She marveled at how wonderful life would be *without* suffering and what it would have been like to be sitting in the fields as

Jesus talked about the God of Abraham and fed all those people with only a little bread and a fish?

"I have read the *New Testament* Melissa; but there were other predictions about the Messiah that Jesus didn't fulfill. Look at all the bad things that have happened to us over thousands of years. Even today, every country hates us. The Messiah will save us from this, he will be our king. Then the world will know."

"You know, even the Muslims believe he really did exist," Melissa continued. "They even believe Mary was a virgin."

Melissa? Jeff craned his head, but Melissa's face seemed faint. *Was it her?*

"No, I don't think he *is* the Messiah, Melissa; but sometimes, in my eighty some years of wondering and thinking about God, I do think about, well . . . what if the stories *were* true, and we have been misled by our teachers for two thousand years? What if he really *was* the Messiah and we *did* miss it? What then? But there has been so much suffering of the Jewish people, even since the ancient times. The Messiah was going to save us from that. Again, Jesus did not."

Suddenly Jeff was walking through a darker green room; and the background lighting began to merge with a deep violet, eventually warming to a soft, red glow. They passed three others, sitting at a round high-top, drinking what looked like mint juleps, all dressed similarly in blue seersucker suits. They were talking about abortion and racetracks. *Bet that's an interesting conversation*, Jeff thought.

"Do these people see me?"

"No, they can't Jeff. They're just passing time, kind of like people-watching." Missy T did that cute smile again, a little mischievous look.

"What kind of people?" Jeff persisted.

"People who are on the way to the *Dark Place*."

Then he saw it, directly in front of him. The dreaded *Black Door*. His heart beat rapidly, and his head spun. Suddenly he was dancing with stars.

Chapter Forty-Five

"Ms. Russell, is it true that you were working under contract with KKD Labs in Gainesville, Georgia?"

"Yes, that is true."

The Atlanta court room in the Richard B. Russell Federal Building was almost silent as a mouse, not a creature was stirring; and the testimony was spellbinding. Samarra Russell *might* receive the death penalty. How ironic, she thought to herself, and she could feel her guilt-ridden heart beating in her chest. She spent her adult life trying to help others; and now so many were dead, because of her. *Was I insane? Am I insane?* But then she thought of young Thomas and his severed finger in the Valentine's box, and the head that would arrive next if she didn't participate. She silently prayed for God's help, again.

"Could you explain your working relationship with KKD Labs, Ms. Russell? Are you aware that KKD has been investigated by the *Gwinnett Post* as a possible clandestine drug operation?"

Not true, she thought. But she was bound to secrecy and dared not reveal the true purpose of the laboratory. It was clandestine, that was for sure, set up by the CIA to lure in potential terrorists, an undercover network trying to preempt any biological or foodborne attack.

"I was under joint-contract with KKD Labs and the Duluth Animal Hospital Research Institute. The Institute and KKD, in conjunction with Centers for Disease Control in Atlanta, are conducting research into possible vaccines for all flu viruses. We were genetically designing a vaccine specific to the 1918 Spanish Flu virus when we realized there might be a universal flu vaccine. That would not be a 'cure' per sé, but would minimize the effects, and in some cases, prevent the symptoms entirely, unless . . ."

The trial was moving along, an end nearly in sight; and Samarra was tired. Samarra was the first victim of the rejuvenated Spanish Flu, and it had taken its toll. The spunkiness that had once been so much of her psyche, was no more. She felt destroyed, and she felt she should be destroyed.

Samarra Russell's husband, Georgia Senator Jack Russell, had been one of the more prestigious U.S. Senators. A member of several intelligence teams, he traveled frequently to Israel where the two countries developed a nanotech spy machine unparalleled in the world. The size of flies, beetles, dragonflies and other small bugs, the nano-devices were almost invisible as they flew or crawled into areas of interest, like jihadist caves, and landed on the wall, ceiling or virtually any surface. The microscopic cameras recorded in high-definition images and sound. Though top secret, several countries were developing the technology. Israel was leaps and bounds ahead in the game. With gecko-like technology, the Israeli spybots could hang upside down, even on glass.

"Ms. Russell?" Samarra was lost in thought but quickly returned to reality. She was beginning to hate reality.

"The Institute researches swine flu mutations, Ken-Ken and Dave research the poultry vectors of the variant viruses."

"Ken-Ken and Dave?"

"Sorry, that's the way most of us refer to the lab. The lab is owned and operated by three guys who have worked with the poultry industry forever, as well as numerous notable universities around the world. Ken Martini, Ken Shubing and Dave Wicher. Dave is world-renown in the field of bird borne virology."

Samarra kept her answers brief, as instructed by her attorney, Mary Bower, also a victim in many ways of the Spanish Flu terrorism. At forty-four, Mary was a young grandmother and lost a grandson to the flu. Her family was angry, at least most of the family, that she was representing Samarra Russell, now the perpetrator of the greatest terrorist attack on U.S. soil and much of the world.

"You mentioned 'unless' earlier. Unless what?"

Samarra was puzzled. The prosecutor continued.

"Let me read to you what you said earlier, Ms. Russell. You said 'That would not be a *cure* per sé, but would minimize the effects, and in some cases, prevent the symptoms entirely, unless . . .'"

"Unless the virus *mutates*. They often do mutate. KKD and the Duluth Animal Institute research poultry and swine flu derivatives, . . . *Did I say that already? . . .* and the Spanish Flu is an H1N1 swine flu."

"Ms. Russell, please allow me to read a description of the Spanish Flu, an eyewitness description from Isaac Starr, a young, medical student at the University of Pennsylvania in 1918:

"As their lungs filled, the patients became short of breath and increasingly cyanotic . . .

"Can you define 'cyanotic' for the court, Ms. Russell?"

"Blue. The skin turns blue from lack of oxygen."

Mary whispered in Samarra's ear. "You don't have to be so descriptive. Just answer the question. 'Blue' works just fine."

"After gasping for several hours they became delirious and incontinent, and many died struggling to clear their airways of a blood-tinged froth that sometimes gushed from their nose and mouth. It was a dreadful business . . .

"Incontinent, Ms. Russell, is defined as: *unable to restrain natural discharges or evacuations of urine or feces.* That means these poor victims; these poor, suffering victims of this terrible flu, actually pooped and peed all over themselves and anyone nearby, isn't that correct Ms. Russell?" The prosecutor was almost yelling.

Samarra started to answer but the prosecutor interrupted.

"Clearing their airways Ms. Russell. Did you know that people literally ripped their own throats open, ripped their trachea out of their throats, trying to get just one more breath of air?"

The room was quiet, the jury and the audience enthralled, and horrified, at the description of the pandemic.

"Ms. Russell, isn't this true?"

"It is . . ." Samarra's voice drifted off. "We have to get a vaccine."

"Yet you, Ms. Russell, took it upon yourself . . ."

"Objection your Honor."

"You, Ms. Russell, made the decision, you alone, to remove the Spanish Flu samples from the CDC, relocate the virus samples to the roof top mechanical room where they were later picked up, got in your fancy car . . ."

"Objection."

"I apologize to the court. You got into your new, one hundred twenty-five thousand dollar G55 AMG Mercedes Benz that goes 0-60 in 5.2 seconds, drove to your *Buckhead* home, parked in your five car garage and decided to take a nap."

The prosecutor was shouting.

"Your honor, what does this have to do with anything? I object." Mary was overruled.

"Is that correct Ms. Russell?!?!?"

"No sir. That's not true. It was a Volvo station wagon."

"Are you saying you don't have a $ 125,000 Mercedes AMG, Ms. Russell?

"No, I have a Mercedes. It was a gift from my husband." It was more of a whimper than an answer, and Samarra seemed in a daze. "I just don't drive it, because it's too big."

"Ms. Russell, does the name 'Bubba' Haskins mean anything to you?"

"Yes. I know Leon Haskins. His wife is a close friend."

"How about 'Bubba?'"

"I hardly know Leon, Sir. I am friends with Jill."

"Ms. Russell. Is that you in this photo?"

The prosecutor pointed to the photo on the electronic screen mounted to the mahogany-sided wall, just to the left of the court recorder. He also handed the photograph to Samarra, a photo from the previous year's Christmas Party at the Buckhead Arts Center. She was standing between Bubba and Jill.

"Yes sir, it is."

"Can you define for the court who the gentleman on the left is?"

"Leon Haskins."

"Did you know that Leon Bubba Haskins is suspected as a co-conspirator in the nuclear bombing of the Buford Dam last New Year's Eve? Did you know that your close friend Bubba owned the air conditioning company that disbursed the Spanish Flu virus through the air conditioning systems at Atlanta's Airport? The same flu virus that has killed, *murdered*, tens of thousands of innocent people? All because of you, Ms. Russell. How does that make you feel?" The prosecutor was derisive.

Samarra's attorney continued to "object," to no avail. The judge was giving the prosecutor total leeway. The prosecutor's voice increased in intensity.

"The Spanish Flu virus that *you*, Ms. Russell, stole from the CDC. How many more do you think will be killed because of your selfish gesture."

"Your Honor, I totally object to this line of vitriolic questioning." Mary slammed her notebook down as the judge again overruled.

Samarra, still weak from her *own* bout with the Spanish Flu, began to shake violently and collapsed behind the witness stand, falling to the tiled floor, head first. The security guard closest to the judge was the first to lend help, trying to stop the bleeding from the gash on her head, and would later testify that Samarra's last words before losing consciousness were something about getting the vaccine and *infidelity*.

The Federal Court adjourned.

Jeff finally woke from his dreams and felt drained. *When they go to the Dark Place, most never return.* He recalled Missy T's warning and was troubled that the dark door seemed to be getting closer with every dream. *Why am I having these dreams?* He composed himself, brushed his teeth and joined Abe up front, just in time to see the road sign ahead:

Lukeville 32 Miles

CHAPTER FORTY-SIX

"Woe to those who call evil good and good evil, who put darkness for light and light for darkness, who put bitter for sweet and sweet for bitter." Isaiah 5:20 NIV

Jami, Jenni and Audry cleaned their Dad's kitchen, preparing for the afternoon cookout. It was Labor Day; and the hotdogs, burgers and barbequed chicken waited quietly in the fridge, oblivious to the coming charcoal fire.

"Why do you think Daddy was so hell-bent on going through Lukeville? Oh my God, there are only about two people who live there."

"Sixty-three people live there. I Googled it. Did you guys notice anything unusual at the truck stop after we left Lukeville?"

"Not really Audry, why?" Jenni *had* seen something but decided not to make an issue. She felt it was her imagination and didn't want to upset her Dad. She knew her Dad well; and had she told him, even in his weakened state, he would have chased down the suspect, beat him with his walking cane and probably gotten killed in the process.

"I don't know, really," Audry continued, "I saw a man getting gas. He had a white car, I think it was a Chevy; and I just thought he looked familiar." Audry didn't *think*, she *knew*; a memory from a parking lot in Duluth one night, when sister Jenni was attacked by . . . the man in the white car.

"Nope, didn't see him," Jenni lied but was well aware of her young sister's intuitiveness about so many things. She now knew that the man she saw getting gas *was* the man who assaulted her and left her to die, a man the gas attendant had called *Señor Ricky*.

"Me neither." Jami chimed. "Didn't see nothin'."

"Are you girls ready?"

Jeff interrupted the three sisters' conversation. He had grown closer to his daughters over the past three months, closer than ever. They had been great caregivers. His fatherhood could have been better, had he not been so into himself, a recent revelation that emerged from a dream. He had dreamed even more than usual lately. The comfort of having his daughters around muted the loss he gradually remembered, memories of Melissa, the giant wave and the strange blip of light that spoke to him, over and over. His eyes still moistened when he thought of his dear wife, or at least she had been his wife *until* . . . His memory lapse; and he wondered why he hadn't seen *Blip* again, since the tsunami.

"We have to get to the diner and help Gray and Andi serve lunch."

"We can't go out looking like this Dad! I have to fix my hair." The twins spoke in unison.

"Fifteen minutes. Then we gotta go." Jeff walked to the TV remote and was pleased with his progress. He could almost walk without his cane, his skeletal system still reeling from the devastating flu.

He turned the TV on and relaxed in the poolside cabana of his Sugarloaf home. He was glad to be recovering but thought briefly again about the man in the white Chevrolet outside Lukeville. He looked familiar, but he couldn't quite place him.

FOX News came to life, *FAUX* News according to the competition; and Erica Robins was interviewing none other than Hutz the Putz. Another memory stirred. Hutz the Putz, the not-so-nice-guy who died, came back and now speaks Hebrew when in trances. *How weird was that?*

"Mr. Hutz . . ."

"Call me Chuck, please."

"Chuck, you've made quite a few enemies in the last year or so, since your accident and remarkable recovery."

"I would say!" Chuck interrupted. *"Trying to kill Audry, Ophelia and me with AK-47s is definitely unfriendly."* He laughed nervously.

"Do you think it's because of your message, Chuck? You're rubbing a lot of different groups the wrong way. You've ticked off, putting it mildly, moms who buy their daughters suggestive clothing, the entire LBGT community, the . . ."

Chuck interrupted again, *"LBGT?"*

"Lesbians, bi-sexuals, gays and transgenders; surely you knew that? You have angered members of most religious communities, including the three monotheistic religions: Judaism, Christianity and Islam. You have offended

the wiccans and most women's groups. What do you have to say about all these accusations?"

Erica liked Hutz the Putz, and this was her third interview.

"I ask people not to kill the messenger. When I get in the trance-state and speak Hebrew, I am convinced now that I am speaking what God is putting in my head, that's all. God is not happy; and it's not just us here in America, it's the entire world. Europe has realigned herself with ancient countries, merging with others to hold back the ongoing financial collapse of the world, North Africans spend seventy-five percent of their income just to eat, natural disasters are occurring all over the world, the Moon has rings for God's sake. And some mothers should be grossly ashamed at the way they let their young daughters and sons dress."

Jeff's mind wandered between the interview and the dreams of Kipper T and Missy T, and the experience behind the dark door. *Had he really gone behind the door?* Was it just a dream? Was *this* a dream, his entire life? He grasped with reality and sometimes pondered that he might really be dead, and this whole thing could be a dream.

"Let me comment on the LBGT thing. No, God is not happy with that, like it or not. He's also not happy with adultery, unlimited fornication, pedophilia, or the latest bestiality craze in Europe. Did you know that in some parts of Europe, the number one cause of injury or death to cats is from men trying to have sex with them? God had many rules pertaining to sex, and man has changed the rules. What was wrong is now right; what was right is now wrong.

"From the messages and visions I get, God did not want a ruleless population. He set rules from the beginning, if you believe the story. Adam and Eve, who many don't even believe existed, had only one rule. The Israelites, thousands of years later, had more than six hundred rules to follow. The God of Abraham, the Jewish God, did draw lines in the sand. We have paid no attention to them. Jesus never said that man should not follow the rules of God. He said just the opposite in Matthew 5:17-20. You can read it for yourself. No, God is not happy with the human race, and his patience has worn thin, I'm afraid. We should all be afraid. We've been warned."

Hutz the Putz had no sooner said these words, than he went into one of his now famous trances, babbling in Hebrew, a language that Jeff and Audry could somehow, someway understand without interpretation. Miss Ophelia was always around to translate for those who didn't understand but was aging fast, her ninetieth birthday just one week away. Chuck repeated himself.

"What used to be right is now wrong. What used to be wrong is now right. Yahweh detests your actions. You have been warned."

Chuck suddenly spasmed, leaned back in his chair as his legs and back stiffened, and he fell backwards, knocking Ophelia to the floor. Within seconds the screen went to commercial break, and the sound changed to the latest coffee commercial directed to senior citizens:

"The best part of waking up . . . is just waking up."

The girls exited the kitchen and walked to the pool, all primped and ready for another day. They wondered what this day would bring, but the man in the white Chevrolet outside Lukeville was on their minds.

CHAPTER FORTY-SEVEN

The Tajikistan night was cooler than the nights before; yet with no breeze, the air was still stifling at ninety-one degrees. The summers had been much warmer the past year or two. Crickets ruled the night air, love songs easily traveling through the maze of thickets, a black-crowned night-heron squawking in the starlit sky above. Naomi and Aludra sat on an oak bench, like they did many nights, talking about their religions and the differences and all the deaths the differences had caused in the world.

"Remember when we used to look at the night sky when we were young? What else was there to do at night?" Aludra didn't look at Naomi and continued to stare into the night. "We would wait for hours to see one shooting star. Do Jewish people call them shooting stars?"

"The whole world calls them shooting stars, Aludra. I guess it's in our genes to look out into the sky and think about what's out there. I mean, *way* out there. If I had gone to the university, I would have been an astronomer."

"Do Jews believe in the Star of Bethlehem?" Aludra continued. Naomi ignored the question until the explosion in the distance, another meteor exploding in the sky; and she thought it kind of resembled the Star of Bethlehem from the Christmas cards she had seen. She did not answer the question.

"The leader of the village has a son who has his eye on you, Aludra. Seems he is somewhat smitten. Very handsome too."

Aludra's face blushed; and she pulled the scarf closely around her head, more reflex than Islamic culture, and thought about the patriarch's young son. At 29, she thought he was probably much younger.

"He gave me a rose and a box of honey dates for my birthday last week. He *is* handsome." Aludra turned to her side, facing Naomi in the almost darkness; and a pink shade of light provided by the half-moon hid her blush. The bench was hard, the night air picking up a slight breeze, finally.

"Naomi, you will think this strange of me; but when I do find a man to marry, and I'm in no hurry," Aludra said defensively, "I do not want to marry a Muslim man. I do not want to be half a person, and that's the way women are treated. If I want to drive a car, I want to drive a car. It's as simple as that." Aludra began to weep, and Naomi held her close, like a grandmother would hold her grandchild; and the smell of youth permeated her skin.

"Why don't you reconsider, Aludra?"

"Reconsider what?" Aludra wiped her eyes on her dark, woolen scarf.

"Why don't you look into the other Abrahamic religions, Judaism or Christianity? They at least treat women better, and the . . ." Naomi's voice trailed off as another duet of moon-meteors lit up the sky along the eastern horizon.

"And the what?"

"Aludra, the truth lies in the scripture breathed by God himself and given directly to Moses and the later prophets. He did not use an angel, neither Michael, the greatest and most powerful of all angels, nor Gabriel. God gave the Torah *directly* to Moses, the history from the beginning of time, from the creation of the formless Earth to the end of the Great Wandering, when the Israelites conquered the land of Canaan."

Aludra quietly considered Naomi's advice. The *land of Canaan* had been the land of her Arab ancestors, descendants of Abraham's first son, Ishmael. She had always been Muslim, had been programmed from birth to be a Muslim, to not trust the Christians and especially the Jews; and the occupation of Canaan had always been one of the reasons to hate. Her own brother had orchestrated the deaths of many Christians and Jews in Europe and America. Her suspicion was that Jews and Christians were probably programmed since birth to believe their religions too.

"I think I want to marry a Christian or Jewish man, Naomi. Islam is a beautiful religion. I know you don't think so, but the way it flows and the wisdom it offers . . ."

"Read the *Bible*, Aludra," Naomi interrupted. "I think you will find it even more flowing and more beautiful, and certainly more peaceful. Read *Genesis 12:3* and recognize the truth in that verse, as has been verified throughout our history. It is good that Muslims love God; but Allah is not his name, at least it wasn't in the beginning. When did he change it? God first said that his name was *I Am*. Did you know that? He revealed his name to Moses. There is plenty of violence in the *Bible*, we know that. It was the way it was then. But the *Bible* and the *Quran* cannot both be true because of all the disparities. Just think about it, Aludra. There are many who believe the *Quran* was dictated to Muhammad by Satan, not the Angel Gabriel; and most Muslims do not know of the *Satanic Verses* that were later deleted from the *Quran*."

The breeze picked up, and the change was pleasant.

"Aludra," Naomi continued and the sky suddenly exploded in light as several meteors passed overhead, "Why do you think so many Islamic nations have cuddled up with Russia and China the past couple of years. These countries are *full* of unbelievers, the people who Muslims would despise even more than Jews and Christians. That is sinister in itself, almost supernatural."

"The enemy of my enemy is my friend."

"What?" Naomi asked.

"The enemy of my enemy is my friend. It's an old Arab saying. Think about it and you will see why they are siding up with their enemies. Russia and China hate the Jews, Americans and Europeans as much as the jihadists do, or almost. And Naomi, all Muslims are not extremists. Most of us just want to worship our way and let everyone else worship their way. It's only the few who are extremists."

"Well 'the few' are estimated at ten to fifteen percent of all Muslims. That would mean that about two hundred million *jihadists* want to kill everyone else. And this warrior-like conquer-the-world logic is directly from *your* holy book, the *Quran*. The Jews and Christians were never instructed by God to conquer the world, to cut off the heads of unbelievers, to convert others by force, to our beliefs. Jesus told his followers to spread the message, the *good news*, to the world. If anyone didn't want to listen, so be it. It was not a death penalty. God does not tell his followers to blow up the Eifel Tower and Big Ben or fly planes of innocent people, God's children, into buildings and mountains."

Naomi paused, and Aludra concentrated on Naomi's words.

"I have read the *Bible*, at least the *New Testament*. It made me think about a lot of things."

"Aludra, you will never fully understand the power of the book if you don't read the *Old Testament* too. The *New Testament* would have never happened were it not for the *Tanach's* predictions.

Before Aludra could ask about the *Tanach*, the women heard stirring in the honeysuckle bushes several meters behind them and turned to see the cause of the ruckus, fear in the eyes of both. It was Ahmed, the patriarch's smitten son. He walked toward them, a single rose in his hand and a box of *something*.

Ahmed crossed the dusty yard, dry as a bone because of the drought, kicking mice out of the way as he walked through the honeysuckles, one of the few plants that would bloom in the dry weather. The mice were hungry and had advanced on his small village just the week before, millions of the tiny rodents scurrying through fields and ruining the rolls of hay intended for the farm animals. Ahmed didn't recall ever seeing such a plague, the smell of the urine and feces masking any hope for the sweet smell of honeysuckles to win this battle of aromas. The villagers had entered an endless battle against the small creatures since the infestation; but so far, the mice were winning. Which meant the fleas were winning. Disease lurked in the darkness.

"Two angels have appeared before me."

Naomi leaned over and whispered in Aludra's ear, "He *is* a Christian."

Ahmed *was* smitten with the beautiful Aludra, and his heart pitter-pattered as he came closer. She had told Ahmed about her culinary training in Paris and how much she loved the city . . . and the guilt she felt because she *did* love the city. Ahmed handed Aludra an Old Testament, written in French.

"Just read the first five books, and see if your interest is piqued." Ahmed handed Aludra the single, red rose, as red as blood, on a long stem.

The night air, still serenaded by the love-drunk crickets, was interrupted by a loud *crack*, a sound that Aludra knew instantly. The red color of the rose suddenly matched the red flowing from Ahmed as the AK-47 round found its target, a Christian infidel. Ahmed fell to the ground, and the two women were spattered with the blood of a good man. In the distance they heard the shout: *Allahu Akbar*. God is Great.

That night, Aludra made up her mind as she and Naomi dragged Ahmed to shelter, hoping and praying silently to their God, that he wasn't dead. She would tell the world the truth about Islam and the evil baggage that accompanies her male-dominated religion.

Vinny waited patiently at the IHOP in Summerville, just outside Charleston, South Carolina. This would be his first meeting with Mahmud since the Buford Dam was blown up. A smile crossed Vinny's face, remembering the night of the nuclear explosion, a night that he camped out a few thousand feet north of the dam, just so he could see the distant fireworks himself. He had been astonished when the bomb went off and the night sky brightened as though it was noon on a sunny day in Saudi. Vinny nearly panicked as the wind from the blast beckoned; and he could actually feel the heat, like the air blowing from a furnace he may have once repaired. His first view of a nuclear explosion was mesmerizing, and this was just a tiny one. He couldn't wait for the coming day, the Day of Terror, when Europe and America would be dropped to their knees by a not-so-small nuke. *The Taking Away.* He was anxious and hoped it would happen soon, though nature seemed to be helping the jihadists kill the infidels. *Allahu Akbar.*

Mahmud walked through the door of the newly remodeled IHOP, Michael Jackson singing *Thriller* on the in-store sound system and a large flat-screen tuned to FOX. He was much thinner than Vinny remembered; and he was glad to see his boss, a man even more ruthless than himself. Mahmud slid into the booth across from Vinny, asking the waitress for a coffee and ice water. The two men ordered eggs, bacon and grits, just to "fit in" but would leave the unclean bacon on the side of their plates. The waitress would later tell the FBI agent that she thought it strange the two men ordered extra bacon and then didn't touch it.

"Vinny my friend." The men shook hands, American style, and added a fist-bump.

"Hey Bubba."

Vinny half mouthed the words as he addressed Mahmud in *Southern*, having mastered the dialect several years earlier when the Islamists decided to take their battle to the Christian-ridden Bible-Belt. They spoke softly in Mahmud's native Farsi, the Persian language of the Iranians and most Afghanis. No one was sitting in the adjacent booths, a good thing, their privacy a gift from Allah. The blue, vinyl seat was warm, as was the weather.

"Everyone thinks you are dead Bubba. They think you were aboard the submarine with Nimrod because your name was on the manifest. You did good Bubba. I guess that's why you're the boss."

"That's good my friend. They need to think that. Do you have the data?"

Vinny handed Mahmud the memory chip with photos of Charleston's largest churches and two synagogues, as well as the military facilities available through *Google Maps*. There were also photos of the Francis Marion Hotel as well as layouts of all floors. Vinny did not mention the missing intel chip from the laptop he had stolen months earlier from Jeff Ross' sports car. He had seen Jeff Ross only once before, except . . . the man with the cane at the Lukeville Truck Stop looked eerily similar.

"Have you tried to contact Jill?"

Bubba Haskins, the name he had adopted three decades earlier, considered the question but only briefly. His marriage of twenty-two years to Jill had been *pretend*, though she never knew, praise Allah, a ruse that had its start in Iran thirty years earlier. *Sneak in as a young man, become a day laborer with fake documents, move into targeted jobs and gradually blend in.* That had been the mantra. Now there were *homegrown terrorists* all through the lands of North America, Europe and Russia. The *Taking* would be soon, as Muhammad, peace and blessings be upon him, would soon return with the Twelfth Imam. They would conquer the world and drive out the Satanists and infidels. *All* will worship Allah in those days, or they will lose their heads.

Mahmud had been fortunate with the funding he received from his Persian fighters in Tehran. That helped him become the most successful minority contractor in Georgia history. Over the years he had grown to care deeply for Jill, not just her ravenous beauty but her beautiful spirit. It was hard to believe she was Jewish, and at first the romance sickened him; but he did what he needed to do.

"No, of course not. It is better that she think I was vaporized and washed down the Chattahoochee. No one has a clue of my involvement."

Vinny knew the last statement was false, because he had followed the Samarra Russell trial. The feds knew of Mahmud's involvement, but they also thought he was dead.

Charleston, South Carolina, because of a horizon marked with the ornate steeples of numerous churches, is often referred to as *The Holy City*. After Savannah, Charleston was one of the first colonies to let Jews worship their faith without any restrictions. Two synagogues were of particular interest to Vinny and Bubba.

Kahal Kadosh Beth Elohim was the fourth oldest synagogue in the United States, founded in 1749. *Brith Sholom Beth Israel* was the oldest Orthodox synagogue in the South. Soon, they would be no more.

"Did you make reservations?" Vinny asked.

"Yes, the new Presidential Suite." They laughed. "Had to book it for a month, but the Japanese have big pocket-books; and they're paying the bill.

The Francis Marion Hotel had been Historic Charleston's landmark hotel since 1924. Newly renovated, the hotel now had 280 rooms. It would be packed on December 21, 2012, as the southern city would be hosting three end-of-the-world conventions and had parties planned from historic downtown to Folly Beach for the entire week. There would be speakers representing the Maya, the Hopi, Nostradamus, Mother Shipton and Merlin. No one would be representing the Apostle John's version of the end of the world, and many evangelicals had protested.

"The explosives will be easily hidden in suitcases. I need Latif or whoever speaks the best English, *Southern* would be better, to move into the suite with his wife. They will attend touristy events around Charleston, go shopping, all the things a wealthy American couple would do. We don't want the suite sitting unoccupied. Latif and his wife . . . Latif *wishes* she was his wife . . . will befriend the hotel staff so there should be no suspicions."

"Why aren't we using a BN?" Vinny asked.

"We have plans for the briefcase nukes Vinny, but we must save them for bigger and better things. You've seen the photographs of Buford Dam and the subsequent flooding. Three thousand dead from one, small BN. It's awesome Vinny, and Allah has given us these great gifts. Let's not waste them. We will take out five synagogues in one morning, and it won't take nukes to do it."

Vinny *had* seen the photographs. He had seen the actual explosion as he waited that night, just a couple thousand feet away. He would never forget the beautiful horror. Even at that distance the light had been blinding. He loved it. Couldn't get enough of it and was anxious about BNs just sitting around waiting to be detected; and then there was the tritium issue. No one really knew for sure if the North Koreans had recharged the nukes. They weren't known for honesty.

"We have close to a hundred operable BNs Mahmud. Let's use them."

"We will Vinny, I promise. We don't have as many as we thought because some tritium triggers have deteriorated too much to initiate the fission reaction. They would be lucky to cause even a small explosion. Plus, you don't need a nuclear weapon to blow up buildings. McVey did it with a single fertilizer bomb, *boom*. Knocked a federal building to the ground, remember?"

An Asian couple slid into the booth behind Bubba and Vinny. The man nodded and smiled, like Asians do, the woman looking down the entire time. Vinny and Bubba smiled back, then continued their conversation in Farsi.

The young couple, thin and disheveled, might have been married had it not *also* been a ruse. They really liked each other and the pheromones screamed out for attention; but anything beyond fake, public intimacy was against *The Rules*.

The man reached across the IHOP table and held the young lady's hand, tenderly stroking it like she was the love of his life.

"Did you hear the two men talking behind us?" He asked in Korean.

"I did," she whispered. "Farsi."

Trained as interpreters for Homeland Security, the couple listened silently. No one would suspect that a South Korean couple would know anything about Farsi. Then the young lady spoke.

"I think the man with the gray hair mentioned tritium triggers."

"I heard," the Asian man replied as he pulled the new Motorola Mi-Pad from his man-bag. In a few seconds he was inputting notes that would soon be in the land of Wi-Fi, speeding at the speed of light toward Washington.

Behind the Korean man, Vinny moved his finger across his trachea, the international symbol for *shut up*. Mahmud said nothing and took a piece of paper from the front pocket of his denim shirt, also removing the pen.

"???" he wrote.

Vinny took the pen and small paper. He wrote in French: We need to go now. Will explain."

Chapter Forty-Eight

The young Asian couple left IHOP, got in their dark green Nissan Leaf, started the electric engine and headed back to Summerville, to their modest apartment where they *blended in*.

"They left suddenly. The old guy flirted with me; he gave me a look and winked at me." The young girl giggled and blushed. The *look* was not a flirt.

Heading west on I-26, the Korean couple took their exit and traveled south. Kwan looked in the rear view mirror again, noticing the black car that was maintaining a position two cars back, behind the Toyota minivan. He said nothing.

Vinny followed the green Leaf as discreetly as possible, but he had a bad feeling about the IHOP couple. Had he known the information about the Farsi conversation was on its way to . . . wherever . . . he would not have been so patient. With all the solar activity, most cell phones were intermittent at best; so if a transmission had been made, it probably would never make it to its destination. He was correct, as the transmission of data from the Charleston IHOP dissipated into nothingness, much like a satellite TV transmission pixelates during interference.

The sun was very active, and hot. Deep within, a coronal mass ejection had been born; and this CME would be like no other, at least in recorded history. Slowly, it worked its way to the surface several thousand miles above.

The group of Jihad's Warriors, indiscreet as usual, met in secret at an Atlanta strip club, shirts unbuttoned. One of the men wore a small gold chain with a gold crucifix. The four men looked *normal* as they moved to a round table in the back of the dingy lounge. The lights were dim, and cigar smoke lingered in the air.

One of the men, *Arzu the Chechen*, moved to the United States when he was two years old, just a couple of years after Ronald Reagan's reign. Almost single-handedly, Reagan brought down the Berlin Wall; and the Soviet Union collapsed into numerous countries, including Chechnya, with a large Muslim population. Arzu would thank the man if he were still alive.

Radicalized after 9/11, the young Arzu frequented jihadist web sites where he became even more radical. Arzu glanced at the groaning man in a seersucker suit, getting a lap dance two tables away. The dark-skinned girl was ravishing, and Arzu found himself aroused.

"Let's hurry and get out of this place before Allah kills us."

Arzu made the comment and wished he meant it, but he didn't. A den of iniquity was calling his name, and the Nigerian dancer smiled his way.

"What would you gents like to drink?" The waitress was barely dressed and would have been stoned to death in some Islamic countries, Arzu thought but said nothing. He was surprised how lovely many of the women were, especially the raven-haired Oriental dancer descending the pole like a firefighter might exit in an emergency; only naked. She smiled at him, he was sure.

None of the men drank, but each ordered a Budweiser. Arzu drifted back to reality but couldn't keep his eyes off the beauty on the pole and the lap dancer two tables away.

"Our chicken is prepped and ready," said the man with the gold chain and crucifix, using the code word for their *targets*. They all exchanged business cards, like business men do. These were not normal business cards though, and each contained a small microchip. The chips contained coded messages of floor plans, schedules and dates of attack for various facilities in the Bible-Belt, including Catholic churches, synagogues and VA hospitals.

As the conversation ended thirty minutes later, Arzu was pleased at the coordination of the coming attacks. Martyrs in Charlotte, Raleigh, High Point, Chattanooga, Charleston and Savannah were cocked and loaded. *The Bible-Belt.*

"The South rocks!" Arzu told the men, and they laughed as they made their way to the exit. On the way out, Arzu was positive the raven haired beauty-on-a-pole admired him. He would be back; and the South *would* rock, literally.

The knock on the door came late. The young Muslim couple knew very few people and had moved into their home in Norcross, just up the street a bit from Duluth only two years earlier. The classic, Southern-style, three-bedroom home was small and located along North Peachtree Street in Old Norcross. The night was warm and muggy, and the new air conditioner could not keep up. Thinking it a neighbor in need, Mrs. Hadad woke her husband. They were good friends with most.

"Gamal, someone needs help. Go to the door."

Gamal was up in an instant and hurried down the carpeted hall. Hadad was the name of the Syrian god of fertility, and this had certainly turned out to be the case as Gamal hurried quietly, trying not to wake the five kids. He opened the front door and recognized the gentleman immediately. He welcomed him in and closed the door. He motioned Latif to follow him to the kitchen.

"Latif, what's up? It's eleven o'clock. I thought you were moving to Charleston."

"The time is near Gamal."

"The time for what? What are you talking about?" Gamal was confused and half asleep.

"The war against the infidel will begin soon. It is your duty to let our people know."

"Latif, I do not understand what you are speaking about? Make yourself clear, please."

"My brother," Latif touched Gamal's arm, "Our mission has been long term. Now we will take over this God forsaken country and convert the people. Our fellow martyrs are stationed all over America and Europe. You know most of our Muslim brethren in the Atlanta area because of your charitable work. The revolution will begin on Yom Kippur and will not end until the people convert or are slaughtered."

"Latif, are you a jihadist?" Gamal was surprised. "We love our neighbors and the Muslims here are not warriors. We are all peaceful. We do not want to be a part of this war. Live and let live. What's wrong with that?"

"Gamal, these instructions come from our Shi'a brothers in Iran. You must, you will, comply."

"What do you want from me?" Gamal's mind was spinning. How did the night go from hot but peaceful to hot and anxious in such a short time?

"Take the message to our brothers. We need to know where the most prominent Christians and Jews live, where they worship, floor plans for their churches and synagogues, what their driving patterns are, do they have children, that kind of information. This will give us the opportunity to take the Prophet's, peace be upon him, glorious message to the people of the Book. Then it will be their choice."

"What choice, Latif?"

"The choice to live or die."

"I refuse!" Gamal almost shouted. His wife joined the two men in the kitchen, dressed in her blue, terry-cloth robe.

"Go put some clothes on woman. This frivolity is about to end. The women will soon be covered." Latif's voice was scolding.

"You can leave Latif!" Gamal stood, "and I still refuse."

Latif stood, spun on his right heel, headed for the front door, saying, "I thought that might be your answer, Gamal. That's why I brought you this."

Latif handed Gamal a small computer flash drive.

"Watch the video. I will be in touch tomorrow."

The green Nissan Leaf continued toward the Asian couple's home, when the black Dodge Charger passed and continued ahead at a high rate of speed, soon disappearing over the distant hill. The couple gave a sigh of relief.

"False alarm," he said, mostly to himself.

As the black Charger passed, it approached the Nissan on the left. With the Dodge's window down, Vinny took careful aim, fired the small air-pistol and a tiny GPS tracking device was quickly attached to the side of the car. It looked like a wad of bubble gum.

Twenty minutes later, Jung and his pseudo-wife were safely in their home, they thought. Locking the doors for the night, they had no idea that Vinny had already turned around and was headed there for a midnight visit.

The front door closed, Latif left and walked down the concrete sidewalk, tinted pink in the moonlight. His car was parked a block away.

Gamal hurried to his laptop, plugged in the flash drive and waited. Within seconds a video appeared with Arabic streaming along the bottom. Gamal's wife read the words, but Gamal just stood with his mouth and eyes wide open. His young brother, only ten, still living in Pakistan with family, was bound and tied like one of the bulls he had seen at last week's rodeo at the arena. He was weeping and trying to beg the two men in the video, but the child's ramblings were muffled by the duct tape over his mouth. Fear was in his eyes.

"Gamal, this message is for you." The voice overlaid to the video was in perfect English. You will abide by the instructions, or your sister is next. And then your own children."

One of the two men, the one with the black and white hood, stepped behind Gamal's young brother, stripped the tape from the child's mouth so he could scream and cut his throat, almost severing his young head. The child tried to scream, but with his trachea now an opening to the outer world, only blood spewed forth. The screen went black and a message appeared.

"This video has self-erased."

CHAPTER FORTY-NINE

"All the stars in the sky will be dissolved and the heavens rolled up like a scroll; all the starry host will fall like withered leaves from the vine, like shriveled figs from the fig tree." Isaiah 34:4 NIV

C had, The Admiral, Wild Willy and Jeff gathered around the air conditioner that cooled Jeff's pool patio. Chad gathered the photographs.

Sheryl was sleeping in one of the guest rooms and didn't seem to be fully recovered from her kidnapping and rescue. Her jaw had been wired together but was now nearly healed. She tossed and turned as her sleep became deeper, and she dreamed of her knight in shining armor who rescued her, single-handedly. Who would've ever thought that Will would fly from Israel just to rescue his good friend. She slipped into dreamland.

"Look at these photos!"

Chad spread the two photos side-by-side. The Admiral put on his reading glasses and grabbed a magnifying glass from his briefcase. The eyes just weren't what they used to be.

"They're the same it looks to me." The Admiral subconsciously rubbed his right thigh, still sore from the attack on Old Peachtree a few months earlier and leaned over the 8X10 photos, studying them carefully.

"Are these Hubble photos?" The Admiral asked, referring to the Hubble Space Telescope that had brought so many wonders from space and into the land of flat screens.

"Yeah, they look the same to me." Jeff said. Wild Willy studied the photos and agreed.

"No. These are from the ALMA project in Chile; World's most powerful telescope."

"OK, now look at the same two photos magnified digitally."

Chad soon had the same two photos displayed on his iPad V. They still looked the same. As Chad zoomed in, the photo on the left changed drastically; and the photo became darker with each enlargement.

"What happened to the stars?" Jeff asked, breathing steady but deeply. At first appearance this was troubling.

"That's what I mean! They're gone!"

"When were these two pictures taken?" The Admiral asked.

"The photo on the left with the missing stars was yesterday at 4:18 AM. The comparison photo was taken two weeks earlier on August 22 at 4:15 AM. In two weeks, six hundred thousand stars and galaxies have just disappeared. Goddard and JPL are working with other observatories, satellites and different wave-length detecting systems; but they are nowhere to be found. It totally defies logic."

"Has this been in the news?" The Admiral asked. He noted that only the stars in the left third of the photo had disappeared, as though something very large was moving across the field of vision, blocking the light.

"Not yet. It's very hush-hush until we can get some kind of handle on it. No one knows, not even our allies unless someone else just happened to be looking at the same stuff as us. It's possible though."

"And this is interesting," Chad continued. "Remember last month when I told you about the jet stream beginning to dip farther south and with increased speed? I saw this happening weeks ago, but the weather channels are just beginning to report it. This is what's causing all the severe straight-line wind storms all over the country."

"And Europe and Australia too, Daddy."

Audry walked out of the kitchen and on to the patio, a chocolate *Yoo-hoo* in hand.

"What color is the wind Uncle Chad? Can you really see it?"

Chad glanced at the other men. "I really can see it sweetie, and it's awesome!"

"What does it look like?" she persisted, her small forehead wrinkled with concern.

"Well, I can see the winds in the atmosphere, high altitude winds that are high-speed. They are almost transparent, sort of like colored water. When the winds are calm, slower than forty knots, the colors are kind of pastel and soft. The higher the wind speed, the darker the color. Lately the colors have been dark." *Really dark* Chad thought but didn't say.

"Is that bad Uncle Chad, the dark colors? Mr. Hutz said the windstorms that are coming will be the worst in history."

Chad knew of Hutz the Putz but had not heard any of his Hebrew ramblings. The four men, friends for years, hadn't formed a hard and fast opinion of Chuck Hutz; but Chad was a skeptic at heart.

The car's horn blew briefly; and the next second Audry had disappeared, running out for a day with her twin sisters. They were spending a lot more time together since her Mom drowned in the tsunami, and Audry liked it, except . . . She wished the thought from her mind and reminded herself not to think about *that* yet. She wasn't ready.

"Tell me about the solar activity, Chad. You mentioned something about an anomaly on the Sun."

"It's not *on* the Sun, Admiral, it's *in* the Sun. The interior of the Sun is estimated to be about fifteen million degrees Fahrenheit. The surface of the Sun is only about ten thousand degrees, a big difference between the two. The two new Solar Observing Stations that are orbiting the Sun are reporting slight increases in the Sun's surface temperature, not much but notable. It has never been observed before."

"So what does that mean?" Jeff asked.

"It could mean many things, including the record setting temperatures of the last decade or so. Even the slightest increase in the Sun's temperature could have devastating effects on Earth. My guess is, the worsening droughts, famine, viral mutations like the one that made HIV transmissible by mosquitos, forest fires and the changing rain patterns could be a result of this minor warming. Then there is the Moon, now eleven hundred miles closer to earth than before the comet hit. It appears to be coming closer, and no one is sure what it means. There are definitely tidal effects." Chad continued.

"It's not unusual for stars to change temperature. It happens all the time. Before stars burn out, they begin to expand and get hotter. The Red Dwarf is reddish in color because it's cooler than the Sun, which is yellow. Stars larger than the Sun are so hot the color changes from yellow to white.

"That's interesting Chad; Wasn't expecting a lecture." They laughed.

"Well, here's the interesting thing. There has been a slight detection of color change in the Sun's surface, a slight shift toward white."

"What do *you* think this means?" Wild Willy piped in. "He knew Chadbo Myers, and they *all* knew he had a theory or two.

"It means," Chad started and paused, "that we better start working on better air conditioners and underground housing. Global warming is here to stay, and man isn't the cause. I'm not saying we don't contribute, but our part is miniscule when compared to Mama Nature's."

CHAPTER FIFTY

"I will make you into a great nation, and I will bless you; I will make your name great, and you will be a blessing. I will bless those who bless you, and whoever curses you I will curse; and all peoples on earth will be blessed through you." Genesis 12: 2-3 NIV

Vinny pulled the black Charger off the road and into a small path leading into the woods, adjacent to the driveway leading to the Asian couple's house, about a quarter mile off the road. It was dusk and would be totally dark in fifteen minutes. The air was still and stifling. In the distance a large dog barked, roaming the fenced-in area behind the house. Soon he was by the green Nissan, still unnoticed by the black Labrador retriever.

Vinny reached into his pouch, pulled out the giant rawhide bone coated with Warfarin and Beggin Strips and threw it as hard as he could, almost to the very back of the young couple's yard. There was a slight bark as the bone dropped into the yard, and the lab was off to investigate. Vinny hurried to the sliding glass door leading into the kitchen, knowing the dog should be an ex-dog within a minute or so. He wasn't there to kill this night, only to retrieve the laptop. The door was too simple to unlock, which made Vinny especially cautious; but it appeared the couple was just careless.

What luck, praise Allah. He lifted the laptop off the small, round dining table, quietly closed the door and walked briskly back to the green Nissan. The dog was nowhere to be seen. Again reaching in his pouch, Vinny removed a four inch by six inch square of C4 plastic explosives with a GPS switching trigger. The GPS trigger was set to explode the mechanism as soon as the green Leaf was three miles away from the house. He hoped both would be in the car.

The Yom Kippur Brigade members, a brand they wore proudly, were really just good old boys, day laborers, janitors and field technicians. Most were bright, American born and raised who somehow ended up in the wrong world, a world they longed to destroy. None had been born Muslim but had learned of the religion in prisons, Internet sites and Aryan web pages. Finally, a religion that wasn't all about the Jews. There were only a few members, but they were growing. The men ordered breakfast at the Summerville Diner, just a few miles from Charleston.

Rosh Hashanah was the next day, followed in a few days by the holiest day in the Jewish year, Yom Kippur. Most of the YK brigade had no clue that Rosh Hashanah was the Jewish New Year and Yom Kippur was the Day of Atonement, and really couldn't care less. They were just Jews as far as they were concerned; and in about a week, a lot of them would be dead. They had never read Genesis 12:3.

"Scott, you are here early today my son. Are we ready for tomorrow?"

Yom Kippur was the following day and Rabbi Joseph Goodfellow was the Senior Rabbi at one of largest synagogues, described as a *Modern Orthodox Synagogue* nestled in beautiful downtown Charleston, South Carolina.

"We have lots to do. I expect a larger service than usual because of all this hysteria about the world ending December 21. I can't believe how many people believe that. I read about a group in Japan that just committed suicide, thirty-six people."

Rabbi Goodfellow paid little attention to Scott's comment and hurried away, always in a tizzy. He headed toward the cantor's office. He wasn't sure why he felt so . . . he couldn't really explain the feeling. Maybe he was just anxious. Crowds were normally not a problem. Like many Christians, Reform Jews usually did not attend services during the year, at least not regularly. They did, however, attend the High Holy Days; and Yom Kippur was the Holiest, the *Day of Atonement*. Known in Hebrew as *Yamim Noraim*, or *Days of Awe*, the ten day period starting with Rosh Hashanah and ending with Yom Kippur was a time when one's name could be written into the Book of Life based on how one behaved the previous year. The ten day period could be a time of reprieve if the sinner was *especially* charitable.

The rabbi was uneasy, and Goodfellow noted the small portable air conditioner-on-wheels that Scott had rented for the overflow crowd. As the rabbi wiped the sweat from the left side of his face, he knew the portable unit would only be a slight help, if any. Everyone had been urged to dress casually this year. He well remembered how hot and muggy the previous year had been, and this year was even warmer. He walked to Scott's office.

"Good morning again, Scott. Have you noticed how warm it already is this morning?"

"Yessir, I am trying to get five more air conditioners for the service tomorrow, but everyone is out of stock! I got a message on my voice mail that there was one HVAC company that may have more. I left a message that we need them desperately. If I don't hear from them in a few minutes, I will call again."

No sooner were the words out of the young engineer's mouth, than Scott's smart-phone started playing the first verses of *Yimei HaChanukah*, a ringtone from the previous December.

"Shalom. This is Scott Rosen."

"Shalom to you too, Mr. Rosen. Thank you for returning my call, and I am sure we can help. We supply portable air conditioning units to area churches and synagogues, including *Kahal Kadosh Beth Elohim* over on Hasell Street. That's the fourth oldest synagogue in the United States."

"Yes, I know. I would like to get five of the larger units as soon as they can be delivered, Mr.?"

"Jenkins. Bubba Jenkins. Most people just call me Bubba. I will have these units crated up, is five all you need? I have seven available."

Scott scratched his head, displacing his gray *Atlanta Falcons* hat and figured they couldn't have too much air conditioning, as hot as it was. "Sure, bring all seven, this morning if possible."

"I will try my best to get them there early. Thanks for your business Mr. Rosen. Maybe we can do more in the future."

"Possibly so, Mr. Jenkins." The line went dead.

Mahmud hung up the phone in the Presidential Suite of the Francis Marion Hotel and laughed out loud. He kind of liked the name *Bubba*. It seemed there were a lot of Bubbas in the Bible-Belt. Vinny had showered and shaved and was ready for an exciting twenty-four hours. He heard Mahmud laughing and wondered what was funny.

"There was an explosion this morning on I-26 near Summerville. Eye witnesses said the green car was passing others at a high rate of speed when the car suddenly vanished in a large explosion. No remains have been identified, and it is unknown how many were in the automobile. Now for other local news. Tomorrow is the holiest day of the year for the area's Jewish popu . . ."

Bubba turned the TV up. This plan was working way too easily. Jews seemed so trusting of Christians. That was a good thing. He called the small warehouse, leased by the Japanese *Select* consortium, and instructed the young worker from the Yom Kippur brigade to *pack the lemons*.

Two hours later, a white panel-truck with large magnetic door signs that read *Have Cool-Will Travel* and the web site address, pulled into the delivery area of *Beth Israel* and unloaded seven air conditioners. The delivery man *insisted* that he roll the 24,000 BTU dual-compressor systems into the sanctuary and locate them in the best strategic place. Scott assumed the delivery man with the French accent meant *the best strategic place* as the best place for proper cooling. Vinny, however, was not concerned with cooling, and located each system close to support towers that would bring the whole building down.

"Thank you for your promptness!"

Scott thanked the delivery man again after the seven portable cooling systems were properly stationed around the sanctuary, along with the cooler Scott already had; and they were checked out thoroughly for cooling output and noise levels. The eight portable cooling systems should handle the crowd, maybe.

The panel truck left the Jewish house of worship, the final portable cooling units now delivered to three Charleston synagogues and two Catholic churches. Deliveries had also been made to four synagogues in Columbia, the South Carolina capital. The driver aimed the truck south on Highway 17, hoping to avoid truck stops along I-95.

Six hours later, air conditioners delivered and *situated*, Vinny drove the panel-truck to a remote boat dock he discovered in a *Google Maps* search, on an especially deep part of the Savannah River. The night was overcast and dark. Night crickets serenaded with their love songs, and an occasional owl could be heard *hooting* in the distance.

The truck rolled down the ramp, gathered speed and two minutes later, floating in the currents to the middle of the river, the truck sank slowly to the bottom, nearly sixty feet below. As it crashed into the muddy surface, the sinking truck made a scraping sound as it hit a large, metal container that was nearly buried, the scraping heard only by the fish and other underwater life. Had the truck been an *animate* object rather than *inanimate*, it may have recognized the Mark-15, a three megaton nuclear bomb, accidently dropped in the Savannah River basin on February 5, 1958, by a U.S. Air Force B-47 strategic bomber. Three million tons of dynamite, not so gently nudged by the sinking panel-truck.

The following morning, more than five hundred of Charleston's Jewish community attended the Yom Kippur services and were already complaining to Scott about the heat.

"Can you make those AC units get it any cooler, Scott? It's eighty-four in here." The cantor was sweating profusely, making his request while wiping his brow with his white handkerchief. *You should shed some fat*, Scott thought but said nothing.

CHAPTER FIFTY-ONE

The Nerpa 155 submarine slowly and quietly made her way toward the eastern Mediterranean and the Suez Canal. They would soon begin the slow ascent toward the surface of the Mediterranean where the Nerpa would unleash all seventeen nuclear tipped missiles.

The submarine's sonar was active in this part of the Mediterranean with an abundance of underwater creatures swimming around the submarine, mostly out of curiosity. A large great-white shark, though few and far between, nudged the underwater behemoth with its snout, but quickly backed off from the electrical charge along the sub's outer skin.

"Anything on the sonar?" Commander Kadyrov asked the technician.

"Just fish, Sir. A large shark approached earlier. There are a few schools of dolphins, but that's it. No sign of naval activity."

Commander Kadyrov smiled. *Almost there*, he thought.

A half mile away, three bottlenose dolphins swam in a pod, circling the curious behemoth. The Nerpa 155 was only a few miles from the Egyptian coast, and dolphins were common.

In what seemed like a flash, the three dolphins were now circling the submarine. The underwater cameras caught the dolphins in action, and two crewmen gathered around the screen to watch.

Two of the dolphins disappeared and seemed to have abnormal growths on their backs, just behind the dorsal fin while one seemed intrigued with the tiny, starboard camera and hammed it up. The crew was mesmerized.

The two Israeli trained dolphins with the *growths* swung into action, one at the bow and the other about mid-stern, and attached their *growths*, coated with the world's stickiest substance, derived from the underwater caulobacter crescentus bug, which could cling to any surface.

"There they go!" the senior tech stated, disappointment in his voice. The three dolphins disappeared as quickly as they had appeared. One of the crewman noticed that the dolphins with the anomaly on their backs now appeared normal.

"The Yom Kippur synagogue bombings in Georgia and South Carolina have outraged the Christian communities throughout the Bible-Belt. Churches have opened their doors for Saturday services for the Jewish populations now displaced. It is a miracle that only 11 people were killed, though many were injured.

"At one historic synagogue in Charleston, the building engineer, Scott Rosen, saved the entire congregation from certain devastation. The sanctuary was surrounded with portable air conditioners when Mr. Rosen checked one of the units that seemed to malfunction. He discovered a receiver device connected to the auxiliary compressor. He alerted Rabbi Goodfellow, and the entire congregation was evacuated. It now appears that Scott Rosen, at risk of losing his own life, again entered the synagogue and used a portable, electronic jamming device to disable the receiver. The Charleston Bomb Squad dismantled seven bombs, all located in the portable cooling units, described as 'significant' and saved the historic building from sure destruction.

"In Georgia, several evangelical Christian groups are gathering with their Jewish brethren; and believe it or not, some Muslims who are disgraced by the violence in the name of Islam. There is a large meeting tomorrow evening in Duluth, Georgia's American Legion Post 251, under the theme, 'No More Turned Cheeks.' As one bass fisherman said this morning, 'They brought their fight to the Bible-Belt, and now all hell's gonna break loose.'

"One local summed it up pretty well with this, 'The loss of Lake Lanier has made the bass fishermen mad, and you don't want to piss off a bunch of bass fishermen.' But it's more than just the fishing that's missing, it's the drinking water. Two reservoirs have been completed in record time, and the pipeline to the Tennessee River is also moving at a record pace. Nothing like running out of water to make you get-a-move-on.

"Savannah . . ."

Abe the Bartender turned the volume up on the TV hanging over the back bar area of *The Divide Disco and Café.* The evening crowds were picking up, and Abe continued to be surprised. He and Pam predicted smaller crowds because of the rioting that had evolved from the original *Occupy Movement* a couple years earlier, but it hadn't happened. Europe was in disarray with countries realigning borders and governments. Fires set by protesters were burning much of the European forests to the ground. *This should be an interesting Halloween night*, he thought.

"Like the costume!" Abe said.

Judi Ellis was dressed like Lady Gaga, except she had a better body, if that's possible, and was a little more modest. At least, that was Abe's opinion.

"Thanks. I like yours too." Judi smiled, coyly.

"But I don't have a costume on, silly girl?" Abe straightened the collar of his *Divide Disco and Café* sport-shirt, and rubbed his hand through his dark hair, receding way too fast.

"Oh, you look pretty scary there, Mr. Abe-the-cutie-Bartender!" She laughed, as did the others sitting around the bar in various Halloween costumes. Abe blushed. "Just kidding, Baby." Judi pinched Abe's butt and gave him a kiss on the cheek. "Hmmmm . . . nice buns!"

". . . dual compressor cooling system. Investigators say that the second compressor in each system was 'compromised.' Let's go to Rich Badey at the Pentagon. Rich, tell us what you know."

Rich Badey had an impressive history. He worked with the finest news agencies during his short career, breaking many stories for CNN and later, FOX. His stint at FOX was one of his favorites, getting to work with all those foxy, foxy *FOX* ladies. He was a man's man, and he definitely loved the ladies; and they loved him. Why wouldn't they? A Pulitzer nominee and recipient of the African-American Writer's Guild for *Best Debut Novel*, Rich tried to remain *humble* and did. Great fame had come upon him since he broke the story of the comet the previous year, while working as an independent investigative reporter.

"Yes Condi, the second compressors in the portable air conditioners used for Yom Kippur services were rented from a company with the motto, 'Have Cool-Will Travel' and distributed by a white or Hispanic man in a white, cargo van."

Abe handed Judi a Dirty Martini, her favorite, and wiped olive juice off his hands.

"Where have you been?" Abe hadn't seen her for months. She had *never* pinched him on the butt either. She was always so reserved. He sort of liked it though. Maybe she'd had a martini somewhere else.

"A girl's work is never done." She giggled. "I've actually been on tour with Dr. Rosenberg."

"The end-of-the-world guy?"

"Well, not really; though many refer to him that way. He's much more than that. He is an expert eschato-o-logist." She giggled again.

"Eschatologist," Abe corrected and started a pot of coffee. Wasn't like Judi to get *tipsy*. "From the Greek word, *eskhatos*. One who studies Bible prophecies concerning the End Times."

"Welllllll . . . Aren't *we* the smart one? Anybody ever tell you you're really cute, Abe the Bartender? *Wait!* I'll be back."

Judi aimed her body toward the lady's room, her gait a little unsteady. Maybe all the end-of-the-world stuff was getting to her, like so many. It was just seven weeks away, December 21, 2012. Destruction coming soon to a town near you, and Abe wondered if anything disastrous *would* happen.

Abe thought he might ask Ms. Ellis to *The Divide's* big 24-hour *Kiss It Goodbye* bash. There were parties all over Atlanta, at least the areas that weren't destroyed in the Buford Dam flood; but Pam had taken special measures to make Duluth's party the best in the area. There would be Greyhound *Buses to Heaven*, waiting to take the raptured to paradise.

Entering the restroom, Judi sneezed four times, her second sneezing spell of the day. Opening her small handbag, she pulled out a pink tissue and wiped her nose. Judi passed out, falling to the tiled floor of the lady's room, before noticing the traces of blood on the pink tissue.

Duluth finally had its first Spanish Flu case.

CHAPTER FIFTY-TWO

T hanksgiving came and went. Everyone was alert to terrorism. The *Bible-Belters*, as they were now called, continued to meet and teach those interested how to be vigilant and how to shoot.

"Hell yes we're gonna profile, fool! What's wrong with you?" The Baptist preacher didn't normally use bad language, and Preacher Tom immediately felt guilt.

American Legion Post 251 had a capacity crowd, standing room only; and many of the men and women wore side-arms on their hips or carried assault rifles. Some had both. The two bartenders, Betty Davis . . . her friends called her Betty Davis eyes . . . and CJ, served hot coffee to the crowd.

"Hell yeah is what I say, too!" The call came from across the room, behind the pool table, now covered with maps and strategies rather than green felt. "They brought their fight to us; we ain't bothered nobody. What the hell's wrong with these people?"

The crowd murmured; and lots of *cussin'* could be heard throughout, not by the preachers and two rabbis but by several of the fishermen and farmers whose land was flooded when the dam blew up. One of the men picked up a montage, photographs of local Muslims in the area, people who *needed* to be watched. Hatred filled the air like a San Diego fog, a hatred perpetrated by fear and fueled by terrorism. Islamic terrorism. There had been plenty of fuel.

"I'll tell you this." The tall, black man took the podium and adjusted the mike, "Their good book says to take over the world, not Europe or Asia, or Israel. I would encourage all y'all to pay close attention to this. We have learned, since we didn't learn through history, that the Islamic goal is to conquer and convert."

"Or kill." The stranger in the back of the room, about six foot tall, muscular and wearing a tank top undershirt, was covered with tattoos. No one recognized him. His skin was pale, at least what you could see of it.

"Might I speak?" the stranger asked as he walked to the podium. He didn't wait for an answer, and no one seemed to want to challenge the man. He looked like an ex-con or something, two earrings in each ear and leather lanyards wrapped snugly around each wrist. His arms and neck were covered with tattoos.

"I wuz in da prison fer twelve years, a'cuseda killin' a famly. I'm free now 'cause a new DNA ev-dence, and God's Great Grace. Lemme tell ya sump'in' you guys don know. Da prisons ah da breedin' grounds fer da terrorists. Dey can be Muslim. Dey can be Christian. Dey can be Hindu. Most ah jus plain mean dough. Meanness is dere religion, but da d'sire ta fit in is strawwwng, lemme tell ya'. Dese boys ah prime fer da pickin', and dey be gettin' picked. Some a dese boys ah *reeall* good on da c'puter too. Dey spend all dere time in de prison liberry, lernin' how ta hack."

The crowd was silent as a church mouse, an occasional cough filling the silence. There were no babies crying. They wondered where this man was from and what kind of accent *was* that?

"Dis here r'ligion, dis Is-lam, is *scary*, man. Dere book, dere *good* book, it tell dem, 'If dey don b'lieve, you cut da heads off.' You people ah payin'a'tention, but most ah not. I been out dere. I seen da malls an da coffee shops. Dey all crowded, like nuttin' be goin' on, like it be Christmas time or sump'in.

"Da time is near, you wait'n see. It be gonna slip up on ev'ryone, like a t'ief in da night, juss like da good book say, da *reeaall* Good Book. You better tell ev'rybody. Ev'rybody better get some guns. It's da devil at wuk heah, don ya unnerstand? You been warned. Dat's what Hutz da Putz say. It be da truth, too."

The tattooed man left the podium, walked out the front door of American Legion Post 251 and never returned. He knew he'd made the devil mad for sure, and he had great respect for the devil. He'd seen what the devil can do, in prison. He knew the devil was a slick dude, so slick he'd already convinced most folk he didn't even exist, something *made up* by the Christians. No, he existed alright. Tattoo man had seen the devil face-to-face, he was sure. That night; that foggy, still and eerie night so long ago at the lake cemetery.

"Who was that?"

The three women asked the question almost simultaneously, but no one responded, and checked their side arms, just to make sure they were there. Wanda, BJ and Beverly were friends from long ago, known as the "Three Wild Women" because of their love of karate and other methods of defense. Wanda was a sharp-shooter with a crossbow and had won numerous awards. All church going ladies, no terrorist would want to run into these three.

Chief Belker walked out the side entry of the Legion Post, and the man had vanished. There were no tail lights leaving the parking lot or driving down Duluth Highway. There was no one walking along the shoulder. Odd . . . He radioed for another officer to take a ride down Highway 120, just to see if a tattooed man might be walking down the highway. Fog set in, thick and wet. The chief walked back inside the Legion Post, just to assure the crowd didn't get too rowdy; but no one was rowdy. Just concerned. And angry.

Thunder boomed in the distance, a low rumble; and the Chief re-entered the side door, which promptly blew off its hinges. The wind suddenly roared. The fluorescent lights flickered three times before it truly was the night the lights went out in Georgia.

CHAPTER FIFTY-THREE

"Jeff?"

Jeff answered his phone on the third Bob Marley *Bad Boy* ringtone. *I need to change that,* he thought. The voice sounded familiar; but his mind was not quite as clear as it had been, before the flu. He still wondered how he survived, now that he had learned all the details. He continued to have dreams about Missy T and Kipper T, and the door to darkness.

"Yes Ma'am?"

Samarra could tell he had no idea who she was. That was disappointing, but why would he? Even though she was married at the time, if that's what you could call it, she always loved the way he looked at her when they would run into each other at the Dunwoody Starbucks, at least until the bombing. The *look* gave her little butterflies, she once told a friend, something that Jack never did.

"Jeff, this is Samarra. I've been meaning to call for months, but haven't. I have been so embarrassed and disgraced for what . . ." Her voice trailed.

"Samarra!" Jeff was hormonized as soon as he recognized her voice.

Samarra Russell, the only *other* woman who held a candle to Melissa; and a Mensa-mate too. Through five years of divorce, Samarra and her husband Jack had been so supportive. Jack was a U.S Senator, and spent most of his time traveling. Jeff wondered if Samarra knew about Melissa's . . . . death. He still could hardly say it, *death*. She *had* to know. He changed his thoughts, not wanting to go *there*.

"Where are you?"

"I'm in the car, with ankle bracelet in tow." She replied.

"Let's have coffee. Starbucks? Can you leave your home?"

Jeff recalled the day at the Dunwoody Starbucks, a year earlier. It seemed like last week. Samarra left Starbucks that day, on her way to CDC; and ten minutes later the brown UPS-looking van exploded on its third pass. Things had been really different since then.

"Actually I'm in Norcross. I hope I didn't wake you Jeff. I just heard about your flu experience, and . . . well, you know." She considered that he might *not* know of her responsibility in his sickness and near death experience. "Can I come by?"

Jeff *did* know. He knew Samarra had been found "not guilty" by *reason of insanity* on all charges. He bought that story. What mother wouldn't go a little batty if someone kidnapped her child, cut off his finger and threatened to cut off young Thomas' eight year old head if she didn't do what the note said. And she had. *Why an ankle monitor?*

"Sure. Let me jump in the shower. Just come on in. Coffee's on the stovetop by the pool." Jeff heard thunder in the background, but the sky was clear and blue; and the temperature for a change was only in the eighties, still warm for December twentieth.

"Thanks Jeff, I will be there in twenty minutes."

Samarra headed north on Peachtree Industrial Boulevard, toward Duluth. The morning sky was clear, except . . . She noticed all the people standing on the sidewalk to her right as she drove by, pointing west at the sky behind her. Looking in the Mercedes' rearview mirror, she saw nothing; but she did hear thunder. *That's strange*, she thought. The sky was clear as a bell. The thunder shook the car, but she continued north.

Ten minutes later, Samarra pulled into Jeffrey Ross' gated mini-estate, exited the dark, gray Mercedes convertible and entered the wrought iron gate to the pool area, just as beautiful as she remembered. Dressed in black jeans and chartreuse tank-top, Jeff was dazzled once again at her beauty. It had been awhile.

He stood, gave her the quick "social" kiss-peck and invited her to the high top table by the waterfall. He was prepared with two cups of coffee and two mimosas neatly placed on the smoked-glass table top.

"I came in the back." She said after the kiss.

Samarra was a stunning woman, beauty and brains. Always a head-turner, she maintained humility and was friendly to all. They met at a Mensa meeting, many years earlier. They had become good friends, and later he became friends with Jack. Jack and Samarra always seemed like the *perfect* couple. Then the child porn and other charges came to light.

An hour of reminiscing later, they had discussed the major connecting events of their lives. Jeff talked about how much he missed Melissa, and how well the kids handled the tragedy. Samarra talked of the heartache she suffered, not just from the trial, but by the grief she caused to the country, actually the world. She talked of all the lawsuits coming her way, from all over the world. She couldn't blame the families of the dead. Now young Thomas was almost ten, getting old enough to ask questions about *what's going on.*

Samarra was religious in nature, unusual for a scientist and Mensa member. Two mimosas later, Jeff decided to ask her.

"One time I asked you why you believed in God. Do you remember what you said?"

"Of course! I said to read the history of Israel. Once you do, you will understand. Is that correct?" She smiled. "So, did you?"

"No. I did get the *Josephus* book though, the one Abe told me about."

"*Antiquities of the Jews*," she said, a statement, not a question.

"Yeah, that's it. Did I ever tell you about the Gideon *Bible* that I found in my suitcase one time, maybe a year or so ago?"

"Nope."

"I returned from a trip, stored my overnighter in the closet, like always. Later I was looking for cologne, or something, that I left in the bag; and a Gideon fell out onto the floor."

"Did he get hurt?" They laughed.

"I can't believe you took the Gideon *Bible*? That's what they want you to do; but since you don't believe *that stuff*, I'm surprised."

"No. I didn't take it. *Why would I*? You know my beliefs."

She did. Jeff had always been perplexed that she, a "learned" woman, a scientist, could possibly believe in this . . . what had he called it . . . *biblical gibberish*?

"Why would I?" Jeff repeated the question out loud, but to himself. He thought about the dreams, Missy T and Kipper T; and the *Blip of Light* that had spoken to him that night . . .

"So, do you still think it's gibberish? Did you read any of it?"

"No, I didn't read it. But the weirdest thing happened to me. After the tsunami at Grand Cayman," Jeff paused to collect his thoughts, and composure, before continuing.

"Just before Gray and Andi found me floating in the Caribbean, after the wave, a bright light appeared in the sky. It was so bright I could see the blood vessels in my closed eyes."

"I think they now refer to that as *Blip*." Samarra said.

"Yeah, that's it. I had seen it before. As a matter of fact, I may have been the first to see it, one night in Villa Rica. Then Abe said he saw it the same night. Now I've seen it four times.

"When the light woke me, guess I was unconscious, it spoke to me. *Seriously*. It spoke to me by name. When Gray and Andi showed up on the jet skis, the light disappeared. It was like it guided them . . ." His voice trailed.

"Like the Star of Bethlehem guided the kings from the East."

"Yeah, like that . . . Yeah, just like that."

Jeff was sorry that he referred to the *Bible* as gibberish, the first time in his life he was sorry about anything like *that*. *What if it's true?* The thought was brief but not as fleeting as in the past. *Could it be true?*

"Anyway, when I came to, there was pressure on my chest, like something was sitting on me. Gray pulled up, boy, were they glad to see me alive! He grabbed the plastic freezer baggie off my chest, as though the contents needed to be protected from water, and you know what it was?"

"Nope."

"*A Gideon Bible*. It was the same one I found in my closet that day; only, I didn't take it to the Caymans with me. I specifically remember putting it on my nightstand. I was planning to read it when I got back. Is that strange, or what?"

"How do you know it was the same one? *Gideons* are everywhere, spreading the Word all over the world. No telling how many people they've saved, just by being in hotel rooms."

"Because I had removed a page from Revelation. The same page was missing."

"Jeff, that is so strange, don't you think?" Samarra believed in miracles and thought this probably qualified.

"Yeah," Jeff said, the thought crossing his mind that maybe, just maybe, the Gideons were after him too. To save him, but . . . from what? The devil? Hell?

"Samarra, can you go to *The Divide* tonight? Big end-of-the-world party." He hoped she said yes but knew there had to be restrictions with the security bracelet..

"Yes. I would love to."

"What about your monitor?" Jeff was pleased at the day's sudden turn of events. The *Breaking News* jingle sounded; but it had become so commonplace, he ignored it.

"We have this Breaking News from Atlanta . . ."

"Jeff, I have a lot of freedom. I'm working on the vaccine. As long as I'm within fifty miles of home, I'm fine. It's a *stipulation*." She smiled, and for the first time in a long time; he felt something for another woman, someone besides Melissa. *It really did feel like butterflies.*

"Jeff? Earth to Jeff." Was he blushing?

"Sorry. It's hard to talk with my heart in my throat."

The comment went over Samarra's head, and she continued.

"I can even go out of the country with enough notice." She watched his reaction, but there was none apparent.

"Jeff, did you hear about Jack?"

He had heard a lot about Jack, the nanotech specialist and U.S. senator, since returning from California. Most was not good.

"No, not that I recall. Why?"

"Well, it's being kept hush-hush." She replied.

Hush-hush, he thought. Not so hush-hush anymore. He listened.

"Someone spotted him at a gay bar in Israel."

"Oh no, you're kidding?" *Why would she be kidding?*

"With a young boy, an underage boy." There was no smile on her beautiful face now. "That was the second incident."

"Samarra, I'm *so* sorry to hear that. I thought Jack was Catholic? Who would've ever thought?"

Jeff's life during the last few years seemed to come with one shocking surprise after another. He would have to process this info. He reached across the table and held Samarra's hand; and she put her other on top of his. She didn't seem particularly upset, but she had been through so much.

"What time do you want to go?" he asked.

". . . so called ice bombs have been falling in the Norcross-Doraville area for the last hour. Several homes have been damaged but no injuries reported so far. The ice bombs are not hailstones, we have been assured by the Weather Channel. Wait, this just in . . ."

Samarra looked fantasic; and Jeff was ready to get to *The Divide* and wait for the Mayan End, something *lighter*.

"The Egyptian Navy has reported two large explosions off the coast of Marsa Matruh in western Egypt. Debris has been spotted, but Egyptian sources are keeping it quiet. An anonymous caller said the debris was from the hijacked Nerpa 155 nuclear missile submarine."

"I brought a change of clothes with me. Can I shower here? It'll take about thirty minutes."

"*Thirty minutes?* Makeup and everything?" Jeff was incredulous. Most women he knew took that long to just think about it.

"I never wear makeup."

There was another boom of thunder, or something, in the distance; and Jeff walked her to her car. Samarra hit the trunk release button, and Jeff grabbed the pink and purple overnight bag.

Re-entering the pool area, they both heard a faint whoosh and then three large thumps as forty-pound ice bombs destroyed the black *Porsche RS Spyder* pulling into the Fahey's driveway, next door.

Chapter Fifty-Four

"**M**an, this place is hoppin'. Look at all the ladies!"
Wild Willy had loved Park Place Café until the bombing last year and felt there would never be another place in Atlanta to match the lovely ladies of Park Place. But he was most impressed. *The Divide*'s disco music and beautiful babes inundated the dance floor, and hearing impaired captions scrolled along the bottom of the flat screens.

"Yep, the best crowd we've had since opening day, even bigger that last year's comet party." Scott replied. He glanced around, looking for Kara Mulherin, his main-squeeze; and he was relieved that she survived the Soufriére Hills tsunami and aftermath while in Haiti. He spotted Judi Ellis dancing with Abe the Bartender, now manager, and was glad she had recovered from the flu so quickly. Everyone held vigils and prayed for her, and it must've worked.

Scott spotted Kara, dancing with one of the residents of Annandale Village in Suwanee, a residential community for developmentally disadvantaged. That's why he loved her.

"Scott, we have a drunk at the bar. Just grabbed the bartender's . . ."

"Too much info for the audience, Dian." Scott interrupted.

Diana Hendricks was the new head waitress, young at twenty-eight but with lots of street smarts. She could spot a drunk over the horizon. Scott saw the man; and sure enough, it was the same guy Diana said would probably get drunk.

Jeff and Samarra walked in the front door, and Scott noted Jeff's arm around Samarra's tiny waist. *My goodness, she is a beauty.* He had never seen Samarra before. It was just a little past seven; and as Scott and Diana headed for the drunk, a news bulletin interrupted WAGA's Home Garden show. The music died and the flat screen volumes went up.

"The Weather Channel has confirmed that the strange storm that hit North Atlanta today may be a rare climatological phenomenon, megacryometeorites, that usually occurs, at least from the few reports available, when the sky is perfectly clear. This storm was unusual because it occurred with very dark clouds and lots of thunder.

"The first reported incidence of megacryometeorites occurred during the seventies in Spain. Eye-witnesses at the time said two large chunks of ice, one weighing almost a hundred pounds, fell from a clear sky. A hundred pounds," the commentator repeated. *"Can you imagine how large that would be?*

"At first, Spanish scientists thought it might be blue ice from an aircraft flying over the area; only, there were no aircraft in the area.

"An associate of Doctor Jesus Martinez-Frias, the Spanish scientist who gave the large ice chunks the megacryometeorite moniker, has said he doubts these are anything but large hailstones."

Samarra and Jeff glanced at each other as they watched the report, but didn't speak. They had both heard the distant thunder earlier in the day, before the Porsche was savaged, and the young girl killed.

Jeff recalled his Mom's warning: *In the end, sonny-boy, there will be hailstorms with hundred-pound hailstones. Yep! That's the truth. Those stones'll cause havoc. That's for sure.*

Susan Storey, the latest in the line of knock-out weather girls, continued.

"There have been several injuries, and two deaths have been reported. There are numerous reports of animal deaths. Extensive property damage has been reported at an apartment complex when at least one of the 10-15 pound ice chunks hit the main gas meter. The gas leak that resulted exploded in a ball of flame when a passing car backfired. In Duluth, Georgia, a Sugarloaf home was hit and a two-and-a-half million dollar Porsche was totally destroyed. The young girl driving the Porsche was killed."

"Man. Take a look at that weather broad. She's freakin' beautilicious." The man was shouting, and slurring.

The verbal assault came from the drunk, now being escorted out the door to the waiting arms of Duluth's finest. He would sleep well in the new city jail.

"Momma, look at the candle. See?"

The young girl stared out the window of the plane as it made its descent into Atlanta's Hartsfield-Jackson Airport. The skyline was beautiful as the distant city-lights adorned the horizon like diamonds on a long, horizontal necklace. The night was moonless. Her *momma* continued to read, paying no attention to her eight year old. She was reading Joel Rosenberg's latest novel, and it was a thriller.

"Momma! Look at the candle!" The girl was emphatic and used her mom's smart-phone to take a picture of the flaming candle, way below the plane. It seemed to be moving.

The jetliner continued its descent, and the crew was rejoicing the near end of a very long day. The flight from Johannesburg to Madrid, and now Atlanta, had been trying. Taking care of 317 vacationers was always trying.

The plane shuttered.

The crowd drank, and waited. It was now December 21 in most of the world as the sun worked its way past the International Date Line. The crowd danced, disco queens twirling in the prettiest of dresses, short dresses; and the warm night was still. The Towne Green was packed. The world was supposed to end when the comet hit last year, but it hadn't. The party continued.

Wild Willy was in deep conversation with The Admiral and Sheryl at a hi-top table by the largest flat screen, as he explained how he single-handedly rescued Sheryl from the Christian militia group that kidnapped her.

"Fortunately Sheryl remembered the GPS button I gave her last year. That's what did it."

"Yeah. I was tied to an old radiator in the warehouse and had received no treatment for my broken jaw. The two men guarding me talked freely of their overthrow plans, so I knew they planned to kill me. I remembered the button and activated it . . ."

"All she had to do was squeeze it," Will interrupted.

"That's correct. I squeezed but didn't know if it was working. About thirty minutes later, I saw a dragonfly land on the radiator. It looked like it was staring at me. Then I remembered Wild Willy's work with Mossad and the tiny nano-bots they were working on, and . . ."

"Not 'working on' them anymore Baby. We got 'em!"

Will interrupted again, a wide grin crossing his face. Sheryl continued.

"I would say! The dragonfly, which looked *so* real, was soon joined by a lady bug-looking thing. The next thing I know, there's a loud explosion at the warehouse door, and in comes Will with the two biggest guns I ever saw. Those two guards peed in their pants, and Will never had to fire a shot. In retrospect, it's kind of funny."

The news, as always, continued; and Condi Zimmerman again interrupted the night.

"Águila Airlines Flight 606 from Madrid to Atlanta has crashed in East Point on approach to Atlanta's Hartsfield-Jackson International Airport. There are no reports of survivors. The plane crashed into a hotel near the airport, so casualties are expected to be high. Two eyewitnesses to the crash claimed to see a trail from a possible missile approach the airplane. Homeland Security denies the reports. We will interrupt when additional information is available.

"Now to the civil war in Egypt. The Muslim Brotherhood . . ."

As the stroke of midnight passed and December 21, 2012, flowed across the east coasts of North and South America, there was nothing. No power outages, no earthquakes, no terrorist bombings. Everyone sang and rejoiced.

Jeff looked at Samarra and asked, "Are you planning on divorcing Jack?"

"I already did. Last month it was final."

Jeff kissed Samarra at that moment, a gentle but lingering kiss; and Samarra leaned against his body. Everywhere, everyone was kissing; but the kisses weren't like *this* kiss.

"Here's to a helluva year." Abe toasted.

Chapter Fifty-Five

"The world is a dangerous place, not because of those who do evil, but because of those who look on and do nothing." Albert Einstein

Eleven months later

"**A**re you awake?" Jeff rolled over in his king size bed and snuggled close. "Are you awake, lovely lady?"

"I am," and she snuggled back, their forms molded together like two spoons snuggling in her Mom's silverware drawer. Was it possible to get closer? She tried.

"And I love you very much Mr. Ross." She looked at her engagement ring, the first time today, and felt like the happiest woman in the world. At least as happy as one could be with several thousand deaths on her hands. *Will I ever get past that,* she wondered?

"Want me to make coffee?" Jeff was up and headed for the kitchen before she answered.

"No. I want you to make love to me. Forget the java, Baby! Just bring those buns over here."

He did and they did. Samarra had never been happier but had a twinge of guilt, knowing she didn't really *deserve* happiness. God was merciful. She looked forward to their spring wedding.

The romance had been a little awkward at first. He had been widowed for almost two years and divorced for the previous four, long enough she thought. She was well over her divorce, *that* was for sure. How long did it take to get over a husband who turned out to be a pedophile who preferred little boys over attractive women? *But am I that attractive,* she asked herself, again. Her self-esteem had hit the pits after the duration and guilt of the trial and her husband's new *progressive* thinking.

"*I never considered you to be homophobic, Samarra!*"

She remembered Jack's sarcastic remark.

"Are you asking me if I would like it more if you liked *little* girls rather than *little* boys? You're a sicko, Senator Russell; and I'm *not* phobic!'" She remembered her answer as well.

Six weeks later, Jeff drove himself to Briscoe Field, now fully recovered from the flu. The business jet was fueled and ready; and soon they were in the air, flying at 32,000 feet, aimed south toward Jamaica. Florida appeared to be on fire.

He thought about Samarra and wished she could be with him. He was always thinking about Samarra, and Jamaica was the most romantic place in the world. How could he feel this way, so in love with this *friend*? A year earlier, he wasn't sure if he even wanted to live. That's what they had been. *Friends*, for years. And now this. He hadn't felt this good since high school. And boy, did she look good *neckid*? He ordered a glass of ice water from the steward, thinking he might poor it on his head, and tried to concentrate on business instead of *neckid*.

Soon his thoughts were back to Chad and the *meeting*, and he recalled the conversation. It had been troubling, to say the least. The normally laid-back Chad . . . everyone knew he was a pothead . . . had not been laid-back at *that* meeting. Pot or not, Chad Myers was a brilliant scientist; but that day he was as animated as animated could be.

"Chad, are you sure about this?" The Admiral had asked.

"Sure as a heart attack. Wish it weren't so, but . . . the physics don't lie."

Chad continued to explain the ramifications of the previous December 21, 2012 astronomical alignment, a year earlier.

"While nothing *apparent* happened last December 21, except for all the loonies killing themselves, I think about a hundred thousand at last count, the planetary alignment caused a significant gravitational effect. This alignment occurs only once every 26,000 years."

"Did this alignment affect only the Earth?" Jeff asked.

"It affected the entire solar system, maybe the galaxy. Data from the VISTA telescope in Chile seems to indicate a closer orbit with Mars."

"Closer orbit?"

"What I mean Admiral, Mars and Earth are closer than they were prior to the alignment. We know these gravitational effects could cause profound seismic activity."

"Like what?"

"Like an increase in earthquake activity, probably increased severity too. Volcanic activity is already increasing, including submerged volcanos. The ocean water temps have risen along the deep ocean trenches. That has led to more melting ice in Siberia, not good; plus that presents another problem.

"The melting ice in Siberia is releasing methane gas in record amounts, gas that has been submerged and trapped under the ice for millennia."

"Methane releases will make it even warmer than it is." The Admiral mused, aloud.

"Yeah, if it doesn't blow up," Chad interjected.

"Isn't there a lot of methane trapped beneath the floor of the Gulf of Mexico?" Sheryl asked.

"That's correct," Chad answered. Methane is much more greenhousy than carbon dioxide, *much* more. *And* explosive. The methane concentration is so high in Siberia that the Russians are burning it off before it builds up to a massive explosion. Unfortunately, something *massive* is likely, possibly equivalent to several megatons.

"The world's supervolcanos are acting up too. Yellowstone's caldera, forty miles across, has risen two feet in the past five months. Carbon dioxide releases have killed several hundred deer and other wild animals. The park is closed."

"Are they evacuating the area yet?" asked Wild Willy. "If that thing goes *boom*, it'll be a really bad day."

"Will, you have such a way with words. How can they evacuate? If Yellowstone has an eruption like the last one 630,000 years ago, every person, plant and animal within a radius of 400 miles will go to heaven, or hell. How do you evacuate half a million square miles?

"That's not all though." Not by a long shot, Chad knew. "The long dormant supervolcano in New Mexico . . ."

"The Valles caldera?" Jeff interrupted.

"Yep. *You so smart*, Mr. Ross. I take back all those nasty things I said about your smartness."

The four men, and Sheryl, laughed; Chad continued.

"Just west of Santa Fe, the 175 square mile Valles caldera is rumbling and rising. This volcano has been dubbed by volcanologists as a *sleeping monster*. During its last major eruption about a million years ago, it blew ash all the way to Iowa and was equivalent to 2,000 Mount St. Helens."

"That would cause a bad hair day!" Sheryl laughed, uncomfortably.

"And then there is the Aira supervolcano in Japan that's acting up. Never in *recorded* history or the geological record have three supervolcanos been active at the same time. The point is this. California may still fall into the Pacific, but it will most likely be Yellowstone's eruption that will cause it. Yellowstone's activity may also be the cause of the increased seismic activity along New Madrid. Everyone that was disappointed when nothing happened December 21, 2012 can relax. All hell's gonna break loose soon. The key word is *soon*. How far away is that?"

The business jet approached the Negril Aerodrome, and Jeff felt the landing gear activate. Fifteen minutes later, he entered his personal suite at Charela Inn, remodeled after the tsunami. The large, tiled balcony overlooked the white sands of Negril Beach, framed by a picture-perfect, crystal-clear sea, embossed with palms. He unpacked his bag, took out the framed photograph of Melissa that he carried with him, and placed it on the Henredon bamboo dresser.

He laid his Gideon Bible beside the picture of Melissa and knew this tradition had to stop. Melissa was in the past, and now he was getting on with life.

Jeff was in love with Samarra, yet the feelings he still had for Melissa were haunting. Being a widower was not a pleasant experience; but finally, it was time to move on. Samarra would never be a *replacement* for Melissa, nor would she want to be.

"*Who woulda ever figured?*" he asked himself often. Samarra Russell would soon be Samarra Ross. He was a very lucky man. Samarra was the most beautiful woman he had ever laid eyes on; and she appeared to be the same inside, a big heart. And a *Christian. Are you sending me a message, God?* He pushed the thoughts from his mind, turned the framed photo of Melissa face down and headed to his SCUBA shop, *The Dive Shop Next To Rick's Café.*

Samarra entered the double-French doors, smiled at Abe the Bartender and Judi, and ascended the two steps to the lunch area. She was meeting Kara and Jill. Kara had recently returned from her mission work in Haiti, distributing Halco light bulbs to those who had electricity.

Samarra couldn't wait to hear the stories. She especially wanted to hear about Kara's budding romance with Scott. She would later find out it wasn't a budding romance, this bad boy was in full bloom, and had been.

She spotted Jill sitting in an over-sized booth by the window, overlooking the Towne Green. *The Divide* was booming, the din of the lunch crowd partly baffled by the American flags hanging from the black-painted ceiling twelve feet above.

"Hey Jill." They hugged, and Samarra slid into the booth.

"Samarra, I am *so* glad to see you. You've been through so much."

Jill was sympathetic and her eyes teared, as usual. She didn't mention anything about Jack, Samarra's pervert ex-husband. They sat down, facing each other, and talked while waiting for Kara, always *appropriately* late. Samarra thought Jill seemed pretty happy, considering the loss of husband Bubba.

"Jill, I have to get this out before Kara gets here. I was devastated to hear about Bubba. I wish so much he hadn't been on the submarine." Samarra watched Jill's reaction, but it *had* been almost two years. Jill was Jill, always smiling and happy, and her expression didn't change.

"Leon wouldn't have missed that night dive for all the tea in China. Have you ever wondered what that means?"

"What?" Samarra asked.

"All the tea in China?" They chuckled. Jill talked on.

"Leon and I were having some *issues*." Jill paused to keep her composure.

"He was fooling around. I found receipts just before the accident. When he was supposed to be at a heating and air conditioning convention in Chicago, I found receipts from Lukeville, Arizona."

"Where?" Samarra interrupted.

"Yes, that's what I thought too. Where in the heck is Lukeville? I found other stuff too." Jill's voice trailed, as she remembered finding notes that were written in Arabic. Notes that she threw away, along with his pictures. Probably another girlfriend. Or . . .

Kara Mulherin interrupted Jill's and Samarra's conversation as she approached the booth. The three friends hugged, sat down and ordered Bloody Marys with celery-salt rims. Laughter and girl-talk would be the theme of their day.

"I hear you're in *love* Kara!" Jill and Samarra looked at Kara, raising their eyebrows in that *how's the sex* look.

"It's great!" Kara replied, "The sex is great. I know how you guys think. It is the *best* ever!"

"Like you would know, missionary woman who's only had sex with one other man. Are you just comparing him to the first?" They all laughed again.

"Yeah, I did feel a little guilty. Why did God have all those sex rules, and then make it so difficult with desire?" Kara asked.

"Desire works for me!" Jill stated; and the three clinked their Bloody Mary glasses in a toast. Kara continued as the other two eagerly awaited. Jill winked at Samarra.

"The first time he made love to me, there really were fireworks."

"Really?"

"Yes. It was the Fourth of July, about midnight. As soon as we started, *finally*, the fireworks started down at the beach." They laughed again, drowning out the din from the lunch crowd.

"Later, Scott asked me, 'Am I the only man who you've ever been with?'"

"And?" Jill asked.

"I said, 'Why does everyone keep on asking me that?'"

The laughter exploded from the booth, and other patrons turned to see what was so funny.

Kara looked at Samarra and asked, "What about you? I hear you and Jeffrey Ross are quite the lovebirds."

"What?" Jill asked, shocked.

"Yep. Mr. *Most Eligible Bachelor* is getting hitched. I never thought he'd get over Melissa, but Jeff would comment about you from time-to-time. I could tell there was some attraction there, but . . . you were married. Scott told me about it."

"That is the best news I've heard in a long time Samarra." Jill was serious, surprised and thrilled at the same time.

"Kara, I don't think I've ever been happier. Jeffrey is the kindest man I've ever met. He leaves chocolates on my pillow for Pete's sake!" Samarra smiled.

"You *sound* like Jeff." Jill said. "He says 'for Pete's sake' all the time."

"I know. He's rubbing off on me."

"I agree with Kara. I didn't think he would ever get over Melissa's death, and the horrible circumstances." Jill and Kara both nodded their heads in agreement.

"We've talked about that a lot. I'm not sure he will ever get over the loss of Melissa. If they had just recovered her body, but . . ."

"There were more than 300 bodies that were never recovered, just from Cayman." Kara knew the facts about the tsunami deaths and was relieved that so many Haitians made it to higher ground. The Haitian lot was a heck of a cross to bear.

"Has he told you that he loves you?" Jill prompted, moving her finger around the now saltless rim of the cocktail glass.

"Loves her?" Kara asked, incredulous. "They're engaged, for Pete's sake."

Samarra held up her left hand, a happiness enveloping her soul.

"Well the next obvious question . . ."

Samarra interrupted. "Yes I do. I do love him. Tremendously. This is a blessing I don't deserve."

Jeff had dinner at Rick's Café, watching the tourists jump from the rocks into the blue sea thirty feet below. The café was adorned with Christmas lights and a lone Menorah in the window by the front door. He loved Jamaica. The odor was prevalent. Ganja. He looked to the left. A table full of tourists was smoking the Jamaican delight, and Jeff thought he might someday try it. Just to see what all the fuss is about.

He finished the Caribbean lobster and filet dinner, motioned his driver, and they were back at Charela in five minutes. It was early, just nine o'clock, and the Jamaican sky was clear as usual. No *Blip* tonight, just a bright, silvery Milky Way scattered across the sky. Walking into his room from the balcony, Jeff found himself wishing that Samarra was here with him. No matter how he resisted, for Melissa's sake, he knew he had fallen hard and fast. It was out of control, and he loved it.

As he started to pick up the phone to call Samarra, it rang instead.

"Hello?"

"Mistuh Jeffy?"

"Yes." Jeff recognized the voice, the young maid who cleaned his suite daily the last three or four times he had visited Jamaica, "What can I do for you Rosalie?"

"Mistuh Jeffy, I need to talk to ya jest a minute Suh."

"I'm getting ready to hit the sack Rosalie. Can it wait until tomorrow?"

"I guess so, Suh." She sounded defeated.

"OK Rosalie. Come on up."

It seemed less than thirty seconds had lapsed before Rosalie, the beautiful, young Jamaican girl, was knocking on the door of The Ross Suite.

"Come in Rosalie. What's up?"

"Mistuh Jeffy, my heart be heavy. It be heavy 'causin I shoulda tell you last year when you visit. I so sorry, Mistuh Jeffy." The young girl started sobbing, and Jeff put his arms around her, hugging her closely.

"What's the matter Rosalie?" Jeff wondered if she might need money, everyone was so poor in Jamaica. He would certainly oblige.

"It's de woman in de picture, over dere." She turned and pointed to Melissa's photograph, now face down on the dresser.

"What about her?" Jeff asked, and subconsciously set the photograph upright. *"What about her, Rosalie?"* he repeated.

"De woman who be yo wife, she be live Mistuh Jeffy. She be livin' near Kingston. Some fishermen found her floatin' in de sea after de big wave, Mistuh Jeffy. At first, I wudn't sho, Mistuh Jeffy, if it wuz her. But now I sho."

Jeff stood speechless.

"Are you sure Rosalie?" He might not believe it, even if he heard it again. *"Are you sure?"* he repeated.

"I sho, Mistuh Jeffy. I sho. She don't r'member nothin' bout nothing,' not even who she be. I ask her myself if she married. She say she don know.

"Dey call her de Lady du Mer, Mistuh Jeffy. De Lady of da Sea."

"The Lady of the Sea," Jeff repeated.

"Yeah, dat right. Yo wife be live, Mistuh Jeffy."

"The National Center for Biotechnology Information in Rockville, Maryland has just confirmed an unprecedented outbreak of rabies in Canada, the United States, Mexico and Europe. Animals not usually associated with rabies, like sheep, cows and horses are attacking their owners.

"The dreaded Morgellon's disease, once thought not to be a disease at all, has raised its ugly head in London with 117 new cases of the painful disorder.

"Meanwhile, a large chunk of the Moon has been spotted by Goddard Space Flight Center's NEO Department, apparently breaking off after the collision with Dark Comet. Chad Myers, an NEO specialist, said they have their 'fingers crossed' that this VLO, or Very Large Object, will stay in orbit around the Moon. Hmmm. Fingers crossed. That's encouraging.

"Wait! This just in: There have been multiple eye witness reports of large explosions in the Korengal Valley region of Pakistan. Pakistan's DAWN

English-language newspaper is reporting that there were three detonations of low-yield nuclear weapons, and a large part of the valley is in flames. Pakistan is threatening war against the United States.

"The Middle East is 'going to erupt any day now' according to <u>DAWN</u>. Since the collapse at the Dome of the Rock in Jerusalem, Israel is on the highest alert status.

"In national news, the Associated Press is reporting that the FBI has arrested Leon Bubba Haskins on charges of conspiring to blow up the Buford Dam last year in Georgia, the country's first nuclear attack.

"And finally, Chuck Hutz is in the news again. In his latest proclamation, in Hebrew as always, his forecast is chilling. His final comment yesterday was: 'You have been warned!'

"This is Condi Zimmerman signing off and wishing everyone a Happy Chanukah and Merry Christmas."

"The great day of the Lord is near—near and coming quickly. The cry on the day of the Lord is bitter; the Mighty Warrior shouts his battle cry. That day will be a day of wrath—a day of distress and anguish, a day of trouble and ruin, a day of darkness and gloom, a day of clouds and blackness."
Zephaniah 1:14-15 NIV

CPSIA information can be obtained
at www.ICGtesting.com
Printed in the USA
LVOW08s1259150617
538247LV00003B/135/P